Romans

Romans

A Commentary

Martin H. Franzmann

CONCORDIA PUBLISHING HOUSE · SAINT LOUIS

Copyright © 1968 by Concordia Publishing House
3558 S. Jefferson Ave., St. Louis, MO 63118-3968
1-800-325-3040 • www.cph.org

Manufactured in the United States of America

Library of Congress Cataloging-in-Publication Data

Franzmann, Martin H.
  Romans: a commentary
  Reprint. Originally published: Concordia commentary—Romans. St. Louis: Concordia Pub. House, 1968
With new introd.
  Bibliography: p.
  1. Bible. N.T. Romans—Commentaries. I. Bible. N.T. Romans. II. Title.
BS2665.3.F723   1986   227'.1077   85-29910
ISBN 978-0-570-04431-4

6   7   8   9   10   11   12   13   15   14   13   12   11   10   09   08

CONTENTS

PREFACE

It is with filial joy that I welcome the republication of Martin Franzmann's commentary on Romans in elegant new garb. I was among his first students at Concordia Seminary, St. Louis, where he arrived in 1946 from a chair at the Wisconsin Synod seminary. He already had a towering reputation as a linguist, scholar, and wordsmith, although he was still astonishingly young in years. Nothing in our experience had prepared us for this precision of scholarship, matched with such poetic loftiness of language. He beguiled us to ponder anew the mystery of communicating the divine Word in human words that would be both fitting and explosively revealing. Martin never relaxed his attitude of reverence before the text that he was enticing us to communicate. His precision might strike an uninvolved observer as pedantry; it was, in fact, the most exact of fine tuning in matching text with reverent and telling comment.

Nothing is more telling of Martin Franzmann's life-long romance with words than the appearance of six of his original hymns and translations in the new Lutheran hymnals. A glance at these hymns will soon reveal Martin's poetic mastery. One of these begins: "Thy strong Word did cleave the darkness." This hymn is fast becoming a classic of modern religious poetry. How utterly characteristic of Martin is this hymn with its adulation of the creative Word of God! The Word he hymned is the Word he served in all he did.

In the late 1950s the literature board of the Lutheran Church—Missouri Synod gave high priority to the publication of Biblical studies for clergy and interested laity. The emphasis would be on full and objective exposure within the context of confessional faithfulness. This emphasis soon focused on a project of producing a new commentary series on the entire Bible. It would be based on the Revised Standard Version and would avoid the obscurities of professional scholarship without being unscholarly. "This commentary, therefore," to quote briefly from the original preface,

> is addressed to the devout who may often be mystified or frightened by the Bible's vastness and depth. The commentary attempts to provide a contemporary understanding of the ancient text rather than to develop practical implications for modern life. Theological, historical, and literary interests are uppermost. However, the writers are aware not only of the difference between the past and the present but also how little basic human problems have changed and how directly helpful the Biblical perspective and commitment remain.

When it fell to me to suggest authors for the New Testament section, I instinctively elected Martin Franzmann for Romans. If any book had warrant to be regarded as uniquely influential in the Lutheran tradition of Biblical study, it was this book with an unbroken line of eminent commentators, leading all the way back to Luther and Melanchthon. If any teacher in our fellowship has a current claim on Romans as his scholarly fief, it was Martin Franzmann. He had been lecturing on Romans for years in his classes and in public settings. What is more, I knew that Martin was a productive scholar. He had recently seen two volumes through the press: *Follow Me: Discipleship According to St. Matthew* and *The Word of the Lord Grows*–both in 1961. Martin did not disappoint me. His manuscript was delivered within the schedule he had chosen and was, in fact, the first volume in the series to be published.

The volume found a ready market and won the respect of readers, who applauded the rare combination of available scholarship, faithful interpretation, and cleanly adapted language. Its long and friendly reception has suggested this new edition. The Word does not grow old; neither does a keenly observed interpretation. The years since the original publication of the commentary have seen the production of a number of impressive new commentaries, both scholarly and popular. That Martin Franzmann's volume stands up demonstrates the integrity and depth of his perceptions.

For one brief period Martin and I were colleagues on the seminary faculty in St. Louis. Although he was now my brother in vocation, I continued to feel myself his son. He had helped me write two theological dissertations in my student days. Both concerned St. Paul, and one was on a passage in Romans. He continued even now to encourage me and to guide me from afar. Then one day I heard that Martin was taking a somewhat early retirement and was moving to England with his charming wife Alice. We deeply regretted the loss of his presence. Yet

9

none of us begrudged his flight at last to the land where he would hear the language of his heart spoken as he had always longed to hear it. When several years later I learned of his death in England, I sang his song in victory: "Thy strong Word did cleave the darkness."

Farewell Martin. Your work lives after you.

WALTER J. BARTLING
Atlanta, Georgia

INTRODUCTION

It is historically natural and fitting that the Letter to the Romans has always been of special interest and import to Western Christendom. For with this letter Paul is looking westward. The hope of coming to Rome was one he had been cherishing "for many years" at the time of writing (15:23). He had met Aquila and Priscilla as early as the year 50. An edict of Emperor Claudius banishing all Jews from Rome had brought that couple, destined to be so dear and so valuable to him, to Corinth, where Paul was then beginning his work. They could tell him of the church (or, more accurately, churches) in that key city of the empire, its life, its problems, and its possibilities, especially its possibilities as a missionary center for the western part of the Roman Empire. It was this last point which was, no doubt, of greatest interest to Paul, whose missionary strategy had as its chief object the founding of churches in the key cities of the empire. That strategy had carried him from Antioch to Corinth and to Ephesus.

The Occasion of the Letter

It was probably in late summer, A. D. 55, when Paul was about to conclude his work at Ephesus and was about to return to Jerusalem with the offering gathered among the Gentiles for the poverty-stricken saints of Jerusalem, that he gave expression to his long-cherished hope of going to Rome: "After I have been there, I must also see Rome" (Acts 19:21). He spoke of that hope again when he wrote to the Corinthians from Macedonia a few weeks later: "Our hope is that as your faith increases, our field among you may be greatly enlarged, so that we may preach the gospel in lands beyond you" (2 Cor. 10:15-16). "Lands beyond you" — this expression coming from a man who had been working his way westward "from Jerusalem and as far round as Illyricum (in northwestern Greece)" (Rom. 15:19) surely points to the West.

The letter itself enables us to fix the time of writing fairly closely. Paul is about to conclude his work in the East, so that he no longer has "any room for work in these regions" between Jerusalem and Illyricum (Rom. 15:23; see 15:19). He is about to go to Jerusalem with the collection gathered in Macedonia and Achaia (Rom. 15:25-27; see 2 Cor. 8 and 9). All this points to the close of the so-called Third Missionary Journey and the winter A. D. 55 — 56.

The place of writing is fairly certain also. Paul spent three months in southern Greece at the close of his Third Missionary Journey. He had promised the Corinthians that he would stay with them or "even spend the winter" with them (1 Cor. 16:6). Corinth would therefore seem to be the most likely place of writing. This is confirmed by three notices in the Letter to the

Romans itself. In 16:23 Paul sends greetings from "Erastus, the city treasurer"; Erastus is associated with Corinth in 2 Tim. 4:20, and an inscription found at Corinth mentions an Erastus as a city official there. In Rom. 16:1 Paul commends to the brethren at Rome a woman named Phoebe, a deaconess of the church at Cenchreae, the eastern harbor town of Corinth (she is probably the bearer of the Letter to the Romans). In Rom. 16:23 Paul mentions Gaius as his host and transmits his greetings to the Romans. One Gaius was a member of the church at Corinth (1 Cor. 1:14); but since Gaius was a very common Roman name, this is not a particularly weighty piece of evidence.

The above paragraph assumes that Ch. 16 is an original and integral part of the Letter to the Romans. Many scholars doubt this and are inclined to see in this chapter a letter, undoubtedly by Paul (with the possible exception of vv. 25-27), addressed to the church at Ephesus, which somehow got attached to the Letter to the Romans when the letters of Paul were collected. The arguments for this hypothesis are chiefly the following:

(1) The letter seems to come to a close at 15:33, with a benediction such as is common at the close of a Pauline letter.
(2) The closing doxology (16:25-27) is placed at various points in the ancient manuscripts; some place it after 14:23, some after 15:33, and some after 16:23. This is thought to indicate that Ch. 16 was not a fixed part of the letter in the manuscript tradition.
(3) Paul greets 26 people in this chapter; it seems unlikely that Paul had so many friends in Rome, whereas it would be very natural for him to have so many friends

in Ephesus; the scene of more than two years' missionary activity.

(4) It seems unlikely that Aquila and Priscilla would change their place of residence so often as this chapter, as a part of the Letter to the Romans, would indicate. They have moved from Rome to Corinth, from Corinth to Ephesus, and thence again to Rome (Acts 18:2, 19; Rom. 16:3); and a few years later they are once more in Ephesus. (2 Tim. 4:19)

(5) The stern warning of 16:17-20 is not prepared for by anything in the first 15 chapters; the tone of the warning seems to be more brusque and authoritative than Paul's usually tactful way of addressing a church he has not himself founded and does not know personally.

These arguments are not conclusive. (1) 15:33 *is* a closing benediction, but a lengthy postscript to the letter is not inherently improbable. (2) The varying position of the doxology points to varying liturgical usage in the churches; they probably did not all read the last chapter or chapters in their public worship. This says nothing about the original length of the letter, for even the manuscripts that place the doxology early contain all 16 chapters of the letter. (3) We have no way of telling how many friends Paul might have had at Rome. It seems unlikely, however, that he would single out some two dozen persons for personal greetings in writing to Ephesus, where he knew, and was known by, all members of the church; that would be tactless, and Paul was not a tactless man. In a letter to an unknown church it would be natural for him to single out those whom he knew personally for special greetings and thus draw nearer to the church as a whole. (4) The movements of Aquila and Priscilla really present no problem. Travel was relatively easy and safe within the Roman Empire, so that people with business interests could move freely in the pursuit of commercial advantages; and besides, Aquila and Priscilla would probably move with the Gospel. (5) We do not know the historical situation well enough to judge whether the stern warning of 16:17-20 would be probable or improbable in a letter to the Romans. Chapters 12 – 15 bristle with strong imperatives; Paul tempers the brusqueness of his imperatives there with a tactful reference to the Romans' Christian maturity and capacity for mutual correction (15:14). He likewise tempers the brusqueness of Rom. 16:17-20 by acknowledging the Romans' exemplary obedience to the Gospel (16:19). To conclude: it is difficult to explain how a letter to Ephesus got so firmly attached to the Letter to the Romans, and there is not a single outright witness for the omission of the chapter in all the manuscripts that have come down to us. Any hypothesis that separates the last chapter from the rest of the Letter to the Romans must be supported by weightier arguments than those hitherto advanced.

The Purpose of the Letter

Paul wrote his Letter to the Romans from Corinth during the winter A. D. 55 – 56. His purpose in writing the letter is delicately but clearly stated in the letter itself. His letter is to prepare for his visit to Rome. But Rome is not his ultimate goal. It cannot be, for Paul has made it his ambition as apostle to the Gentiles "to preach the gospel, not where Christ has already been named," lest he "build on another man's foundation" (Rom. 15:20). The apostle's task is to lay foundations, not to build on foundations already laid by others

15

(1 Cor. 3:10). The foundation has long since been laid in Rome. Paul's language in the Letter to the Romans indicates that the church there had been in existence for some time; the faith of the Roman Christians is already being proclaimed "in all the world" (1:8); their obedience is known to all (16:19); Paul has longed for many years to come to them (15:23). Non-Christian sources indicate that there was a church in Rome at least as early as A. D. 49 and probably earlier. Neither Paul nor any other early source points to any single outstanding personality as founder of the Roman church; Christianity probably came to Rome through the agency of a number of nameless men such as the "visitors from Rome" who were present in Jerusalem at Pentecost (Acts 2:10) and later returned to Rome, bringing with them the Word of God "sent to Israel, preaching good news of peace by Jesus Christ." (Acts 10:36)

The "visitors from Rome" present at Pentecost were in all probability Jews, and the church at Rome was no doubt strongly Jewish in its beginnings. At the time when Paul wrote to the Romans, the church was no longer predominantly Jewish; indeed, Paul speaks of it and to it as a basically Gentile church (1:13-15; cf. 1:5-6; 11:13, 28-31). But there remained in it, no doubt, a strong Jewish-Christian element. The presence of this element helps to explain why Paul in this letter expounds his Gospel by setting it in contrast to Judaism (the works of the Law, circumcision, descent from Abraham) and why he speaks at such length (Chs. 9 — 11) of the relationship between the Old Israel and the New Israel, the church.

Paul plans to spend some time in Rome, to enrich and be enriched by his association with the Roman

Christians and to proclaim the Gospel there (1:11-13; 15:24). But he is looking beyond Rome to Spain (15: 24-28). Paul hopes to be "sped on his way" there by the Romans (15:24). The expression "to be sped on one's way" seems to have become almost technical for the support, both moral and material, given to missionaries by established churches or individual Christians (Acts 20:38; 21:5; 1 Cor. 16:6, 11; 2 Cor. 1:16; Titus 3:13; 3 John 6). Paul evidently hopes that Rome may become his missionary base in the West, what Syrian Antioch had been for him in the East.

This explains why the Letter to the Romans, a letter written merely to *prepare* for his visit to Rome, is so deep and massive a treatment of the Gospel, which Paul proclaims and now intends to proclaim in the West. Everything that we know of Paul's missionary preaching and his missionary methods (for example, his practice of revisiting already established churches and his continued contact with them by letter or by means of personal emissaries) makes it clear that he did not aim at creating a vague, emotional, and enthusiastic movement but rather the firmly rooted, grounded, and established church of God, in which the Word of Christ dwelt richly. What he looked for and strove for in a church that was to be his base in the West was a full and thoroughgoing common understanding of the Gospel. At his former base in the East, this common understanding was something he could presuppose. Antioch had been deeply influenced by Barnabas, and Paul himself had preached and taught at Antioch for a full year before the Holy Spirit sent him forth on his wider mission to the Gentiles (Acts 11:26; 13:1-3). What a year's ministry had accomplished in the East, a brief visit and a single letter had to ac-

17

complish in the West. That letter had of necessity to be a full and rich one.

The Content of the Letter

The theme of the letter is announced in 1:16-17; it is the Gospel as the power of God for salvation. This theme is developed in four great movements of thought that unfold the creative power of the Gospel, (1:18 – 15:13). This body of the letter is preceded and followed by sections that make clear Paul's relationship, as apostle, to that Gospel and the relationship of the Romans to the Gospel's westward movement. The following outline may serve as a guide.

OUTLINE

Introduction

Romans 1:1-15

GREETING: THE BEARER OF THE GOSPEL, PAUL THE APOSTLE   1:1-7

¹ Paul, a servant *a* of Jesus Christ, called to be an apostle, set apart for the gospel of God ² which he promised beforehand through his prophets in the holy scriptures, ³ the gospel concerning his Son, who was descended from David according to the flesh ⁴ and designated Son of God in power according to the Spirit of holiness by his resurrection from the dead, Jesus Christ our Lord, ⁵ through whom we have received grace and apostleship to bring about the obedience of faith for the sake of his name among all the nations, ⁶ including yourselves who are called to belong to Jesus Christ;

⁷ To all God's beloved in Rome, who are called to be saints:

Grace to you and peace from God our Father and the Lord Jesus Christ.

a Or *slave*

1 Paul's greeting follows a common ancient letter form: "The sender (v. 1) to the recipient (v. 7a), greetings (v. 7b)." But it differs in two points from the ancient formula: (1) the first element, the naming of the sender, is greatly expanded—an expanded self-designation found only in ancient *official* letters; (2) the whole formula is given a completely Christian content.

The formal self-identification of the sender becomes the personal confession of the apostle. Paul confesses that he is in his person a testimony to the creative power of the Gospel, that the God who said "Let light shine out of darkness" has shone in his heart, as he says elsewhere (2 Cor. 4:6). He is now a servant, or slave, of Jesus Christ, he who "formerly blasphemed and persecuted and insulted Him" (1 Tim. 1:13). With this word "servant" Paul confesses that he belongs to and is totally at the disposal of his Lord. It is an expression of humility, a title that Paul shares with all believers (Rom. 6:22; 14: 4, 8). But there is in this title also a high claim. Great and singularly favored men of God were in the Old Testament called servants of God: Moses (Joshua 1:2), Joshua (Joshua 24:29), David (Ps. 78:70), and especially the prophets (Amos 3:7; Jer. 7:25; Dan. 9:6). And Jesus had applied this high title to the disciples and apostles whom He had called and sent (Matt. 10:24-25; John 13:16). With the self-designation "servant," Paul is joining the ranks of those to whom the Word of the Lord came, men who were chosen to be the proclaimers of the Word and will of God. There is no personal pride in this for Paul; he is confessing what God by His call has made of him. The call of God that had summoned Abraham and Israel and the prophets to their place and to their task in a history controlled by God (Gen. 12:1-3; Ex. 3:10; Is. 6:8-9; Jer. 1:4-5) had come to Paul and given him his

work to do. He was "called to be an apostle," an authorized and empowered messenger of Christ, one through
whom Christ works, one in whom Christ speaks (Rom.
15:18; 2 Cor. 13:3), so that men are confronted in the
word of the apostle with the dread decision between
life and death. (2 Cor. 2:15-17)

With his third self-designation, "set apart for the
Gospel," Paul may be alluding to his rebellious past as
Pharisee and persecutor of the church. For the name
Pharisee means literally "one set apart." The Pharisee
was set apart from the broad mass of his people for a
scrupulous devotion to the fulfillment of the Law. God
had reversed this Pharisee's course and had set him
apart for the proclamation of the Gospel. Not all the
Roman readers would catch the allusion to Paul's
Pharisaic past; but all would, as men who lived with
the Old Testament, recognize in the words "set apart"
the consecrating hand of God. (Cf. Gal. 1:15-16; Jer. 1:5)

2 It was God's call that made Paul a servant of Jesus
Christ, an apostle, and a Pharisee set apart for the
Gospel. The call was God's, and the Gospel that Paul
proclaims is His, God's own gracious and redeeming
Word to man (cf. 1 Thess. 2:13; Acts 10:36). The Gospel
is news of God's new creation in the world's last days.
But new as it is, it has behind it a long history. It is the
culmination of God's revelation; it is the fulfillment of
His promises. Paul shares with all the men of the New
Testament the believing conviction, implanted by Jesus
Himself, that the Old Testament is the foreword to the
New, that the life and death and resurrection of Jesus
all took place as the fulfillment of the ancient promises
of God, that "all the promises of God find their Yes in
him" (2 Cor. 1:20). These promises of God Paul cherishes
as "holy scriptures," as God's Word in written form, in

which God's prophets still speak to the New Testament people of God (cf. 15:4; 16:26). The Letter to the Romans itself again and again testifies to Paul's reverence for the ancient oracles of God.

3 The Gospel of God speaks of God's Son. Only the Father knows the Son and can reveal the Son (Matt. 11:27; 16:17), and He has revealed Him in history. The Gospel is news, genuine news of a divine action in history. The Son of God entered history as a descendant of a solidly historical Jewish king, David, to whom God had given the promise of a greater King to come (2 Sam. 7:12-16). Paul gives but the barest summary of the Gospel here; but even in this summary the grace of the Son of God, who loved us, becomes apparent: He is descended from David "according to the flesh." This need not be said of any man; *we* are born "according to the flesh," or we are not born at all. When the New Testament church says this of Jesus Christ (Paul is probably quoting an early creed-like summary of the Gospel), the church is saying: "He came from the realm of God to us of His own free will; He took upon Himself the flesh of man for us men and for our salvation."

4 God set His seal upon His Son's and Servant's work and highly exalted Him (Phil. 2:9). The obedient Son was marked out by God as Son of God in power. The "Spirit of holiness," the veiled Godhead that shone through His flesh during His days among men, broke forth in unmistakable splendor in the risen Son. God marked Him out as Son of God in power by raising Him from the dead. Paul speaks in a curiously subtle way here in the original, with a suggestiveness that no translation can really reproduce. Where we are forced to speak of "*His* resurrection," Paul speaks simply of

24

"*the* resurrection"; he is thus suggesting here what he says plainly elsewhere, that the resurrection of Jesus was an event which involved mankind, that Jesus is "the first fruits of those who have fallen asleep" (1 Cor. 15:20), the Beginner and the Guarantor of the resurrection for all, the one Man in whom all "shall . . . be made alive." (1 Cor. 15:22)

"Son of David," "Son of God in power," "Jesus," the Son of God in the flesh, "Christ," the anointed King of the promise — there is only one name that can sum up all the glory of the grace that is in these titles. That name is "Lord," the name above every name. Only the working of the Spirit of God enables men to call Jesus Lord (1 Cor. 12:3). And men moved by the Spirit cannot speak that name objectively; they *confess* it: He is "*our* Lord." (Cf. Rom. 10:9)

5 This Lord Jesus Christ blazed on Paul near Damascus and claimed him as His chosen instrument (Acts 9:15); through Him God's call reached Saul the Pharisee and made him Paul the servant and apostle. That was pure grace, the free favor of God counter to all man's deserving. Paul regularly speaks of his apostleship as grace given him (1 Cor. 15:10; Eph. 3:8; 1 Tim. 1:12-14), and he means the *work* of his apostleship when he speaks of it as grace, not just the honor of being an apostle (cf. Rom. 12:3; 15:15). He speaks of his work as the messenger of Christ here; his task is "to bring about the obedience of faith" by proclaiming his Lord. The combination of "obedience" with "faith" is a telling one. Paul knows of no obedience, in the religious sense, which is not faith. Faith is created by the proclamation of the Gospel of the Son of God, who came in freedom into the flesh and was designated Son of God in power by His resurrection from the dead; it is created by the

25

proclamation of a divine action that is none of man's doing or deserving. Faith is therefore pure receiving; faith is pure relatedness to the redeeming act of God, an act present and at work in the apostolic Word that proclaims it. But the apostolic Word also proclaims the Son as Lord, with the right and the power to rule. His grace lays total claim to men (cf. 2 Cor. 5:15), and faith is therefore always obedience. When the Son of God in power confronted Paul, Paul bowed before Him in the *obedience* of faith; he said "What shall I do, Lord?" (Acts 22:10). Paul can on occasion use "faith" and "obedience" interchangeably. (Cf. Rom. 1:8 with 16:19; 10:16; 2 Thess. 1:8)

Paul's work as apostle is for the salvation of men; for that very reason it glorifies his Lord, being done "for the sake of his name" (cf. Acts 9:16; 21:13; 3 John 7). And since the Lord whom he proclaims is "Lord of all and bestows his riches upon all who call upon him" (Rom. 10:12), Paul's mission is a universal one, "among all the nations." 6 The fact that God's Gospel has created "the obedience of faith" in men in Rome so that they now belong to Jesus Christ is therefore of direct and lively concern to Paul, for Rome is the crossroads of all nations. 7 He is in this letter seeking contact with them, these men whom God has loved and called and made His own, just as He once called Israel and made him His own people, His beloved child, set apart for Him (Hos. 11:1). "God's own," "set apart for God" — that is the basic meaning of the word "saint" in the Bible. A man becomes a saint not when he has attained moral perfection but when God's call has consecrated him for God's uses; moral excellence is the result of sainthood, not the condition for it.

To these saints Paul sends his usual greeting,

"Grace and peace." Grace is the free favor of God, His undeserved favor revealed and active in Christ for the salvation of men. Peace is the state of whole and sound well-being, the divine health, which God's grace creates, bestows, and perpetually renews. Grace and peace come to men as the gift of the God who has revealed Himself as Father in the sending of His Son, the Lord Jesus Christ. (For "Father," see the "Abba" of 8:15; for the combination "Father" and "Lord," cf. 1 Cor. 8:6.)

In the greeting Paul speaks with measured eloquence. Ideas are marshaled carefully, in threes: There are three self-designations ("servant," "apostle," "set apart"); three modifiers of the Gospel ("God's," "promised beforehand," "concerning God's Son"); three titles of Jesus ("Son of David," "Son of God," "Lord"); three descriptive phrases modifying apostleship ("to bring about the obedience of faith," "for the sake of his name," "among all nations"). The language is pithy and rich in suggestion; the whole New Testament Gospel is presupposed by it, and Old Testament associations cluster around it. Paul is telling the Romans not *who* he is but *what* he, by the grace of God, is. This is the first hint of the purpose of the letter and of the purpose of Paul's coming to Rome: here is a man whom God has caught up into His motion in these last days. Here speaks a man who moves on God-impelled ways to carry out the purposes of God. His movements are dictated by the movement of the Gospel of God. This is an apostolic Word.

27

Thanksgiving and Prayer   1:8-15

*Thanksgiving for What the Gospel Has
Created in Rome*   *1:8*

*Prayer that God May Fulfill the Apostle's
Wish to Come to Rome*   *1:9-15*

**⁸ First, I thank my God through Jesus Christ for
all of you, because your faith is proclaimed in all the
world. ⁹ For God is my witness, whom I serve with
my spirit in the gospel of his Son, that without ceasing
I mention you always in my prayers, ¹⁰ asking that
somehow by God's will I may at last succeed in coming
to you. ¹¹ For I long to see you, that I may impart to
you some spiritual gift to strenghten you, ¹² that is,
that we may be mutually encouraged by each other's
faith, both yours and mine. ¹³ I want you to know,
brethren, that I have often intended to come to you
(but thus far have been prevented), in order that I
may reap some harvest among you as well as among
the rest of the Gentiles. ¹⁴ I am under obligation both
to Greeks and to barbarians, both to the wise and to
the foolish: ¹⁵ so I am eager to preach the gospel to
you also who are in Rome.**

Paul is an apostle "set apart for the gospel of God";
that makes him a man of prayer. Apostles devote themselves "to prayer and to the ministry of the word" (Acts
6:4), for as apostles "by the will of God" they seek continually and consciously to align their wills with the will
of God. Thanksgiving and prayer are therefore the usual
opening of a Pauline letter. These same elements are
found in ancient pagan letters too; as in the greeting,
Paul follows current forms and puts into them his own
vital apostolic content.

8 Thanksgiving is always first; thanksgiving, Luther says, is the fire in the censer that makes the incense of our petitions rise with a fine and joyous buoyancy to the throne of God, and Paul himself urges men to make their requests known to God "with thanksgiving" (Phil. 4:6). Paul gives thanks for *all* the Christians in Rome; this peculiar stress on the "all," here as in the greeting (v. 7, *"all God's beloved"*), is probably due to the fact that Paul had many friends at Rome, whom he greets by name in Ch. 16, and also to the fact that the Roman Christians were organized, apparently, as a number of house-churches (cf. 16:5, 14-15). Paul wants to greet and reach all his brothers in Rome, not only his personal friends, not only one or another of the house churches.

He gives thanks for their faith; faith is so central to the Christian life that Paul can use it to describe the whole Christian life. In Gal. 1:23 he says that when he persecuted the church (Gal. 1:13), the churches spoke of him as trying to destroy the faith. The faith of the Romans must have been an active, working, and witnessing faith, the kind that James calls for (James 2:14-26), for it has made news. Paul values the churches of Rome as allies to aid him in his apostolic task of bringing about the obedience of faith among all the nations. Again the purpose of Paul's writing to Rome shimmers through.

9 Paul's preaching and suffering men can see; only God knows of his unceasing prayers, and only He can witness to them. Paul makes clear in passing that his prayers for all churches everywhere are an essential part of his work; they are a part of his priestly service in the Gospel (the word used here for "serve" has suggestions of a priestly ministry; cf. 15:16), which he performs in his spirit, inwardly, to God.

10 Paul has long ("for many years," 15:23) desired to come to Rome: the strength of his longing and the fervency of his prayers that he might reach Rome are apparent in the choked-up vocabulary of his prayer here. But he who is an apostle by the grace of God, by the will of God, and by the call of God prays that he may come "by God's will." His plans are under the will of God, not his own to make as he wills.

11 This does not make him a will-less automaton. Paul longs very fervently to see the Christians at Rome, but his personal longing is wholly one with his apostolic will. He desires to *serve* the churches of Rome by enriching them with some gift that the Spirit has given him, for their strengthening. What gift Paul may have had in mind we can only guess. He lists a great variety of such gifts in Rom. 12:6-8 and 1 Cor. 12:4-11, but these lists are obviously not intended to be exhaustive. The entire purpose and thrust of the Letter to the Romans suggests that the spiritual gift meant here might be a prophetic revelation that would create in the Romans a deepened sense of their missionary opportunity and responsibility. (Cf. Acts 13:1-2)

12 An apostle is not, for all his authority, *over* the church (cf. 2 Cor. 1:24); he is *in* the church, a member of the body, among members who all "have the same care for one another" (1 Cor. 12:25). Therefore, if Paul edifies the church, he will himself be edified. The spark of missionary fervor he kindles in the men of Rome will grow into a fire that warms him too. They will be "mutually encouraged by each other's faith"; here too, "faith" is a living, acting, busy thing that works in love from man to man.

13 Mutual edification in the church is not Paul's only aim; he would be active in strictly apostolic activity also, as missionary. He wishes to "reap some harvest" in Rome; the figure of the harvest for missionary achievement was probably familiar to the church from the words of Jesus (Matt. 9:37-38), and Paul himself uses the figure elsewhere (1 Cor. 3:6-9; 9:10-12; 2 Tim. 2:6). This work would be a continuation of Paul's particular mission to the Gentiles; the churches of Rome are characterized hereby as Gentile churches.

14-15 "I am under obligation" – "so I am eager"; the obligation which rests on Paul (he uses the even stronger term "necessity" in 1 Cor. 9:16) is the velvet yoke of the controlling love of Christ (2 Cor. 5:14-15). It does not, therefore, destroy his freedom; rather, it creates true freedom.

The apostle who is under obligation to Greek and barbarian (that is, to men of Greek language and culture and to men of foreign speech), to the wise and the foolish, is also eager to preach the Gospel to the men of Rome. Paul is writing to the Romans in the Greek language; he reckons them among the Greeks. Who these barbarians are Paul does not say; perhaps he is thinking of the men of Spain (15:24, 28). But he looks first to Rome, his gateway to the West. With this Paul has reached the point where he must deal in full and at length with that which impels him Romeward and westward, the Gospel. He now states the theme that is to occupy him for the rest of his letter.

The Gospel That Goes Westward

Romans 1:16 — 15:13

Theme: The Gospel as the Power of God for Salvation,
the Revelation of the Righteousness of God to
All Believers   1:16-17

¹⁶ For I am not ashamed of the gospel: it is the power of God for salvation to every one who has faith, to the Jew first and also to the Greek. ¹⁷ For in it the righteousness of God is revealed through faith for faith; as it is written, "He who through faith is righteous shall live." [b]

[b] Or *The righteous shall live by faith*

16 "I am not ashamed of the Gospel." Why should Paul speak, even negatively, of being ashamed of the Gospel, which gives his life its content, purpose, and direction? He is probably recalling Jesus' warning, "Whoever is ashamed of me and my words, of him will the Son of man be ashamed when he comes in his glory" (Luke 9:26). Paul's missionary experience lies behind these words too; his experience had brought home to him how resolutely a man must take Jesus' warning to heart. He knew how the Gospel looked to outsiders, to those who had not yet been brought to the obedience of faith by it. He had seen how the Jew stumbled at the Gospel of a crucified Messiah and called Jesus the Accursed. He had seen how the Greek shrugged off the Gospel and called it foolishness (1 Cor. 1:23). He would meet both Jew and Greek again in Rome. And so one can see why his high confidence in the Gospel of God should be expressed negatively here: "I am not ashamed."

He is not ashamed, for he knows that the Gospel is not the product of Judaic dreams, to satisfy Judaic hope and pride; he knows that the Gospel is not a plausible system of thought competing with other plausible systems. He knows that this offensive and foolish Gospel is power; no one can know it as wisdom who has not first felt it as power (1 Cor. 1:24). It is God's own power, no less; and it is power in the service of God's mercy, a power for salvation. The word "salvation" is for us a worn coin; for Paul and his readers, fresh from their Old Testament, it still had a sharp image and a clear superscription. It meant radical deliverance out of a desperate situation. What Israel had experienced at the Red Sea, when all help was cut off before and behind and only a vertical miracle from on high could save, that was salvation. Of it Moses could sing:

The Lord is my strength and my song,
and he has become my salvation. (Ex. 15:2)

"Gospel" means news, tidings of salvation. News enters men's lives and changes them. The news of a decisive victory that sets a country free is a liberating word for each man who hears it and believes it; it is a power in his life and determines his whole future. The

33

news of God's saving action is a saving power "to every one who has faith." This faith is not, strictly speaking, a condition man must meet in order to be saved by the Gospel. Faith is simply acceptance, receiving. When I believe, I accept God's saving act as done for me. I let it count for what it is in my life—I breathe the free air God's liberating act has created. This does not, of course, exhaust the meaning of faith; but this sense is basic to the whole meaning of faith in the life of man.

And this news is for "man" simply, for all men. It comes "to the Jew first"; to the Jew the promises were given for mankind (he was "entrusted with the oracles of God," 3:2), and so the news of the fulfillment comes first to him. To the Jew came John the Baptist, to the Jew came Jesus, and the apostles brought their witness first to him; they preached "beginning from Jerusalem" (Luke 24:47). But the Gospel was intended for all; it had to break the bounds of Palestine. When the Seed had fallen into the ground and died (John 12:20-24), the hour of the Greeks struck too. The apostolic witness went beyond Jerusalem and Judea to Samaria and to the ends of the earth (Acts 1:8), and Paul himself was God's chosen instrument in carrying forward this great movement of the Gospel (Acts 9:15). He remained mindful of this "to the Jew first"; wherever he came, he preached first in the synagog (Acts 13:14-16, 46), and in his work among the Gentiles, too, he never lost sight of the ancient people of God (Rom. 11:13-14).

17 What makes the Gospel a power? In it revelation takes place; it is powerful because it has the force of revelation. In revelation, according to the Bible, God enters men's lives and determines their lives. Paul's very next words illustrate this meaning of revelation;

when "the wrath of God is *revealed*" (v. 18), it enters men's lives and determines them; men are struck by the wrath. And so, if the Gospel has the force of revelation, it is not only news of an event. In news there is a report of an event that has taken place; in revelation the event is not only reported but *presented*, made a present reality, effectually active in the life of man. The saving revelation of the Gospel takes place "through faith for faith." Only faith can receive it and be blessed by it; that is, only he who is open for God's action, willing to let God's saving action count supremely in his life, comes under the saving power of revelation. But man is not of himself free to be thus open; therefore revelation is also "for faith." Revelation sets man free and enables him to accept the act of God as done for him.

Revelation has a content that makes it a power to save. Paul here calls the content "the righteousness of God." He does not unfold the meaning of this term until later (3:21-31). But this much is clear even now: (a) since "the righteousness of God" is the content of the news (Gospel), it means an action by God; (b) the content of the Gospel has already been described by Paul as the life on earth of the Son of God, His coming into history as the Son of David, His exaltation by His resurrection from the dead (1:3-4); "righteousness of God" and "Jesus Christ our Lord" are intimately connected; (c) it is the revelation of the "righteousness of God" that makes the Gospel a power to *save*; if it connotes an action, it is a gracious, redeeming action that is meant. Why Paul spoke just of "righteousness" in describing the saving act of God will become apparent later (3:21-31), after Paul has portrayed man under the wrath of God, fallen man as he is, confronted by his Judge.

Paul had in his opening confession professed his

submission to the God of the Old Testament, who had spoken through the prophets, to the authority of the Holy Scriptures of the Old Testament (1:2). He now gives evidence of his submission; he rounds out the announcement of his theme with an "it is written." He quotes the words of Habakkuk (2:4): "The righteous shall live by faith." (This reading, given in the footnote, is to be preferred as being more in harmony both with Paul's own Greek and the Hebrew of Habakkuk.)

Habakkuk in his day wrestled with riddles. He saw in his own people destruction and violence, strife and contention raging unchecked and going unpunished:

So the Law is slacked,
    and justice never goes forth.
For the wicked surround the righteous,
    so justice goes forth perverted. (Hab. 1:4)

And when he cried to the Lord, the Lord's answer was another riddle: The violence of the wicked in Israel would be punished, but God's instrument for punishing them would be "that bitter and hasty nation," the Chaldeans, "guilty men, whose own might is their God!" (Hab. 1:6, 11). How could God use these men, men who spat in the face of the high majesty of His righteousness, as the rod of His anger? Habakkuk had to wait for his answer; and the answer, when it came, was not a simple solution of the riddle that plagued him. The Lord told him:

Behold, he whose soul is not upright in him shall fail,
    but the righteous shall live by his faith. (Hab. 2:4)

This word of the Lord did not make the future clear for Habakkuk and Habakkuk's people; the Lord gave no indication as to when and how His deliverance would come. But He made the future bright with His promise of life to the righteous. That promise asked for faith; that is, the Lord asked His people to lay their life in His hand, unquestioningly, in the face of the insoluble riddles with which His governance of history confronted them. He who thus lays his life in God's hand is righteous; he is in the right relation to the God of the covenant and promise. He is taking the Lord at His word and is facing the present and the future in the strength of that word. He shall "live" — live in the full sense of the word, live in communion with the God whose word he has trusted. That is faith as it was given Habakkuk to know it; in the strength of that faith he can say:

> I will quietly wait for the day of trouble
> to come upon people who invade us. (Hab. 3:16)

He can say even more; he can speak words that anticipate Paul's cry of joyous defiance in Rom. 8:31-39. He can see all the material props and guarantees of faith, all the blessings that a gracious Lord can give, swept away and yet hold firm in the Lord and rejoice in Him:

> Though the fig tree do not blossom,
> nor fruit be on the vines,
> the produce of the olive fail
> and the fields yield no food,
> the flock be cut off from the fold
> and there be no herd in the stalls,
> yet I will rejoice in the Lord,
> I will joy in the God of my salvation. (Hab. 3:17-18)

Paul is obviously not offering proof for his statement concerning the Gospel and faith by citing the verse from Habakkuk; he is, however, confirming it by pointing up the fact that God's actions are all of a piece: both in His promise through the prophet and in His fulfillment in the Son there is the same unbreakable connection between faith and righteousness and life. Only by submitting unreservedly to the judgment of God and by accepting in beggar's fashion the salvation of God does a man stand in a right relationship to God; only so does he come to know Him as the God of his salvation.

THE GOSPEL CREATES A NEW STATUS FOR MAN 1:18 — 5:21

The Old Status: Man Under the Revelation of the Wrath of God 1:18 — 3:20

The Wrath of God upon Pagan Idolatry 1:18-32

[18] For the wrath of God is revealed from heaven against all ungodliness and wickedness of men who by their wickedness suppress the truth. [19] For what can be known about God is plain to them, because God has shown it to them. [20] Ever since the creation of the world his invisible nature, namely, his eternal power and deity, has been clearly perceived in the things that have been made. So they are without excuse; [21] for although they knew God, they did not honor Him as God or give thanks to him, but they became futile in their thinking, and their senseless minds were darkened. [22] Claiming to be wise, they became fools, [23] and exchanged the glory of the immortal God for images resembling mortal man or birds or animals or reptiles.

38

²⁴ Therefore God gave them up in the lusts of their hearts to impurity, to the dishonoring of their bodies among themselves, ²⁵ because they exchanged the truth about God for a lie and worshiped and served the creature rather than the Creator, who is blessed for ever! Amen.

²⁶ For this reason God gave them up to dishonorable passions. Their women exchanged natural relations for unnatural, ²⁷ and the men likewise gave up natural relations with women and were consumed with passion for one another, men committing shameless acts with men and receiving in their own persons the due penalty for their error.

²⁸ And since they did not see fit to acknowledge God, God gave them up to a base mind and to improper conduct. ²⁹ They were filled with all manner of wickedness, evil, covetousness, malice. Full of envy, murder, strife, deceit, malignity, they are gossips, ³⁰ slanderers, haters of God, insolent, haughty, boastful, inventors of evil, disobedient to parents, ³¹ foolish, faithless, heartless, ruthless. ³² Though they know God's decree that those who do such things deserve to die, they not only do them but approve those who practice them.

18 The Gospel is the power of God for salvation, for radical rescue out of a desperate situation. And the situation of man is a desperate one; man is under the wrath of God. God's wrath, His fearfully destructive reaction to evil, strikes all ungodliness and wickedness (literally, "unrighteousness") of men. It *strikes* them, for it is "revealed against them." When God reveals Himself, He is going into action; revelation means, not "There it is, see it!" but "Here it is, have it, feel it!"

39

When God reveals Himself, whether in wrath or in mercy, He takes over. This revelation of wrath, which is going on now, is "from heaven"; it is as inescapable as the revelation of God's wrath in the Judgment at the end of days (2:5). All days since the coming of the Son of God are "last days" (Heb. 1:2), and all the revelation of wrath in these days is the upbeat of that final dreadful music of damnation.

The ungodliness and wickedness of men which invokes God's wrath is this: they suppress the truth. They hold down and hinder the working of the truth of truths, the encountered reality of God. To know that truth is to be controlled by it; to know God is to be in fellowship with Him and to serve Him in righteousness. Men do not want righteousness and therefore they do not want the truth; they want the lie that promises them freedom. **19** They *do* suppress the truth; they are not ignorant but rebellious; not atheists, without God, but anti-theists, against God. For God has shown them the truth, Himself.

20 The Creator, who is still at work in nature and in history, continually attests Himself to men. His still-enduring power and His deity are continually before their eyes in the things that He has made. The invisible God is visible to the mind of man in His works. **21** God is thereby inviting men to fellowship with Himself; He is bidding them bow before His Godhead and give thanks to Him for His goodness (cf. Acts 14:17). Men refuse; giving thanks to God would be acknowledging their dependence on Him. Men who give thanks are no longer "like God" (Gen. 3:5), autonomous, sovereign, free. Men *willed* to be free of God; they are therefore without excuse. They have no plea that they can make in their defense before the judgment seat of God.

Man refuses to be bound by God, even if he is to be bound by cords of love. When the tie with God is broken, man's whole existence goes askew. The thinking of man now has no anchor point to save it from futility. Man will not have the light to walk by; he shall not, by the judgment of God, have the light to see by. 22 The emancipated mind, delivered from the wholesome awe and discipline of communion with God, is free to pursue wisdom, free to go down the road of infinite bewilderment and unhemmed questioning that leads to folly. 23 But emancipated man cannot quite endure the freedom he has chosen; he needs a deity of some sort after all. He documents the folly of his freedom by taking to himself *ersatz*-gods, images of man and beast.

24 God is not mocked; man in flight from God does not escape the hand of God. God uses the very wickedness of men, that wickedness by which they suppress the truth, to punish them in their ungodliness. He stands over their wickedness with an inexorable "I am the Lord thy God," as the Judge whom they can neither evade nor escape. Men do what they want to do; but God makes of what they want to do a hell of His imposing. He gives them up, judicially, to their sin. "In the lusts of their hearts," in doing what they want to do, they become the executors of God's wrath upon themselves. God gives them up to the defilement of their unleashed sensuality, so that they cease to have any honor in one another's eyes; the culture or the society that tolerates marital infidelity and prostitution (with a "Pooh!" to the Sixth Commandment) still has no place of honor for the paramour and the prostitute, especially not when a career of sensuality has riddled their bodies. 25 Paul spells it out again: this

is their punishment for their ungodliness. The lie of idolatry for the truth of God, worship of the creature for adoration of the Creator – this mad exchange dooms the exchanger. "Blessed for ever!" The glory of God the Creator looms large in the Holy Scriptures that were Paul's life-element; Paul had heard the Creator's "Let there be light" sound forth again when God revealed His Son to him (2 Cor. 4:6). The apostle's adoration of Him breaks forth irrepressibly here in a typically Judaic doxology confirmed by a solemn Amen.

26-27 A second time the awesome "God gave them up" is heard. God gives man up to "dishonorable passions." Man has destroyed the natural relationship between himself and his God; his life has become perverted at its heart and core. God's wrath brings home to man the horror of this religious perversion in the perversion of his sexual instincts, in the horror of homosexuality. Paul is not muckraking or going far afield to find materials for the indignant moralist when he speaks of these things; these horrors were in the very texture of the life (including the religious life) and culture of the world to which he spoke; he had to speak of them. They were vividly before him as he wrote; he wrote from Corinth, notorious for its viciousness even among the tolerant Greeks.

28 Defilement of the body, debasement in unnatural passions – these are the heavy hand of God on irreligious man. That hand bears hard also upon the communal life of man. When man refuses to acknowledge God, to honor Him and give Him thanks, man is turned in upon himself and insulated against his fellowman. God uses this false bent of man as the instrument of His wrath. Men who were created to live for one another in mutual ministration are condemned to the hell of living against one another. **29-31** All seventeen of the vices listed here by Paul have this in common: they rend the fabric of society and make an agony of the common life that should in God's intent have been a blessing for mankind. **32** Man knows God and denies Him. Man knows God's will (His "decree") and does not do it. He reaches still for all forbidden fruit, even though his conscience cries out "No!" and tells him of the death that is at the core of the stolen fruit, and he makes heroes of those strong individualists who dare to gather most forbidden fruit of all.

Paul is not accusing each man in the Roman world of every sin which he enumerates. But he is telling all men: These are the diseases of your culture, the blight upon the history in which you play your part. He bids each man see in them the symptom of his own deep disease – to see, for instance, in his "envy" (v. 29) the same disease that in another man erupts in murder. He gives each man eyes to see in his history the revelation of the wrath of God. He is calling on all men to repent.

The Wrath of God, the Judge, upon the Man
Who Judges His Fellowman   *2:1-11*

¹ Therefore you have no excuse, O man, whoever you are, when you judge another; for in passing judgment upon him you condemn yourself, because you, the judge, are doing the very same things. ² We know that the judgment of God rightly falls upon those who do such things. ³ Do you suppose, O man, that when you judge those who do such things and yet do them yourself, you will escape the judgment of God? ⁴ Or do you presume upon the riches of his kindness and forbearance and patience? Do you not know

43

that God's kindness is meant to lead you to repentance? [5] But by your hard and impenitent heart you are storing up wrath for yourself on the day of wrath when God's righteous judgment will be revealed. [6] For he will render to every man according to his works: [7] to those who by patience in well-doing seek for glory and honor and immortality, he will give eternal life; [8] but for those who are factious and do not obey the truth, but obey wickedness, there will be wrath and fury. [9] There will be tribulation and distress for every human being who does evil, the Jew first and also the Greek, [10] but glory and honor and peace for every one who does good, the Jew first and also the Greek. [11] For God shows no partiality.

Paul has been picturing mankind's disease in its most striking and evident form, in terms of the crass idolatry and the blatant immorality of the pagan world. Many of Paul's contemporaries, both Gentile and Jew, would assent to his indictment of the pagan world; many a pious Jew and serious-minded Greek would concur in his proclamation of divine judgment upon a culture and a history that was religiously and morally out of joint. These serious men would thereby exempt themselves from the judgment of God proclaimed by Paul and would feel secure in their ethical superiority to the libertine, the pervert, and the antisocial criminal. Paul aims to stop every mouth, including the mouth that utters ethical judgments, and to make all the world, including the ethical world, accountable to God (3:19); otherwise he cannot bring about the obedience of faith. As long as man still has the righteousness and pride and strength to judge his fellowman, he is not ready for the beggary of faith, he is not ready to receive the radical rescue of the righteousness of God.

1 Paul therefore proceeds to proclaim the judgment of God upon these judges of mankind. "Therefore," since you judge another, Paul tells the judge, you are under judgment too; in judging your fellowman you assent to God's decree and call it valid, right, and good. If God's decree holds, then you are doomed, for you do what you condemn and are pronouncing sentence on yourself. You, too, suppress the truth. – Paul does not *prove* to these men that they are guilty of the sins which they condemn. His word is no objective analysis of man's lost estate; it is a divine indictment of man, whoever he is. Revelation is addressed, not to our intellect but to our conscience (cf. 2 Cor. 4:2; 5:11) and strikes home at a level deeper than the level of logic. 2 God's law wants doers and His judgment strikes men's deeds; His judgment is not affected by the pious, serious, ethical words with which men cover up their deeds. His judgment falls "rightly," in accordance with the facts, according to the truth.

3 Paul knows how adroit we ethical gentlemen are at evading the truth. He hunts us down in the coverts of our self-deception. Each man considers himself *the* great exception; his sin is somehow less sinful because it is his, and he will escape the judgment of God. This is a completely irrational egoism; and once it is put into words, it stands convicted by its folly. But it is impious folly, for it assumes that God will, after all, be something less than a righteous Judge, an all-seeing Judge, a Judge from whose avenging presence none can flee.

4 The other attempt at evasion is more openly impious. Man sees in God's long patience with the sinner a toleration of his sin, and he grows secure in this de-

45

lusion. There is contempt for God in this misreading of
His purposes. It ignores the fact that God's forbearance
is meant to give man room and scope for repentance,
not "one more midnight to be free" (cf. 2 Peter 3:9, 15).
5 This toying with God's patience, this desecration of
His love, is the mark of a hard and impenitent heart.
God's patience may yet be long and His forbearing call
to repentance may persist through a lifetime. But there
comes a final day when all lifetimes are ended, and
then the effect of this fearful desecration of God's love
will be seen. That misused love of His will have become
a charged accumulation of wrath which the righteous
Judge will visit on the desecrator's head. 6 For God
will on that day render to every man, not according to
his judgments on his fellowman but according to his
works. On that day all delusions and self-deceptions
end; those who have evaded the Judge in His forbearance shall then face Him in His strict, impartial
judgment.

7 "To every man according to his works." It is noteworthy and instructive that Paul gives no description
of man's works here; he has no list of "bad deeds" or
of "good deeds." He speaks more precisely and fully
of the motives that produce the works than of the prod-
ucts. In the case of those who are rewarded with eternal
life, the work produced is called simply "patience in
well-doing," a persevering and consistent doing of what
is good. Their motive is called a "seeking"; they have
sought "glory, honor, and immortality." One is reminded
of Jesus' word, "Seek first his kingdom and his righteousness" (Matt. 6:33). These seekers sought their
glory in the God of glory; their life has been centered
in God, who alone can bestow honor and give immortality. They shall find eternal life in Him. 8 The empha-

sis on motive is even stronger in the case of those who come under the ultimate wrath and fury of God. They have *obeyed* wickedness; wickedness has been the center of their life, the focus of their loyalty. They have obeyed wickedness where they might have obeyed the truth, the revealed reality of God who confronted them and invited them. They suppressed the truth (cf. 1:18) because they were "factious"; their life was one long quarrel with God and therefore a continual resistance to His revelation. — The word translated as "factious" in the Revised Standard Version can also be rendered as "selfish" or "selfishly ambitious." This is perhaps better, for it takes us to the root of man's "factiousness"; man holds to his party line against God because he seeks his own and wants to have done with God. He is like the son in the parable who demanded what was coming to him and left his father's house for a distant country. (Luke 15:12-13)

"Wrath and fury" shall be the portion of these factious men. A combination like "wrath *and fury*" makes it clear that we cannot think of the wrath of God as a sort of impersonal retributive force, as some have suggested. The fact that Paul often speaks simply of "the wrath" without mentioning God (e. g., 5:9) cannot be used in support of this interpretation, for Paul speaks also simply of "the grace" (e. g., Eph. 6:24; Col. 4:18), and there is nothing impersonal about Paul's conception of grace. There is, of course, nothing freakish or arbitrary about God's wrath; the high and sober majesty of God, the Judge, is in it. But it remains as personal and as passionate as His love.

9-10 Good to the doers of good, evil to the doers of evil; that is the just judgment of God. Paul expatiates on this in vv. 9-10; the only really new element in these two verses lies in the words "to the Jew first and also to the Greek." Here for the first time since 1:16 the Jew is explicitly mentioned. Many scholars are of the opinion that Paul has been addressing only the Jew from 2:1 on. Certainly the Jew is included in this indictment, but there seems to be little warrant for confining it to the Jew. Paul speaks in broadest generality ("man, whoever you are," "O man," "every human being") and here, where he mentions the Jew, he also mentions the Greek. In the following section (2:12-16) he is dealing with both Jew and Gentile; it is not until 2:17 that he addresses the Jew alone. It seems better, then, to interpret as was done above, referring the indictment to ethical man generally.

"There will be tribulation and distress . . . for the Jew first." Israel was God's firstborn, His son called out of Egypt, the recipient of God's promises and the witness of their fulfillment. If the Jew misused this his priority in the grace of God, he has a priority in punishment. Paul is taking up the cry of Israel's own prophets; through Amos God had told the Jew:

> You only have I known
>   of all the families on the earth;
> therefore I will punish you
>   for all your iniquities. (Amos 3:2)

His *knowledge* of God's will, which made him judge others, will not exempt him from judgment; it puts him first and foremost under judgment, along with the disobedient Greek. 11 God will judge man as man. He plays no favorites; no Jew who obeys wickedness receives eternal life; no Greek who is patient in well-doing comes under His wrath.

The impartial judgment of God on every man according to his works is really one great question addressed to man as man: "You knew Me; did you honor Me and thank Me by doing My will?" But God Himself has made a great division in mankind; the distinction between Jew and Greek is of His making. He made His covenant with Israel alone and gave the Law, the embodiment of knowledge and of truth, to Israel alone. The one great question therefore gives rise to two subordinate questions. Concerning the Gentile the question is: What of the nations without the Law? Did they know God, and could they, too, have done His will? Can God justly judge them as He judges Israel, every man according to his works? The Jew knew God, there is no doubt of that; the only question left concerning him is: Did he do God's will? Paul takes up these questions in vv. 12-24.

The Question Concerning the Gentile   *2:12-16*

12 All who have sinned without the law will also perish without the law, and all who have sinned under the law will be judged by the law. 13 For it is not the hearers of the law who are righteous before God, but the doers of the law who will be justified. 14 When Gentiles who have not the law do by nature what the law requires, they are a law to themselves, even though they do not have the law. 15 They show that what the law requires is written on their hearts, while their conscience also bears witness and their conflicting thoughts accuse or perhaps excuse them 16 on that day when, according to my gospel, God judges the secrets of men by Christ Jesus.

12 Did the Gentile know the will of God? Paul is still proclaiming the wrath of God on all ungodliness

49

and wickedness of man; he is silencing every plea and bidding all the world plead guilty in the court of God. He proclaims that judgment according to works means judgment on the sinner; all who have sinned will perish, each man being judged on the basis of the revelation which God has given *him*. The deed is what counts and decides, no matter whether it was done by a Jew who had the Law or by a Gentile who had it not. 13 The Judge will "justify," pronounce righteous and acquit, those who have *done* what the Law demands; whether a man has heard the Law Sabbath for Sabbath in the synagog or learned its every jot and tittle in the schools will not decide. The deed will decide; the deed is the great leveler between the Gentile and the Jew.

14 But this does not erase the fact that the Jew is guided in his action by a direct and expressed word of God, the written Law; compared with him, the Gentile sins "without the Law." Is the Gentile, then, responsible for his deeds with anything like the Jew's responsibility? He is, Paul says. God has attested Himself and His will to the Gentile too. The actions of the Gentiles bear witness to this; they do "by nature," without ceasing to be Gentiles, without becoming Jews, what the Law requires. Their actions testify that they behold the guarding hand of God laid on their parents' honor, their neighbor's life, his marriage, his property, and his good name. They are "a law to themselves," not in the popular sense of that phrase with its suggestion of self-will and arbitrariness but in its literal sense: each Gentile is to himself what the Law of Moses is to the Jew.

15 The finger of God has written on his heart what God's law requires of him. Paul does not say that this is the equivalent, in fullness and clarity, of the Law

of Moses; what he does say is that it makes the Gentile responsible for his sin. The Gentiles' deeds are thus a witness to the fact that they know the will of God. The operation of their conscience is a second witness to the fact that they have within them something that enables them to call right right and wrong wrong. The voice of conscience may be howled down by the voices of their mad desires. It may be reasoned out of court by the perverse logic of their base minds. But it is still *there:* the thoughts they think upon their deeds are still "conflicting thoughts," some for the prosecution, some (less likely and less often) for the defense. **16** Each Gentile has a conscience; he carries about in his heart a secret miniature of the Last Judgment, as it were. It will no longer be a secret when the Last Judgment comes. On that day God will judge the "secrets of men"; all hidden motives, all secret motions of the conscience, will be laid bare before His eyes. Judgment according to works is clearly not a judgment on the bare, external deed; a man is judged by the deeds with which he has expressed the hidden motions of his heart.

"*My* Gospel," Paul says, proclaims this judgment, a judgment which God will execute "by Christ Jesus." Paul had heard his Gospel of the grace of God that triumphs over sin maligned by Jews as leading to the conclusion, "Let us do evil that good may come of it" (3:8). He had seen how even men within the church had drawn the conclusion which he himself indignantly rejects, "Let us continue in sin that grace may abound" (cf. 6:1; Phil. 3:18 f.). He solemnly asserts, therefore, that "his" Gospel is the Gospel of God, the Gospel of that divine grace which can forgive and overcome sin but cannot ever compromise with sin. The Christ who is the content of the Gospel as the Savior of mankind

51

appears in that Gospel also as the Judge of man (cf. 2 Cor. 5:10). It becomes apparent here that Paul's rehearsal of the revelation of the wrath of God on man concerns the church; for Christians, the wrath of God is not merely something which has preceded their present deliverance (3:21). The revelation of the wrath of God is the constant presupposition of their faith, the persisting dread alternative to their being justified through faith. Paul is the servant and apostle of the Christ who spoke judgment upon salt that loses its saltness (Matt. 5:13) and kept His disciples mindful of the fact that a man's life moves on a path that takes him to his Judge. (Matt. 5:25-26; 7:1; 16:27)

The Question Concerning the Jew   2:17-24

[17] But if you call yourself a Jew and rely upon the law and boast of your relation to God [18] and know his will and approve what is excellent, because you are instructed in the law, [19] and if you are sure that you are a guide to the blind, a light to those who are in darkness, [20] a corrector of the foolish, a teacher of children, having in the law the embodiment of knowledge and truth—[21] you then who teach others, will you not teach yourself? While you preach against stealing, do you steal? [22] You who say that one must not commit adultery, do you commit adultery? You who abhor idols, do you rob temples? [23] You who boast in the law, do you dishonor God by breaking the law? [24] For, as it is written, "The name of God is blasphemed among the Gentiles because of you."

17 The Jew knows the will of God; there is no doubt of that, least of all in the mind of the Jew himself. He wears with pride the name that sets him apart from the nations, he rests in high confidence upon the Law, which the Lord had declared to him alone (Ps. 147:19 f.), he exults in the God who is peculiarly his God, the God of Israel, and clings to Him with a tenacity that both amazes and irritates the nations among whom he dwells. **18-20** The Jew knows God's will from the Law and speaks a glad assent to it; in the possession of this "embodiment of knowledge and of truth" he feels himself to be the destined teacher of mankind: *he* will set to rights the ruined, feckless, groping lives of men. (These words depicting the high self-consciousness of the Jew are no doubt part of Paul's autobiography; these were the axioms and slogans by which Saul the Pharisee had lived.)

21-22 Only, none of this answers *the* question: Did he *do* the will of God? Paul's answer to this question is the same as Jesus' had been: "They preach but do not practice" (Matt. 23:3). The Jew's possession of the Law and all his proud devotion to it do not keep him from those common pagan sins, theft and adultery. They do not even keep him from idolatry. True, he abhors idols, the images of gods that are no gods. But, does he love the Lord his God with all his heart and all his soul and all his might? Does not the silver and the gold in pagan temples draw his heart away from the Lord? He expresses his contempt for idols by robbing their temples, but in that act he gives his heart to the idol Mammon. **23** The Law is his boast, but it is not the light he walks by; he dishonors his God by breaking the Law God gave him. **24** The sorry history of his people is reenacted in his life. What Isaiah (52:5) and Ezekiel (36:20) once said of the captive people of God must be said to the Jew now; they both rob God of His honor.

53

For a people of God delivered up into captivity for its sins (cf. Is. 51:17-21; Ezek. 36:17) and a teacher of the Law whose life is a crying contradiction of that Law both invite the blasphemy of the Gentile upon the name of God.

The Gentile is a law to himself; the Jew has and knows the Law of God. Both, when they sin, suppress the truth. Both are accountable; both are without excuse.

Circumcision and the Law   2:25-29

[25] Circumcision indeed is of value if you obey the law; but if you break the law, your circumcision becomes uncircumcision. [26] So, if a man who is uncircumcised keeps the precepts of the law, will not his uncircumcision be regarded as circumcision? [27] Then those who are physically uncircumcised but keep the law will condemn you who have the written code and circumcision but break the law. [28] For he is not a real Jew who is one outwardly, nor is true circumcision something external and physical. [29] He is a Jew who is one inwardly, and real circumcision is a matter of the heart, spiritual and not literal. His praise is not from men but from God.

25 But it is not only the possession of the Law that makes the Jew a Jew. Long before the Law was given through Moses, God made His covenant with Abraham and set upon it the sign and seal of circumcision. In circumcision God incised upon the flesh of man His covenant will, His pledge of "I will be your God." In an unrepeatable act, with an ineradicable mark, God pledged Himself to every member of His people; the circumcision of the male hallowed him and his house.

54

Each male member of His people, slave or free, received this Word-made-visible that expressed God's
gracious and elective will; he received it, moreover,
in infancy, before any willing or doing of his own. If the
Law demanded doing, circumcision was pure gift. Could
the Jew thus marked and honored by his Lord be made
to stand on a level with the Gentiles in the Judgment?
Would not this enduring sacrament shield him from the
wrath of God?

Paul's answer is: Circumcision is the sign both of
God's gift to the Jew and of His claim upon the Jew;
the covenant of which it is the sign puts a man under
both the promise and the commandment of God; the
Jew speaks his Amen to the promise of God by obeying
the law of God. The Jew's own Law and Prophets had
already told him this (Deut. 10:16; Jer. 4:4; 6:10). Circumcision is no magic spell but the dealing of the living
God with responsible man. If man breaks the Law, his
circumcision cannot save him; it indicts him. **26-27** The
obedient Gentile, uncircumcised though he is, stands in
God's judgment as a Jew. More than that, since he has
been obedient where the Jew has failed, he is in his
person the living condemnation of the Jew who with
the Law before him and God's mark upon him yet breaks
the Law. There is no partiality with God. **28-29** The true
Jew is not a statistical, ethnic quantity; one cannot
count and classify true Jews as one counts and clas-
sifies other nationals. Within the chosen people the line
is drawn between the Jew in the flesh and the Jew in
heart, between the Jew whom men can see and praise
and the Jew on whom the Lord's good pleasure rests.
Paul is alluding to the root meaning of the name Judah,
from which the name "Jew" is derived; that root meaning is "praise." When Judah was born, his mother

55

cried out, "I will *praise* the Lord" (Gen. 29:35), and Jacob's blessing on his son Judah, the bearer of the promise, was "Your brothers shall *praise* you." (Gen. 49:8)

The Jew's Objections and Paul's Reply   *3:1-20*

¹ Then what advantage has the Jew? Or what is the value of circumcision? ² Much in every way. To begin with, the Jews are entrusted with the oracles of God. ³ What if some were unfaithful? Does their faithlessness nullify the faithfulness of God? ⁴ By no means! Let God be true though every man be false, as it is written,

"That thou mayest be justified in thy words,
and prevail when thou art judged."

⁵ But if our wickedness serves to show the justice of God, what shall we say? That God is unjust to inflict wrath on us? (I speak in a human way.) ⁶ By no means! For then how could God judge the world? ⁷ But if through my falsehood God's truthfulness abounds to his glory, why am I still being condemned as a sinner? ⁸ And why not do evil that good may come?—as some people slanderously charge us with saying. Their condemnation is just.

⁹ What then? Are we Jews any better off?ᶜ No, not at all; for Iᵈ have already charged that all men, both Jews and Greeks, are under the power of sin, ¹⁰ as it is written:

"None is righteous, no, not one;
¹¹ no one understands, no one seeks for God.
¹² All have turned aside, together they have gone
    wrong;
no one does good, not even one."

ᶜ Or *at any disadvantage?* ᵈ Greek *we*

56

¹³ "Their throat is an open grave,

   they use their tongues to deceive."

   "The venom of asps is under their lips."
¹⁴ "Their mouth is full of curses and bitterness."
¹⁵ "Their feet are swift to shed blood,
¹⁶ in their paths are ruin and misery,
¹⁷ and the way of peace they do not know."
¹⁸ "There is no fear of God before their eyes."

¹⁹ Now we know that whatever the law says it speaks to those who are under the law, so that every mouth may be stopped, and the whole world may be held accountable to God. ²⁰ For no human being will be justified in his sight by works of the law since through the law comes knowledge of sin.

According to the Book of Acts Paul regularly began his work in a city by preaching in the local synagog. Paul's Letter to the Romans gives us a vivid picture of his preaching to the Jews. Only, it was not quite so calm and set a thing as "preaching" in our sense of that word. Paul "argued with them from the Scriptures" (Acts 17:2) — and they argued back. This section of the letter (3:1-20) is probably a reproduction of the objections that Paul had to meet as he wrestled with his kinsmen for their souls, seeking to "destroy arguments and every proud obstacle to the knowledge of God, and take every thought captive to obey Christ." (2 Cor. 10:5)

Paul used no quotation marks or other punctuation to distinguish speaker from speaker in this dialog, and so there is considerable difference of opinion among interpreters as to the distribution of parts and a corresponding difficulty in determining the exact course of the argument. The arrangement suggested by the paragraph indentations in the Revised Standard Version is as plausible as any. According to it, there are three objections by the Jew, stated in vv. 1, 5, and 9a. Paul's reply follows in each case in vv. 2-4, 6-8, and 9b-20. This last section, with its cluster of quotations from the Old Testament and two weighty summarizing sentences (19 f.), rounds off not only the dialog with the Jew but the whole major section which begins at 1:18.

1 The Jew may well object: "If possessing the Law is in itself no advantage to the Jew and if circumcision does not 'automatically' benefit the members of God's covenant people, what advantage *does* the Jew have?" He is asking the question in order to evade the call to repentance that is contained in Paul's proclamation of God's exceptionless wrath and His judgment on every man according to his works. 2 Paul seeks by all means to save some (1 Cor. 9:22). He therefore deals patiently with the question and takes it seriously. How very seriously he takes it appears later, when he devotes three whole chapters to the question of Israel's disobedience to the Gospel (Rom. 9—11). In 9:4-5 he enumerates the full array of all God's gracious gifts to Israel; here he concentrates on the one great advantage, on the fact that the Jews were "entrusted with the oracles of God."

We need not confine "oracles" to the Law; it is a broad term covering all God's speaking to Israel in deed and word, in law and promise, all that now lay enshrined for Israel in the Holy Scriptures. Paul may even have intended the term to include God's ultimate Word to His people, when in the last days God no longer sent servants but the Son (Matt. 21:37), in whom "all the promises of God find their Yes" (2 Cor. 1:20). With these utterances of God the Jews were entrusted; what

58

God spoke to the children of Abraham was intended for a blessing on all the families of the earth. (Cf. Gen. 12:3; 18:18; 22:17-18; 26:4)

3 The Jew would naturally object: "But you have told us that our possession of the Word of God helps us only if we obey it and do it. What becomes of this advantage then?" Paul's reply is surprisingly gentle. He speaks only of "some" who have proved unfaithful to their trust; he is remembering the "remnant chosen by grace" (11:5) in Israel, those who remained faithful. The failure of the others does not call into question the validity and the power of the Word that came to Israel. God's whole will was in that Word and is in it still. He still is faithful to His given Word. In it He still says, "I will be your God." 4 To deny that this Word, present and still speaking, is an advantage is to utter blasphemy. For that would be denying the bedrock affirmation of the Old Testament and the New, the affirmation that God is true, that His Word holds, whatever else may break. Where His will and the will of man collide, it is for faith axiomatic that the will of man is false. This faith speaks in the word of the Psalmist who will not attempt to conceal or excuse his sin but confesses it freely to his Judge (whatever the consequences for himself may be), in order that God may be seen to be the righteous God and all men may be still and know that He is God. (Ps. 51:3-4)

5 The second objection of the Jew attaches itself to Paul's answer to the first objection: "Granted that God always 'prevails when He is judged,' that He always and consistently shows Himself to be the faithful, sure, reliable God; does not the history of our nation, blackened as it is by our infidelity and apostasy, show forth God's 'justice,' His faithfulness to the covenant, which

we broke? Can He then in justice inflict wrath on us for what in the last analysis still glorifies Him?" (Paul apologizes for uttering this thought, even when he is putting it into an opponent's mouth. He is speaking, he says, "in a human way" about God, as if there were after all a court in which God could be brought to trial.)

6 In his answer Paul appeals to what was for him and for every pious Jew a fixed certainty: God will judge the world. If the Jew's plea holds good, there is no sinner under the sun who cannot make the same plea. For God's sovereign control of man's sin-ridden history always leads that history to goals which glorify Him. If, then, sinful man is excused by the fact that even his sin glorifies God, God can judge no one; the argument robs God of His acknowledged function as Judge. **7** Paul illustrates by citing his own case. (Many good ancient manuscripts read "for" instead of "but" at the beginning of v. 7; this seems preferable.) Paul, the Pharisee turned Christian, would be to the Jews the classic example of the "falsehood" of man. He was, in the Jews' eyes, a traitor to the God of his fathers, doomed to judgment if ever a man was. If the Jew can plead that his sin is excusable because it indirectly glorifies God, Paul can make that plea too: why should even he, the renegade, still be condemned as a sinner?

8 The Jews saw in Paul's Gospel of the God who justifies the ungodly (4:5) the tearing-down of all serious morality; to proclaim such a gospel was, in their opinion, inviting men to do evil that good might come of it. Paul rejects such an interpretation of his Gospel as pure slander. "But," he says, "if you plead as you do, you cannot object to my Gospel even in the distorted form which you give it, since my Gospel in that distorted form *does* 'glorify' God just as you are 'glorifying' Him."

60

He will not let this distortion of his Gospel stand; he solemnly announces the judgment of God on those who blacken the face of God by caricaturing the Gospel of His grace.

9 The Greek text of the Jew's third and last objection (9a) is uncertain; the translation and interpretation of it are therefore somewhat doubtful. The translation given by the Revised Standard Version in the body of the text ("Are we Jews any better off?") is possible and is adopted by many scholars. But it seems rather tame as the Jew's *concluding* question, for it is hardly more than a repetition of his first question in 3:1. The translation given in the footnote ("Are we at any disadvantage?") seems better suited to the context. As a parting shot the Jew, unconvinced, asks with bitter irony, "So, then, we are actually worse off than the Gentiles? The chosen people of God come in last in the race?" Paul's answer (9b-20) is what he has been maintaining all along: All men alike face the wrath of God, all men stand equally guilty before the tribunal of God.

But there are two new and important elements in Paul's last answer. The first is this: Paul here speaks for the first time of sin in the singular, as a power exercising dominion over men (v. 9); this conception plays a great role in subsequent chapters (cf. 5:12, 21; 6:6, 7, 12, 14, etc.). This brings out the utter hopelessness of man's situation. Man who has suppressed the truth is not merely man in error. Man literally "*obeys* unrighteousness"; he has committed himself to a power which holds him fast. Thus we again see God's judicial sway over man's sinning, that rule of wrath which appeared in the threefold "He gave them up" (1:24, 26, 28). Man is entrapped by what he has in freedom chosen. **10-18** The second new element is that Paul cites the Old Testament

61

Scriptures to indict the ungodliness and wickedness of man (Ps. 14:1-3; 5:9; 140:3; 10:7; Is. 59:7-8; Ps. 36:1). The quotations begin and end with man's violation of the First Commandment, with his ungodliness. Man does not "understand," he will not be told by God. He does not seek the God who offers Himself to man for fellowship (v. 11). Man does not know the way of peace on which the will of God would set him; there is no fear of God before his eyes to make him bow before his God and obey Him (vv. 17-18), as Abraham in the fear of God obeyed (Gen. 22:12, 18). This basic violation of the will of God spells man's moral ruin; they have all "gone wrong" (v. 12) in turning aside from their God. Man's words have become instruments of evil (vv. 13-14); his deeds spread ruin and agony over the face of his world. (Vv. 15-16)

19 This is an indictment the Jew cannot evade; this is his Bible speaking to his people. He must submit to judgment in the same court and on the same terms with the Gentile. And if the Jew's defenses are down, then every mouth that pleads in man's defense is stopped, and all the world is accountable to God. Paul speaks of these passages from the Psalms and Isaiah as "the Law"; this is in keeping with Judaic thought, which treated the Law as the heart of the Bible, to which all the rest was commentary. But there is also an inner justification for the locution here, for the voice of God that exposes and convicts the sinner is "Law" in the fullest sense.

20 In his concluding sentence Paul introduces two new thoughts that he will treat more fully later, "works of the law" and "through the law comes knowledge of sin." Paul has spoken (2:17 ff.) of the Jew's failure to do the Law. Now he indicates that even when the Jew "does" the Law after his fashion, that piecemeal righteousness does not remove him from the curse and the compulsion of sin; it does not make him righteous in God's judgment. What actually happens when man, as God's fallen and rebellious creature, as "flesh," is confronted by the Law is that he comes to know sin. Sin becomes a realized and powerful reality in his life. With this thought, which is diametrically opposed to Judaic thinking on the Law, Paul deals at length in Ch. 7.

It is no mere chance that the "clearest Gospel" of the Letter to the Romans is prefaced by the fullest, the most profound, and the most incisive proclamation of wrath and judgment that the New Testament contains. The Gospel is the power of God for *salvation* to everyone who has *faith*. Neither "salvation" nor "faith" can be understood aright unless they are seen against the dark background of the wrath of God on all ungodliness and wickedness of men, as 1:18 — 3:20 proclaims it. This proclamation makes it clear that all men, Gentile and Jew, are in desperate need of deliverance, of the absolute miracle of salvation, and that they can only *receive* it, passively, in faith. The old status of man under sin and under wrath is, for man, irrevocable and fixed. If he is to have a new status, he can obtain it only if God, his Judge, creates it.

The New Status: Man Under the Revelation
of the Righteousness of God   3:21 — 5:21

Justification Through Faith: The Manifestation
of the Righteousness of God in the Death of Christ   3:21-31

21 But now the righteousness of God has been manifested apart from law, although the law and the prophets bear witness to it, 22 the righteousness of God through faith in Jesus Christ for all who believe.

63

For there is no distinction; [23] since all have sinned and fall short of the glory of God, [24] they are justified by his grace as a gift, through the redemption which is in Christ Jesus, [25] whom God put forward as an expiation by his blood, to be received by faith. This was to show God's righteousness, because in his divine forbearance he had passed over former sins; [26] it was to prove at the present time that he himself is righteous and that he justifies him who has faith in Jesus.

[27] Then what becomes of our boasting? It is excluded. On what principle? On the principle of works? No, but on the principle of faith. [28] For we hold that a man is justified by faith apart from works of law. [29] Or is God the God of Jews only? Is he not the God of Gentiles also? Yes, of Gentiles also, [30] since God is one; and he will justify the circumcised on the ground of their faith and the uncircumcised through their faith. [31] Do we then overthrow the law by this faith? By no means! On the contrary, we uphold the law.

21 "But now" — God Himself has spoken, where all mankind must fall silent (v. 20) before His wrath and judgment; He has spoken a great "nevertheless." In the face of man's desperation, He has said, "Nevertheless, you shall be righteous, and you shall live." (Cf. Eph. 2:4, "But God . . .") He *has* manifested His righteousness; that completed act gives the "now" its significance. The Greek may view the "now" with a melancholy resignation born of his sense of the fugitiveness of time and the transience of all things in time, the Jew may see in the present merely a dark preliminary to the great age to come; for Paul and the whole New

64

Testament the "now" is filled. It is the "now" of the time of God's favor, the "now" of the day of salvation (2 Cor. 6:2). It ushers in a greater future, to be sure, but for all the incompleteness (8:23 f.) and the suffering (8:18) that mark it, it has a weight, a value, and a splendor of its own (cf. 5:9, 11; 6:22; 7:6; 8:1; 11:5, 30-31; 13:11; 16:26). Paul speaks of this manifestation of the righteousness of God in the perfect tense; it has taken place, once for all, with enduring results. The once-for-all historical manifestation of God's righteousness lives on and works on in the continued revelation of that righteousness in the Gospel. (1:17, "is revealed," present tense.)

THE OLD TESTAMENT AND THE NEW REVELATION

The revelation of the righteousness of God means life for man (1:17 "shall live"). But man is not required to earn this life; this manifestation of the life-giving righteousness of God has taken place "apart from law." The Law with its "This *do*, and thou shalt live" plays no positive role here. The Law as part of the Old Testament Scriptures ("the law and the prophets") bears its witness to this act of God, to be sure; whenever God speaks, He reveals *Himself*, and so all His previous speaking remains a witness to Him as He stands revealed now in the last days in the supreme manifestation of His righteousness. Paul has already spoken of the Old Testament Scriptures as constituting one great promise of the Gospel which was to come (1:2). He finds in a book of the Law (Genesis) the pattern and prediction of all God's dealing with man (Ch. 4). He sees in the institutions prescribed by the Law a foreshadowing of all that was to be a full reality in Christ (Col. 2:17): the sacrifice of Christ is the substance of which the Old Testament sacrifice was the shadow, He is "our"

65

Passover (1 Cor. 5:7), the sacrifices and the worship of God's ancient people find their fulfillment in the sacrificial life of the new, transfigured people of God (12:1-2). Paul can picture the New Testament people of God as an enlarged Israel (11:17-24), and he sees in the love which the revealed righteousness of God has made possible the fulfillment of the Law given to Israel. (13:8-10)

22 But this revelation of God remains "apart from law." Here God says not "Thou shalt" but "I will"; this revelation asks not for works but for faith, the very opposite of works (cf. Acts 16:30-31). Faith in Jesus Christ is at work here. In Him the righteousness of God has been manifested and is *there* "for all who believe."

23 The revelation is universal. It is as wide and comprehensive as man's need of it, and the need is universal. Paul sums up the burden of his proclamation from 1:18 to 3:20 in one weighty sentence: all men without distinction, Jew and Greek alike, have sinned; the glory of God which is the promised portion of those who do good (2:10) does not rest on them.

24 Paul has hitherto spoken of the righteousness of God as revealed in the Gospel, whose content is the career of the Son of David and the Son of God (1:17; 1:3 f.). He has indicated that it is an act of God, an act in Christ Jesus, a saving act. Now for the first time he describes the nature of this act more fully and makes clear its connection with the incarnation of the Son of God. Now we can see why he spoke just of the *righteousness* of God in speaking of the saving act of God, for the desperate plight of man is that he is under the wrath and judgment of God, his Judge, because of his ungodliness and his unrighteousness ("wickedness,"

1:18). Only an act of God can restore him from ungodliness to communion with God, only an action of his Judge can free him from the curse and the power of his unrighteousness. And that is what the revelation of the righteousness of God does — God justifies, pronounces righteous, unrighteous man; He "justifies the ungodly" (4:5). This is a judicial action, but it is "apart from law," indeed, it violates all legal justice. Legal justice can recognize the fact that man is righteous; it cannot make him righteous. God makes man a gift of His acquittal, gives him, effectually, the status of righteousness, lets him stand and count as righteous in His eyes. He bestows righteousness on man (cf. Phil. 3:9). That is pure grace, gratuitous favor, against all man's deserving.

This acquitting and restoring grace is lavish, generous, without reserve. It is in the last analysis wholly inexplicable, being hidden deep in the abysses of the love of God. But it is neither sentimental nor arbitrary, it does not drown sin in tears, neither does it simply ignore sin. The God of grace *deals* with sin effectually and at a fearful cost to Himself. God in His grace remains the God of justice. The God of grace does not cease to be God the Judge. His freely-given acquittal has a solid basis in the redemption which He Himself has provided, "the redemption which is in Christ Jesus."

REDEMPTION

"Redemption" means that a price was paid to ransom from death the forfeited life of mankind. One modern translator, Moffatt, has translated redemption with "ransom" in this passage. The ransom paid was the life of Jesus Christ. Paul goes on to speak of His shed blood in the immediate context. Elsewhere he speaks of Christ as the redemption in person — "Christ Jesus, whom God made . . . our righteousness . . . and redemption" (1 Cor. 1:30), and that, too, in a context which emphasizes the cross (1 Cor. 1:18, 23). Jesus had spoken of His life as the ransom given for many (Matt. 20:28), and Paul echoes this saying in 1 Tim. 2:6.

Many have found the idea of an actual redemption, a ransoming with a price, by the substitution of a Life for the lives of many, an offensive one, unworthy of the God of love. The idea of "redemption" is therefore limited by them to the idea of release from servitude without any idea of purchase. Paul does use the word family of which "redemption" is a member simply in the sense of "deliverance," without any direct suggestion of a price paid to secure the deliverance (e. g., Rom. 8:23), as the Old Testament also does. But where, as here and in Eph. 1:7 and 1 Cor. 1:30, the death of Christ is in view, the full sense of redemption is surely present. It should be noted that Paul also uses the ordinary Greek word for "purchasing" with reference to man's redemption, with the price either expressly mentioned (1 Cor. 6:20; 7:23) or strongly implied (Gal. 3:13; 4:5). The idea of substitution, which lies at the heart of redemption-by-ransom, finds drastic expression in Paul's letters: Christ was made to be sin for us (2 Cor. 5:21), He became a curse for us (Gal. 3:13). It is doubtful, moreover, whether any Greek-speaking reader could fail to associate the idea of price with the word which Paul uses for redemption. Words of this family were commonly used for the freeing of slaves by purchase and for the ransoming of prisoners of war. These considerations forbid any softening-down of the austerity of the New Testament revelation concerning the death of

Christ. God's grace was a costly grace. He "ransomed" men from their ruined past "with the precious blood of Christ" (1 Peter 1:18-20) and did not spare His Son (Rom. 8:32). God gave Him the cup of judgment to drink (Matt. 26:39; John 18:11), He smote the Shepherd (Matt. 26:31), He forsook Him on the cross. (Matt. 27:46)

25a But if we dare not take away from that revelation, we dare not add to it either. We dare not make of the God of grace an irate pagan deity whom someone else must mollify. For it is the God of wrath and judgment who Himself supplies the redemption. *He* sent His son to do the redeeming work that makes men sons of God (Gal. 4:4 f.). *He* put forward Christ Jesus "as an expiation by His blood." Paul changes from the legal image of ransom to that of sacrifice; no one image can express the fullness of the meaning of the cross of Christ. The idea of blood sacrifice was familiar to Paul and his readers from the Old Testament. They knew that sacrifice was possible because God ordained it and that it availed because He accepted it: "The life of the flesh is in the blood; and *I have given it* for you upon the altar *to make atonement for your souls;* for it is the blood that makes atonement, by reason of the life" (Lev. 17:11). The grace of God permitted the life of the slain victim to be substituted for the forfeited life of the sinner. Thus the broken relationship between God and His people was restored. All Old Testament blood sacrifice was but a token and a promise of the one great sacrifice to come. Here in Christ Jesus the one sacrifice of reconciliation was made, here the grace of God reached the goal to which all sacrifice had pointed — the restoration of communion between God and man. This sacrifice avails for all, not only for the Israelite, for its benefits are "to be received by faith."

EXPIATION — PROPITIATION

The term used by the Revised Standard Version translators ("expiation") seems too narrow to express the full scope of the term Paul employs. "Expiation" concentrates on the effect of the sacrifice on the sin and the sinner: the guilt of sin is canceled, and the sinner is made pure, fit for association with his God once more. It says nothing, at least not directly, of the effect of the sacrifice on God. Now, sin, in the Biblical view of it, is never merely *something* gone wrong with man but the whole man gone wrong, man in revolt against his God ("Against Thee, Thee only, have I sinned," Ps. 51:4). This personal aspect of sin is left largely unnoticed in "expiation." Moreover, Paul has been dwelling at length on God's personal and passionate reaction to man's sin, God's wrath and fury. The term Paul uses, however one may interpret it in detail, suggests the averting of this wrath of God, "propitiation," as the Authorized Version puts it. Some shrink from using the term propitiation because it suggests to many minds the pagan idea that *man* can somehow "bribe" his god and obtain his favor by means of sacrifice. It must be admitted that the term *can* be misunderstood. Whatever term is used, the Godward reference of the sacrifice ought to be made clear, and the fact that Christ "gave Himself up for us, a fragrant offering and sacrifice *to God*" (Eph. 5:2), should not be ignored. Perhaps a translation like Goodspeed's "sacrifice of reconciliation," or "atoning sacrifice" will do. Perhaps it is best to use the time-honored term "propitiation" and keep it clear of false associations by giving close heed to *all* that the New Testament has to say about the sacrifice of Christ.

As has been noted, Paul's term suggests the averting of God's wrath, reconciliation, propitiation. The Septuagint, the Greek translation of the Old Testament, which became the Bible of the Gentile church, uses the term for the mercy seat, the golden cover of the ark of the covenant in the Holy of Holies (Ex. 25:17-22). This was the place of God's presence, the throne of the invisible God, the place from which He spoke through Moses to His people (Ex. 25:22). On the great Day of Atonement the blood of sacrifice was sprinkled upon it (Lev. 16:14). In the only other New Testament passage in which the word occurs (Heb. 9:5), it is used to designate this mercy seat. In accordance with this some interpreters take Paul's word to be a bold figure indicating that Christ is "the place of propitiation," the place where God is reconciled to man by sacrifice. Others find this metaphor too harsh and inappropriate (one would expect the *Cross* to be compared to the mercy seat) and give the term a more general reference, translating "means of propitiation," or "that which propitiates," or "means of atonement." On either interpretation two things remain clear, the idea of sacrifice (underscored by the words "by His blood") and the idea of propitiation.

25b-26 God went the way of grace to the utmost when He pronounced the sinner righteous and restored him to communion with Himself. In going the way of ransom and of atoning sacrifice He asserted to the full His righteousness, in every sense of the word "righteousness"; He pronounced the sinner righteous in virtue of a redemption provided by His Son, in virtue of a sacrifice which He Himself provided. God's manifested righteousness is at one and the same time, in one and the same act, both the righteousness of the Judge who punishes sin with death and the redeeming righteousness of the Savior who bestows righteousness

71

as His gift upon inglorious man. The history of the world had, as it were, called into question the righteousness of God the Judge, for the history of man had largely been the history of God's forbearance. Even in Israel men could say, and say it with some show of right, "Everyone who does evil is good in the sight of the Lord . . . Where is the God of justice?" (Mal. 2:17); and Epicurus could dream of careless gods who neither punish nor reward. But now at the supreme hour of history, in the great "now" of deliverance, He has in the cross shown forth beyond all doubt His righteousness as Judge; He has shown that all His "passing over" of men's former sins was just that, a *suspension* of judgment that had this hour in view. Now it is clear: He spared mankind, He did not spare His Son but gave Him up for all (8:31). When He justifies the man who has faith in Jesus, makes him stand and count as righteous in His eyes, there is no "as if" in that verdict; it is a serious verdict because it is executed verdict.

27 There is no room left now for "boasting." Any boasting, any assertion of the wisdom or the righteousness of man, was shut out once for all when Jesus went down into the depths alone, drank the cup alone, paid the world's ransom alone. He alone by His sole blood has inaugurated the new covenant in the world's last days. His work is the one work that avails henceforth. What the Law with its promise to the performer of good works had left open as a possibility which man could in his pride misuse, namely, a righteousness which is man's attainment and a basis for man's boast, has been shut out. There is room only for the faith which receives everything from God and gives all glory to God. In coming to faith the Greek sheds his sorry wisdom, leaves his idols (1:22-23), and bows down before his God.

In coming to faith the Jew strips off the filthy rags of all his righteousness (Is. 64:6), drops his high pretensions to be teacher of mankind, and finds at last the God of Abraham who justifies (4:5). **28** The "principle of faith" is an exclusive principle, intolerant of compromise. No compromise is possible between faith and works of law. We hear the echoes of the battle Paul once fought for the churches of Galatia (cf. Gal. 2:16; 3:2). Paul's confident "we hold" is the word of one who in an agony of love and fury has fought and won the battle for a Gospel uncontaminated by the Law. **29** Paul knows what was involved in that battle; the very Godhead of God had been at stake. If the Law given to the Jew is God's first and last word, then God is God of the Jews only; He has lost His glory as the God of all. **30** But He *is* God of all, Lord of Jew and Gentile; His first word was the promise of a blessing for all nations and His last word is the manifestation of His righteousness, "apart from law," for *all* who believe, His free and costly acquittal of all, Jew and Gentile alike, through faith alone.

31 "Apart from law," "apart from works of law" — does not this sharp antithesis between "faith" and "law" overthrow the Law, rob it of all force and authority as the uttered will of God? Paul's assent to the Old Testament Scriptures, to the Law and the Prophets, is not a matter of form, indicating merely a certain reserved respect for the authority of the ancient oracles of God; he means it. His answer is therefore not, "We respect the Law, of course"; his answer is, "We *uphold* the Law." And uphold it he does; he makes it stand and makes it count. He has just taken the First Commandment more seriously than ever he did as a Pharisee (vv. 29-30). He has proclaimed his Gospel against the background of the Law's verdict on men (3:10-19); he has set men before the God of judgment. The terms in which he has proclaimed salvation (justification, redemption, sacrifice) get their color from the Law. His Gospel proclaims that God will judge through Christ each man according to his works (2:16). And the sequel also shows how seriously these words, "We uphold the law," are meant. Paul will speak of the witness of the Torah (the books of the Law) to the righteousness of God received by faith (Ch. 4) and of the function of the Law in the service of God's redemptive purposes (5:20-21). He will show that freedom from the Law is not freedom to transgress the Law (6:15); that liberation from the Law is not a self-willed act of man's but God's own releasing act in Christ, to set men free for service to Himself (7:4-6). He sees the goal of Christ's redeeming work in this: "That the just requirement of the law might be fulfilled in us." (8:4; cf. 13:10)

Justification Through Faith: The Case of Abraham   *4:1-25*

"What *then* shall we say about Abraham?" For Paul the figure of the patriarch comes naturally into his proclamation of the good news at this point; the word "then" shows that he feels compelled to speak of Abraham here. He *is* in fairness bound to speak of Abraham, for he is engaged in a dialog with the Jew (cf. 2:17 – 3:20; 3:29-31). And for the Jews it was a settled conviction, drawn from their Bible, that if ever a man was justified, right with his God, and in the sunshine of His favor, that man was their physical forefather Abraham, "the friend of God" (cf. James 2:23; 2 Chron. 20:7; Is. 41:8). The Jews had made a hero of their father Abraham; they made pilgrimages to Abraham's grave at Hebron and graced this venerated figure with legends that remade

74

him in the image of the legend-makers. They thought of him as a man of works. Even his faith they thought of as a work, a meritorious performance: they told of the ten trials through which he passed successfully and how his unshaken fidelity to his God was credited to him by God as a meritorious work. Abraham was for the Jews a man of the Law. By a special dispensation the whole Law was revealed to him, they said, a thousand years before its promulgation on Mount Sinai, and Abraham kept it all. He belongs to the number of the righteous who never sinned. As for the promise, Judaic legend declared that he received the promise and the covenant which guaranteed the prerogatives of Israel as a reward for his merits. Indeed, his merits were, according to the Jews, so great that they could be credited to his descendants even now.

This was the picture that, for the Jews, stood at the beginning of the history of the people of God, and it determined the Jews' conception of their relationship with God. This Jewish picture of Abraham, the picture of a man justified by his works, would rise up to contradict at every point Paul's picture of the silenced sinner justified giftwise by God's grace through faith, so that all "boasting," any assertion of the merit of man as a claim upon God, is excluded. Paul's claim that he was upholding the Law (3:31) would sound like hollow mockery to the Jews; to them Paul, in proclaiming justification through faith without the works of the Law, was departing radically from the norm which God Himself had established at the beginning of the history of His people, the people to whom He gave the Law.

But Paul's interest in Abraham goes deeper than that. He is not only contraverting Jewish legends and correcting Jewish misconceptions; he is holding to the

75

Old Testament, the Bible of the Jew, which is for him, as it was for Jesus, the very voice of God. The Gospel of God is for him the fulfillment of a promise of God recorded in the Holy Scriptures of the Jew (1:2). He claimed the Law and Prophets as witnesses to the righteousness of God revealed in His Gospel (3:21). His proclamation of justification through faith was for him no overriding of the Law; it made the Law stand and made the Law count as it had never stood and counted before. Paul's Gospel takes the Law, the inscribed will of God, seriously (3:31). If the Gospel that Paul proclaimed was not "according to the Scriptures" (1 Cor. 15:3), it could not be, for Paul, a valid word of God.

"According to the Scriptures" was for Paul no merely formal norm. He was not content to find in the Old Testament select passages to suit his purpose. He was concerned about the deep organic unity between God's former self-disclosure to His people and His last supreme self-proffering to mankind in His Son. Abraham is the beginning and the father of the separated people of God, the first whom God called to be His saint. If the new saints created by Paul's Gospel do not stand before God as Abraham stood and do not answer to God's call as Abraham answered in his day, they are not members of the true, the separated people of God. The case of Abraham will decide whether Paul is proclaiming the mighty acts of the Creator and Redeemer, the God of Abraham, or is indeed as the Athenians once suspected, introducing alien gods. (Acts 17:18)

These three concerns (the controversial, the Scriptural, and the theological) were not compartmentalized for Paul; they were all part of his one apostolic drive, to bring about the obedience of faith among all nations. He was taking the Gospel to Spain as the fulfillment of

God's promise to Abraham. He had no business in
Spain if his Gospel was not the fulfillment of that promise. He had no right to compete with the synagogs in
Spain if they, not he, spoke truly of Abraham "our
forefather according to the flesh." He had no right to
establish in Spain a new people of God, comprising both
Jews and Gentiles, if the Gentiles had no part in father
Abraham or could have part in him only by way of circumcision and the Law, that is, by becoming Jews.

ABRAHAM JUSTIFIED THROUGH FAITH, WITHOUT WORKS   4:1-8

¹ What then shall we say about ᵉ Abraham, our
forefather according to the flesh? ² For if Abraham
was justified by works, he has something to boast
about, but not before God. ³ For what does the scripture say? "Abraham believed God, and it was reckoned to him as righteousness." ⁴ Now to one who
works, his wages are not reckoned as a gift but as
his due. ⁵ And to one who does not work but trusts
him who justifies the ungodly, his faith is reckoned
as righteousness. ⁶ So also David pronounces a blessing upon the man to whom God reckons righteousness apart from works:
⁷ "Blessed are those whose iniquities are forgiven,
    and whose sins are covered;
⁸ blessed is the man against whom the Lord will not
    reckon his sin."

ᵉ Other ancient authorities read *was gained by*

1-2 The case of Abraham is indeed crucial. For if
Abraham was justified by works, he has something to
boast about, and there would be, just here at the crucial
point in God's dealings with mankind, a crying contradiction to Paul's "boasting is excluded," his "apart from

77

works of the law." But before God Abraham has no grounds for boasting. 3 "For what does the scripture say?" The voice of Scripture is the voice of God; there, in Scripture, His will and verdict may be heard, not only in the utterances of God recorded there, but in the simple narrative itself. The narrative, in the one place where it speaks of Abraham's righteousness (Gen. 15:6), speaks not of Abraham's doing but of his believing. What else was there for him to do, this childless nomad, grown weary in waiting for the fulfillment of the promise of descendants and a land (Gen. 15:2-3)? Here God was acting, Abraham was passive. *God* reckoned his faith to him as righteousness. The word for "reckon" in Hebrew has in it much more of emotion and of will than there is in our English word. This should be borne in mind for the understanding of the next verses, for Paul goes back to the Biblical sense of the word in order to overcome the Judaic interpretation of Gen. 15:6, which made a meritorious work of Abraham's faith and understood "reckon" in the commercial sense of "setting down something to someone's account, crediting him with it." 4 In the case of one who works, Paul says, reckoning is a simple and objective calculation of what is the worker's due; no *will* to give enters into the calculation. 5 But where we have to do with trust, with faith, there we have a "reckoning" in the full Hebrew sense of the word; there the will of the Reckoner counts supremely. In the case of the God of Abraham, that will was a will of grace and giving; Paul makes that plain by his description of the faith of Abraham. The believer "trusts in Him who justifies the ungodly." Paul regards this as the normal character of faith. Faith looks to God, the gracious Reckoner, for that which is "legally" impossible; it looks to Him for righteousness "apart from the law."

78

6-8 Paul cites a second witness to confirm the testimony of Genesis regarding the relationship between righteousness and faith and works. He cites David. David calls blessed the man whom the Lord forgives, against whom He will not reckon his sin (Ps. 32:1-2). Here again God is at work. God is in charge; man is the recipient. Paul calls this nonreckoning of sin a reckoning of righteousness to a man. God's forgiveness, His nonreckoning of sin, does not leave the forgiven man at dead center, in a sort of neutral zone. God's forgiveness is a whole and personal forgiveness; it restores a man to God. Jesus forgave like that. He ate with those whom He forgave, entered into full and free fellowship with them (Luke 15:1-2). The scribes and Pharisees, those men of the Law, quite understandably found that horrendous.

ABRAHAM JUSTIFIED THROUGH FAITH,
WITHOUT CIRCUMCISION   4:9-12

⁹ Is this blessing pronounced only upon the circumcised, or also upon the uncircumcised? We say that faith was reckoned to Abraham as righteousness. ¹⁰ How then was it reckoned to him? Was it before or after he had been circumcised? It was not after, but before he was circumcised. ¹¹ He received circumcision as a sign or seal of the righteousness which he had by faith while he was still uncircumcised. The purpose was to make him the father of all who believe without being circumcised and who thus have righteousness reckoned to them, ¹² and likewise the father of the circumcised who are not merely circumcised but also follow the example of the faith which our father Abraham had before he was circumcised.

Judaic teachers held that the promise of Ps. 32:1-2 held only for Israel and referred it to the forgiveness bestowed upon the people of God on the Day of Atonement; no other nation partook of it. The blessing held only for the circumcised. Then too, there were men in the early church who still preached circumcision as necessary to salvation (Acts 15:1; Gal. 3:3; 5:2-3). Could there be a reckoning of righteousness to man without benefit of circumcision? That question was a live one for the Jew, and it disturbed Christendom. The question of the circumcision of Abraham is therefore of importance for the men to whom the Gospel comes.

9 Abraham comes under the blessing pronounced by the psalmist; Gen. 15:6 shows that. But must one be circumcised to become partaker of that reckoned righteousness? **10** Again the case of Abraham is decisive. How did Abraham receive the blessing of reckoned righteousness? He was as yet uncircumcised, Paul says; he is arguing from the sequence of events in Genesis. The reckoned righteousness (Gen. 15) and the circumcision (Gen. 17) are two chapters apart; the rabbis set the interval between the two events at 29 years. **11-12** Circumcision did not create Abraham's status as righteous before God. Circumcision, God's seal, certified that status, a sign and seal impressed upon the flesh of Abraham and all his house. And it was no more a meritorious performance on Abraham's part than was his faith, for Abraham "*received* circumcision as a sign or seal." Thus, according to God's purpose, father Abraham becomes the father of the whole people of God, father of the uncircumcised Gentiles who receive God's righteousness through faith and father of the Jews who are Jews indeed, not only outwardly through circumcision but also inwardly, who follow in the footsteps of their father's faith, the faith he had while still uncircumcised.

ABRAHAM JUSTIFIED THROUGH FAITH,
WITHOUT THE LAW   4:13-15

¹³ **The promise to Abraham and his descendants, that they should inherit the world, did not come through the law but through the righteousness of faith. ¹⁴ If it is the adherents of the law who are to be the heirs, faith is null and the promise is void. ¹⁵ For the law brings wrath, but where there is no law there is no transgression.**

13 Paul is thoroughly Jewish in his language, and yet his thought is worlds apart from that of Judaism. He describes the promise given to Abraham and his descendants in a phrase that the Jewish rabbis used: "That they should inherit the world," and at the same time he brushes aside the Judaic interpretation which made the promise given to Abraham God's reward to Abraham for his keeping of the Law, his good works. The promise was in fact given, not to an Abraham who worked but "through the righteousness of faith," that is, to an Abraham who believed and thus received a reckoned righteousness.

14 The promise is God at work. The promise is God's free and sovereign gracious will to bless man, His offering of Himself to man as Shield and great Reward (Gen. 15:1). If the promise is made dependent upon the Law, which bids man work and promises a blessing to the worker, then the promise is no longer promise. The promise then can give nothing, and faith can receive nothing. **15** For the Law brings not righteousness but wrath. Man fails utterly in the face of the Law's demands.

81

Through the Law sin becomes an experienced reality
in his life (3:20); man becomes a transgressor and thus
comes under wrath of God, his Judge. There can be
no prospect of a great "But now!" (3:21) of deliverance
when the Law alone determines man's relationship to
God. But where the promise of God, the grace of God,
the Christ of God determine that relationship, there
there is no transgression either. There the promise given
to God's people through Micah is fulfilled for all people:

> Who is a God like thee, pardoning iniquity
>   and passing over transgression . . .?
> He will again have compassion upon us,
>   he will tread our inquities under foot.
> Thou wilt cast all our sins
>   into the depths of the sea. (Micah 7:18-19)

There there will be men who, believing in the God who
justifies the ungodly, will in the beggary of faith turn
to God their gracious King (Matt. 5:3) and in meek dependence of faith will inherit the earth. (Matt. 5:5)

THE FAITH OF ABRAHAM   4:16-22

**[16] That is why it depends on faith, in order that
the promise may rest on grace and be guaranteed
to all his descendants — not only to the adherents of
the law but also to those who share the faith of Abraham, for he is the father of us all, [17] as it is written,
"I have made you the father of many nations" — in the
presence of the God in whom he believed, who gives
life to the dead and calls into existence the things that
do not exist. [18] In hope he believed against hope, that
he should become the father of many nations; as he
had been told, "So shall your descendants be." [19] He
did not weaken in faith when he considered his own**

body, which was as good as dead because he was about a hundred years old, or when he considered the barrenness of Sarah's womb. [20] No distrust made him waver concerning the promise of God, but he grew strong in his faith as he gave glory to God, [21] fully convinced that God was able to do what he had promised. [22] That is why his faith was "reckoned to him as righteousness."

16 Faith, promise, grace — these three constitute an indivisible trinity. Only where a man ceases from the attempt to work his way up to God, only where in faith he lets God come all the way to him, only there can God's potent promise do its gracious work, its universal work for all the believing sons of Abraham. Then the promise is freed from all conditions and provisos that restrict it to one people or demand the impossible of man; then there is a certainty of faith, a certainty for all. 17 Then all nations can call Abraham "father Abraham," can stand where Abraham stood before the God in whom he believed.

Abraham believed. Paul does not define the faith of Abraham. No one in the New Testament seems to be much interested in a *definition* of faith. Paul gives instead a sort of case history of faith, which is more vivid and more revealing than a definition. What is this posture of man, the only possible response to the promise of God, the means by which he receives the acquitting verdict of the God who justifies the ungodly, the only possible correlative to God's grace? Faith is anything but dream and desire; it is no losing oneself, with half-closed eyes, in dimly dreamt-of possibilities. Faith is open-eyed realism; it faces the reality of God, who is revealed as the Creator, whose possibilities begin where man's possibilities end — at death, at nonbeing. Faith knows that death is for Him no unpierced and unpierceable blank wall, that He alone can work where there is nothing to work with, that He called to heaven and earth when heaven and earth were not, and lo! they stood forth together (Is. 48:13). His creative Spirit works and triumphs where chariots and horses, the solid sure devices of the men of might, fall down and fail (Is. 31:3). **18** In this God Abraham believed "in hope against hope." Against all human possibilities of hope, but in sure trust in his God's creative power, he believed the fantastic promise that he should have descendants innumerable as the stars. (Gen. 15:5)

19 Faith looks at God with open eyes, faith does not "suppress the truth." Faith does not "suppress the truth" about man either, faith is open-eyed toward man's impotence. Believing Abraham faced the fact that as a father he was dead and gone and that there was no life in Sarah's womb. If he was to be the father of a multitude of nations and if kings of people were to come from Sarah's womb, that was a possibility with God alone. All human knowledge and experience contradicted this promise of God, the response of man as man could only be — laughter (Gen. 17:17). **20** But believing man is taken captive by the disclosed reality of God, by His revelation. Believing Abraham held to the promise of God despite all the contradiction of his senses, his knowledge, and his littleness of faith. He lived by the word that proceeded from the mouth of God and grew strong on it. In his impotence he "gave glory to God." He did what sinful man has constantly refused to do, he "honored God as God" (1:21). He let God be God, let Him count as God, let Him have full weight as God in his poor, hopeless life. **21** He was fully convinced that the Creator had the power of His Godhead in His words; that when he said, "I have made you the father of many nations," the thing was done. 22 Therefore God reckoned his faith to him as righteousness, for here was man before God as God would have him, the creature before the Creator, the "ungodly" man looking to his God for justification.

ABRAHAM'S FAITH AND OURS   4:23-25

23 But the words, "it was reckoned to him," were written not for his sake alone, 24 but for ours also. It will be reckoned to us who believe in him that raised from the dead Jesus our Lord, 25 who was put to death for our trespasses and raised for our justification.

23 What's Abraham to us or we to Abraham? How does his "primitive" faith concern us, upon whom the end of the ages with God's culminating revelation in His Son has come (1 Cor. 10:11)? This record of Abraham's faith, Paul says, was written for our instruction (cf. 15:4); his faith is a prototype and exemplar of our own. **24-25** A faith that can be reckoned to us as righteousness will have in it the three impulses that lived in Abraham's faith: an open-eyed and overawed recognition of the Godhead of God, an open-eyed appraisal of the desperation of man, and a desperate laying-hold of the proffered redeeming Word of God, His promise. We believe in the God who raised Jesus our Lord from the dead (Paul uses the human name "Jesus" alone here, to indicate the dying manhood which our Lord shared with us). The resurrection of Jesus is the resurrection of man, for He comprehended us all in His loving Lordship. (Cf. 1 Cor. 15:20-22)

85

It is, moreover, the resurrection of *condemned* man, man under the wrath of God; for Jesus "was put to death for our trespasses," and His dying was the death of all (2 Cor. 5:14). In raising Him from the dead, God was "justifying the ungodly" for whom He died; God was saying to a doomed mankind, "You are righteous, you shall live." There is in our faith, therefore, the same realistic recognition of the death of man that was in Abraham's faith, and the same expectation of the creative miracle of God's grace which raises the dead and calls into being righteous men. The death and resurrection of our Lord Jesus are past events, they live on only in the Gospel that proclaims them. We meet them only in the Word, the promise of God. Our faith, like Abraham's, "comes from what is heard" (10:17) and lives by holding to that heard and heeded Word of God.

Our New Status Before God:
Peace Without End   *5:1-11*

¹ Therefore, since we are justified by faith, we *ᶠ* have peace with God through our Lord Jesus Christ. ² Through him we have obtained access *ᵍ* to this grace in which we stand, and we *ʰ* rejoice in our hope of sharing the glory of God. ³ More than that, we *ʰ* rejoice in our sufferings, knowing that suffering produces endurance, ⁴ and endurance produces character, and character produces hope, ⁵ and hope does not disappoint us, because God's love has been poured into our hearts through the Holy Spirit which has been given to us. ⁶ While we were yet helpless, at the right time Christ died for the ungodly. ⁷ Why, one will hardly die for a righteous man — though perhaps for a good

ᶠ Other ancient authorities read *let us*
ᵍ Other ancient authorities add *by faith*   *ʰ* Or *let us*

man one will dare even to die. ⁸But God shows his love for us in that while we were yet sinners Christ died for us. ⁹Since, therefore, we are now justified by his blood, much more shall we be saved by him from the wrath of God. ¹⁰For if while we were enemies we were reconciled to God by the death of his Son, much more, now that we are reconciled, shall we be saved by his life. ¹¹Not only so, but we also rejoice in God through our Lord Jesus Christ, through whom we have now received our reconciliation.

Our new status before God is no neutral state. Being justified does not mean merely that we have "gotten off" unpunished. It does not mean that we must make our way ourselves, as best we can, from here on out. Jesus pictured justification by faith as the return of the prodigal son to his Father's house; that was what happened when Jesus received sinners and ate with them. Now, the son's return to the Father's house meant more for him than life on a bleak subsistence level, although that was the most the son had dared hope for. It meant a return to full sonship; it meant the Father's kiss, the ring, the robe, feasting, music and dancing (Luke 15:11-32). Paul's words on justification, from the triumphant "but now" of 3:21 onward, have been vibrant with this sense of joyous splendor; but it is in the first half of Ch. 5 that he gives it full expression.

1 "We have peace with God through our Lord Jesus Christ." This is the Pauline counterpart to the warmth and splendor of the Father's welcome for the returning son in Jesus' parable. For "peace" is no mere cessation of hostilities; it is not only the antithesis to "war" or "strife." The Old Testament has given the word "peace"

87

a positive content that is reflected in the New Testament use of the word. "Peace" in the Old Testament signifies soundness, wholeness, health; where there is "peace," things are as they ought to be. Where the relationship between God and man is concerned, "peace" means that things are as a gracious God wills them to be — divinely normal. "Peace" can therefore sum up all that the Lord, the God who made a covenant with Israel, can give, all that faith can look for. The close and crown of the blessing which the sons of Aaron are to lay upon the people of Israel is "and give thee peace" (Num. 6:26). The promise of a "covenant of peace" includes all that the Lord in His forgiving and restoring love can give His people; the blessings of paradise ("I will bless them and multiply them"), the gracious presence of God in the midst of His people (Ezek. 37:26-28). The Messiah, whose birth brings the light of God's new creation to a people dwelling in a land of deep darkness, the new King, who multiplies the nation and increases their joy, who makes them free and glad again and establishes a reign of justice and righteousness over them, is called the Prince of Peace (Is. 9:2-7). The angel sang of this peace at the birth of Jesus (Luke 2:14). Jesus sent out the Twelve as bearers and givers of this peace when He sent them to the lost sheep of the house of Israel (Matt. 10:12-13; Luke 10:5-6). When Jerusalem rejected Jesus, Jerusalem rejected this peace (Luke 19:42). It is a peace in this sense that Paul speaks here, "peace . . . through our Lord Jesus Christ."

2 This peace fills the present. Having this peace means access to God, access to the God whose grace is a perpetually active grace, a field-of-force into which we are brought and in which we can stand and play our part in history according to the will of God. "By the

grace of God I *am* what I am," Paul says elsewhere, "and his grace toward me was not in vain. On the contrary, I *worked* . . ." (1 Cor. 15:10). This peace opens up the future. "We rejoice in our hope of sharing the glory of God." "He who conquers, I will grant him to sit with me on my throne," the exalted Christ tells His people, "as I myself conquered and sat down with my Father on his throne" (Rev. 3:21). This, too, is "through our Lord Jesus Christ."

3 But we justified men are not wafted to the skies on flowery beds of ease; we pass through a difficult and dangerous present to that future and assured glory. What of our sufferings? Do they not put a question mark before this "peace"? "We rejoice in our sufferings," Paul says. That is a hard saying, but the experience of millions who have taken Paul and Paul's Lord at their word attests its truth. We rejoice in our sufferings because we *know*. We know that the God who has delivered up His Son for us is in charge of all history. He is in charge of our sufferings too (Rom. 8:28) and works for our good in them too; yes, in them particularly. These sufferings discipline us and temper us. They produce "endurance," that resilient and athletic temper which is so sure of the future that it can live of the future and bear manfully the pressure of the present. It sees the present as the stairway to future glory and resolutely climbs the stairs one by one by the light that falls on them from the opened door at the head of the stairs. 4 This step-by-step living of the future leaves its mark on us; it produces "character"; the flustered raw recruit becomes the tempered veteran. With every step we take, we know more surely that the light at the head of the stairs is a light we can walk by; it does not fail us. And that is hope, no half-hearted wistful longing for a better

89

day but a resolute taking-refuge in God at every step of the way in the mounting and triumphant confidence that He will take us all the way.

5 We take refuge in the God whose love is the ultimate certainty in our lives. That love has been poured out into our hearts; that is something that has happened to us. We did not somehow achieve a noble conception of the love of God. No human religious genius gave us that conception. It was the creative working of the Spirit of God that implanted that love in our hearts, and it is the Spirit that gives us the unshaken assurance of it. That Spirit is, again, God's gift to us. Our hope does not put us to shame, for it is a divine work in us. **6** It is the Spirit that floods our hearts with the love of God, and the Spirit works with facts. He overwhelms us with the love of God by pointing to the Cross. Christ's act is the revelation of God's love, and there is for Paul no cleavage between Christ and God. They are one, so that the love of the Son of God, who loved us and gave Himself for us (Gal. 2:20), is the revelation of the love of God. This love which the Spirit reveals is love that originates solely in the will of God. There was nothing in us to inspire it; we were helpless, incapable of good, incapable of response. We were ungodly when that love sought us out, and we did not even want God's love. "At the right time," at the time of our utmost desperation and at the extreme of our revolt, Christ died for us.

> O loving wisdom of our God!
> When all was sin and shame,
> A second Adam to the fight
> And to the rescue came.

7 This is a love that is beyond our conceiving, alien to our experience. The greatest love that our experience knows, the best that grows in man's gardens, is a love that is willing to sacrifice itself for a good and gracious man, for a worthy cause. This does not happen often, and it "just barely" happens. Even this much goes against the grain of our humanity. 8 But God has documented His love in an act that lies on another plane altogether. Christ died for us while we were yet sinners, still men in revolt against God, still holding in wild contempt the high majesty of the God who all the while invited our worship and thanksgiving (Rom. 1:19-21). 9 Since God has come all the way to us in our rebellious impotence, since the incredible has happened, since we stand acquitted by the atoning blood of Christ, the peace we have with God is peace without end. The wrath of God that looms up at the end of all men's ways, to judge them and destroy them, does not loom up at the end of our new way; the Christ looms up, and He will save us from the wrath to come.

10 Paul adds yet one more description of our past estate. To "helpless," "ungodly," and "sinners" he adds "enemies," to mark once more the singularity of the love of God. "While we were enemies," the death of God's Son restored us to God's favor, we were reconciled to God. "Reconciliation" describes God's act in the Cross in personal terms, just as "justification" describes it in terms of law and justice. One act of God is thus described from two points of view, both valid, both necessary. Jesus, too, described His mission as God's Son and Anointed in both terms: He spoke of the King who forgave His servant "all that debt" (Matt. 18:23-35); He spoke also of the Father who welcomed home the undeserving son (Luke 15:11-32). The first is justification, the second is reconciliation. Christ's death has reconciled us to God; He rose from that death to be our living

Lord, at the right hand of God, interceding for us (Rom. 8:34). If His death means our reconciliation, His life shall be our ultimate deliverance. 11 The past is the history of God's unparalleled love; the future is the full assurance of that love's last reach, the great deliverance from the judgment. No suffering can make of the present a gray and deadly stretch with no meaning and no joy of its own. The present is filled with rejoicing; we exult in the God who in our Lord Jesus Christ has lifted up His countenance upon us and gives us peace.

The Old and the New: Adam and Christ   5:12-21

¹² Therefore as sin came into the world through one man and death through sin, and so death spread to all men because all men sinned — ¹³ sin indeed was in the world before the law was given, but sin is not counted where there is no law. ¹⁴ Yet death reigned from Adam to Moses, even over those whose sins were not like the transgression of Adam, who was a type of the one who was to come.

¹⁵ But the free gift is not like the trespass. For if many died through one man's trespass, much more have the grace of God and the free gift in the grace of that one man Jesus Christ abounded for many. ¹⁶ And the free gift is not like the effect of that one man's sin. For the judgment following one trespass brought condemnation, but the free gift following many trespasses brings justification. ¹⁷ If, because of one man's trespass, death reigned through that one man, much more will those who receive the abundance of grace and the free gift of righteousness reign in life through the one man Jesus Christ.

¹⁸ Then as one man's trespass led to condemna-

tion for all men, so one man's act of righteousness leads to acquittal and life for all men. [19] For as by one man's disobedience many were made sinners, so by one man's obedience many will be made righteous. [20] Law came in, to increase the trespass; but where sin increased, grace abounded all the more, [21] so that, as sin reigned in death, grace also might reign through righteousness to eternal life through Jesus Christ our Lord.

Paul has ascended to high places (5:1-11); from this vantage point of exultant certainty he looks back and surveys once more the whole ground that he has traversed. All that he has said of wrath and righteousness, of sin and grace, of Law and Gospel, of man's old status under the judgment of God and his new status under the acquittal of God, he sums up once more in the one monumental comparison and contrast between Adam and Christ. From this high citadel we are permitted to look into the ultimate depth and breadth of man's sin and to see the whole sweep of God's triumphant counterthrust to sin in Christ. Here, too, we find made clear the ultimate purpose of the Law in God's long counsels of salvation.

The section 5:12-21 is in every way the crown and capstone of the building which Paul has been constructing from 1:18 on. This is reflected in the style of this section also. Whereas 5:1-11, written in the "we"-style, is a lyric chorus of praise to Him who loved us and gave Himself for us, 5:12-21 is in the third person throughout; it is a concise, straightforward proclamation that sets forth with the greatest objectivity, like an inscription cut in stone, the eloquent facts of God's action in Christ for all the world. Paul ends this major section (1:18 − 5:21) as he began, with an almost austere emphasis on the fact that the Gospel is the Gospel of *God*, the power of *God*, the action of *God*; that revelation comes from God to man and in no wise depends either on man's hot desires or on his warm response. God's redeeming act is *there*, independent of our willing or running, there for all mankind.

This section is admittedly one of the most difficult in the whole Letter to the Romans. Part of the difficulty lies in the form. Paul begins by stating one half of the comparison and contrast (between Adam and Christ) which he intends to carry through, "As sin came into the world through one man" (v. 12). Before he completes the comparison, before saying "So through one man righteousness came into the world," he makes two parenthetical statements, both essential to the clear enunciation of his thought. The first parenthesis, vv. 13-14, is designed to support the opening statement that death came upon all men through one man's sin. The words at the end of this parenthesis, "Adam who was a type of the one who was to come" (v. 14), remind the reader that the second half of the comparison is yet to come; Paul has suspended, not broken, his line of thought. The second parenthesis, vv. 15-17, consists of three statements designed to make clear the great inequality and difference between the two members of the comparison, Adam and Christ; all three assert that there is a great divine "plus" on the side of Christ, that He is in the last analysis incomparable. Then in vv. 18-19 Paul finally carries out the Adam-Christ comparison and contrast. In vv. 20-21 he takes up the question, bound to arise at this point, of the significance and function of the Mosaic Law which "came in" midway between Adam and Christ. In outline form:

94

I. *The First Member of the Comparison-Contrast:* "As sin came into the world through one man," v. 12

   First Parenthesis: The history of the period between Adam and Moses, the time without the Law, as evidence that Adam's sin brought death on all men, vv. 13-14

   Second Parenthesis: The restriction of the Adam-Christ parallel; the triumphant "plus" on the side of Christ, vv. 15-17

II. *The Comparison-Contrast Adam-Christ Carried Out:* "One man's trespass . . . one man's act of righteousness . . . ; one man's disobedience . . . one man's obedience," vv. 18-19

III. *The Significance and Function of the Law,* vv. 20-21

12 The opening word "therefore" indicates that what follows has been prepared for by what precedes and grows naturally out of it. That Christ is the Key Figure in the history of God's dealing with mankind has been stated again and again: through Christ Paul received grace and the apostleship which made him the bearer of the Gospel (1:5); through Christ he gives thanks to God (1:8); through Jesus Christ ("by," Revised Standard Version; but the Greek word is the same one that is elsewhere translated "through") God judges the secrets of men on the Last Day (2:16); through Jesus Christ we have peace with God and access into the grace wherein we stand (5:1-2); we shall be saved through ("by," Revised Standard Version) Him from the wrath to come (5:9); through Him we rejoice in God, through Him we have received our reconciliation. (5:11)

95

"Therefore" He may be, formally, compared with another key figure in the history of God's dealing with man; He may be compared with Adam, a figure wholly different from Christ and yet of similarly universal significance for mankind. Through this one man sin came into the world. Here again, as in 3:9, sin is pictured as a sort of personal power. When Adam listened to the serpent's alienating voice, that power invaded the world. The history of man thenceforth is a history determined by sin, as both the Old Testament and the New testify. When Paul uses the word "world," he thinks primarily of the world's inhabitants, of men (cf. 1:8; 3:6; 3:19); but there may be a hint even here of the thought which Paul elaborates in 8:19-21, namely, the thought of Gen. 3:17-19 that the ground is cursed for man's sake, that man's world is involved in the doom of fallen man. That doom is death. Through one man's sin death came into the world and so spread to all men. Death is a heritage that is distributed evenly to all the sons of Adam.

But what does Paul mean by "death"? Adam did not drop dead when he had taken the fateful step and death entered the world, and the world since Adam has been filled with people who are very much alive. Adam ultimately died, of course, and all his children die. But even the fact that all men sooner or later die is not the whole and real content of what Paul here means by death. He speaks a little later of a "reign of death" (v. 14) and of a "reign of sin in death" (v. 21). This takes us closer to his meaning; death is obviously not only the end of life but the opposite of life in the full sense of the word "life," the kind of life of which Paul speaks when he cites Habakkuk to the effect that "the . . . righteous . . . shall live" (1:17). Death is a reality *in* the lives of men, a power that holds sway over men's most vital acts. Man's sin was that he did not want to be limited by God; he wanted to be "like God." His punishment is that he must henceforth live a life limited at every point by death. Death means that men are born into lives of desperation and die deaths of desperation. Man cannot fear and love and trust his God; he must suppress the truth of God because he sees in God the Death-dealer. Man cannot love and give, as God intended him to; because he is limited by death, he creates his own hell by getting and hating. Man's avarice and his worrying are tokens of the reign of death over his life; he must in his desperation get what he can and have while he can — "getting and spending we lay waste our powers." Man's wild, ungovernable sex impulse is another mark of his desperation, his protest against the fact that his life is a dying life. His desire for acceptance and prestige, his self-seeking ambition, are part of man's desperate quest for an antidote to death. The death of man as man's doom means that man lives at a "dying rate" as he moves toward the time when death shuts up the story of his days. This same judgment on the quality of human life is implied in Jesus' command to let the dead bury their dead (Matt. 8:22; cf. John 5:24 f.) and to lose one's life in order to gain it. (Matt. 10:39; 16:25; cf. John 12:25)

Death became the doom of all men "because all men sinned." Many scholars interpret this to mean: "All men *after Adam* sinned and thus repeated and confirmed in their own lives the act and the doom of Adam." This is in itself possible and in itself true; Adam's sons do go the way of Adam and do reenact their father's sin, to a degree at least. But that can hardly be Paul's meaning here. For one thing, the obvious sense of vv. 13-14 is that the sin of Adam, and it alone, accounts for the reign of

97

death in the period between Adam and Moses "before the Law was given," in the period when men did *not* sin after the manner of the transgression of Adam. For another, Paul in v. 17 restates the thought in the form "because of *one man's* trespass, death reigned through that *one man*," and again in v. 18 in the form *"one man's* trespass led to condemnation for all men," and yet again in v. 19 "by *one man's* disobedience many were made sinners." All this is in parallel and contrast to the sole deed of Christ who by His righteousness and obedience reversed the doom of all. As surely as Christ's great act of deliverance was solely His and not the act of all and yet involves and affects all, so surely the transgression of Adam was his own act and yet involves and affects all. The closest formal parallel in Paul's writings is 2 Cor. 5:14, when Paul states the significance of the death of Christ thus: "One died for all; therefore all have died." Applying this to Christ's negative counterpart, to Adam, one could say without violating Paul's thought: "One sinned for all; therefore all have sinned." Adam sinned as the head and inclusive representative of his race. The rhyme in the old New England Primer puts it harshly, but succinctly:

> In Adam's fall
> We sinnèd all.

13-14 Where is the evidence for this iron, unbreakable connection between the sin of Adam and the dying of mankind? Paul finds it in the history of the period between Adam and Moses. From the giving of the Law through Moses onward man was, in Israel, once more standing before his God as Adam stood, with an express commandment to guide him and the threat of death to warn him. In Israel man sinned once more as Adam sinned; he *transgressed*. In Israel, God's chosen people, sin was "counted," rigorously laid to man's account, imputed to him as it had not been since Adam. Man within the blessing of the covenant was, in a sense, a repetition of man in paradise. Between Adam and Moses, then, there lies a period unique in the history of mankind, a period where there "was no law" (in the sense that there was a Law before it and after it). Here, if anywhere, there should be a lightening in man's dark sky, some breaking of the stranglehold of death, if man's dying is not given with his birth and is not his inescapable heritage from Adam. "Yet death *reigned* from Adam to Moses even over those whose sins were not like the transgression of Adam." Death was in charge of those centuries. The gray fog of death lay unbroken on men's lives through all those years; the history of each man ends always with the words: "He died."

So Adam stands at the beginning of man's history, determining the history of all men by the deed that he has done, by the answer he has given God. In that respect he is the "type" of Christ, "the one who was to come." In Adam there was prefigured, in black, the bright and shining figure of the woman's Seed (Gen. 3:15), who would by His sole act do for all mankind what Adam had done, that is, determine all man's history henceforth, who would be the Beginning, the Head, and Representative of a new mankind. Paul seems to be alluding to the promise given in Gen. 3:15. The word translated "was to come" is often used of that which must and will be because God has promised it (cf. Col. 2:17; Matt. 11:14; Rom. 8:18). Paul echoes the wording of Gen. 3:15 in Rom. 16:20 (and there only in all his writings), an indication that the passage was running through his mind. In 7:11 his language echoes

that of Gen. 3:13; and in 8:20, where Paul is again dealing with the events of Gen. 3, he speaks of the fact that
creation was subjected to futility "in hope" — and Gen.
3:15 seems to be the only verse in the account of the
Fall which holds out any hope for fallen man and for
his fallen world.

The parallel between Adam and Christ has been
indicated, and the statement that Adam is the predic-
tive counterpart of Christ has been justified. One might
expect the comparison to be carried out forthwith. But
Paul is not the servant of Adam; he is the servant of
Jesus Christ and works to bring about the obedience
of faith to His glory (1:5). A flat, unqualified comparison
between Adam and Christ would leave too much unsaid
and would be an obscuration of the unique and gracious
splendor of Paul's Lord. Paul therefore prefaces the
comparison with a qualification which safeguards the
uniqueness of the Second Adam in the history of man.

15 The parallel is, after all, only a formal one; Adam
is only a negative and incomplete type of Him who was
to come. On Adam's side there is the trespass of one man
and the resultant death of "many." (Paul here uses
"many" in the Hebrew way, not in contrast to "all"
but simply in contrast to "one"; "many" is therefore
not essentially different from "all" in this context. Note
how in vv. 18-19, parallel statements, he uses "all" in
the first case and "many" in the second.) On the side
of Christ, however, there is the grace of God and the
free gift in grace of the one man Jesus Christ. The fullness of Paul's language matches the content; on the
side of Christ there is an "abounding," an overflowing,
an overwhelming and triumphant "much more." What
happened in the case of Adam's trespass was God's
reaction, His wrath; what comes upon man in the case

100

of Christ is God's prime native will and action, the action of the God who of His native grace gives life to the dead and calls into existence the things that do not exist. The one has the inevitability of doom, the other has the free exuberance of creation.

16 On Adam's side there is the one trespass and the resultant, necessary condemnation; on the side of Christ there is the miracle of justification, of God's free acquitting verdict in the face of the accumulated trespasses of mankind. **17** On the side of Adam there is one man's trespass and the uncontested reign of death through that one man (note how Paul again and again hammers home the universal effect of the *one* primal sin). On the other side there is again a "much more"; not the reign of a power over men but men themselves reigning, men royally alive, men who have received the abundance of God's grace and His free gift of righteousness. Through the one man Jesus Christ the hungerers and thirsters for righteousness have been filled and the poor have entered upon the promised kingdom of God (Matt. 5:6, 3). One is the iron logic of law; the other is the uncaused and divine creative miracle of grace.

Why does Paul labor so to mark this plus on the side of God and Christ? To judge from the whole of Paul's writings, one motive was to give God His glory; Paul would have no shadow fall upon the face of Him who shined in his heart with the light of His new creation. To proclaim His wrath and His love as evenly balanced and equal potencies in Him would be to blaspheme Him. John can say that God is love, and Paul and all the prophets and apostles say Amen to that. But neither John nor Paul nor any man in whom God's Spirit works would dare to say that God is wrath. Another motive was pastoral. Paul knows that man in this age must still do perpetual battle with sin, that he remains both saint and sinner all his days. Paul would assure embattled man that there is no touch-and-go balance between his sainthood and his sinnerhood, that the justified man's righteousness is a victorious certainty. To doubt that is the *sin* of fear of which John Donne spoke when he prayed to God the Father:

> I have a sin of fear that when I have spun
> My last thread I shall perish on the shore;
> But swear by Thyself that at my death Thy Son
> Shall shine as He shines now and heretofore.
> And having done that, Thou hast done;
> I fear no more.

18 "Then" resumes the comparison begun in v. 12. For all the disparity between Adam and Christ, the parallel holds. Paul can now state it very briefly, in two weighty sentences. Each man is the head of the race, each determines the fate of the race. One man's trespass means condemnation for all men; God's judgment on his trespass shapes the history of all mankind. One Man's act of righteousness (Paul can sum up Jesus' whole career in that one phrase! cf. Matt. 3:15) means acquittal for all men. The righteous Servant (Is. 53:11) makes many to be accounted righteous; they are righteous in God's eyes, and they shall live.

19 "Act of righteousness" is an eloquent description of the life and death of Christ, but it leaves untold, for Greek and English ears at any rate, one most important aspect of His life and death. The Gospel is the good news of the *Son* of God; it is the record of the Son's obedience to the Father, an obedience unto death, even the death of the cross. And so Paul states once more the sin of Adam and the righteous act of Christ in terms of their personal relationship to God, in terms of disobedience and obedience. He places side by side the man who grasped at equality with God, disobeyed, and thus brought guilt and death upon his race, and the Son of God who "did not count equality with God a thing to be grasped, but emptied himself, taking the form of a servant . . . and became obedient" (Phil. 2:6-8). Through His obedience, which took Him down into a criminal's death for all, "many will be made righteous." They shall believe in Him, be baptized in His name, and stand all clothed in Him before their Judge.

20 Adam and Christ are *the* key figures in the history of man before his God. Great as the Law is in its austere and high inviolable majesty, it has no significance that is comparable to theirs. Moses is not epoch-making in the sense that Adam was, and Christ is, epoch-making. "Law came in." It "slipped in," as a dictionary of New Testament Greek puts it, to occupy a secondary place and to perform a secondary function. It was not God's first word to the guilty sons of Adam; that word was the promise of Him who was to come (cf. Gal. 3:15-22). It was not God's last word to the sons of Adam either; that Word was Christ, the Redemption and the Righteousness of God in person. Between these two words the word of the Law was spoken; here it has its subordinate, and negative, role to play. It came in "to increase the trespass," to call forth and mark the sin of man as what sin at bottom always is, man's revolt against his God. This took place in Israel. At one point in mankind, in Israel to whom the Law was given, man was set before his God as Adam had been set. The house of Israel was the vineyard of the Lord of hosts, and the men of Judah were His pleasant planting; and the vineyard, tended

103

and protected by the Lord Himself, yielded wild grapes. Where the Lord looked for justice, the answer was bloodshed; and where the Lord looked for righteousness, "Behold, a cry!" (Is. 5:1-7). Here in Israel sin increased, and here sin was counted as nowhere else in the history of the nations (cf. Amos 3:2), just here where the Law was given and known — and honored.

Israel passed through the fire of God's judgment, and to this humbled Israel God sent His Son and asked the keepers of the vineyard to give God what is God's. The men of Israel who had the Law and honored it ("We have a law and by that law he ought to die," John 19:7), just they, cast the Son out of the vineyard and killed Him (Matt. 21:33-39). But just where sin increased, where Adam's trespass was reenacted on a national scale, the "much more" of the grace of God in Christ prevailed — grace abounded all the more. The Son of God, who went in freedom to His death, bore in that death the sins of those who destroyed Him. He interceded for them, drank the cup for them, paid the ransom for them, and rose again and sent His messengers of peace to them.

21 Sin had reigned in death; the constant dying life of man had been the constant witness to the sovereignty of sin. But the reign of sin went down before the reign of grace. Grace did what the Law, which promised life to the fulfiller but did not have the power to make alive the dead sons of Adam (Gal. 3:21; Rom. 8:3), could not achieve. Grace set up a reign whose gift to man is righteousness; grace now reigns "through righteousness." That reign means life, unbroken, full, eternal life; for the righteous shall live. That grace, that reign, that righteousness, that life — all are through Jesus Christ our Lord.

The Gospel Creates a New Life in Man   6:1 — 8:39

Until now Paul has concentrated on the new status the Gospel creates for man. This is all God's doing. The culminating section of the first major unit, 5:12-21, is a statement, made with the utmost objectivity, of the righteousness and obedience of Christ and of the judgment and the grace of God. There is no activity of man's here. Man receives the acquitting verdict of God in the passive desperation of faith; he "is justified by faith apart from the works of the law." (3:28)

But the creative force of the Gospel as the power of God for salvation is not exhausted in creating a new status for man. Even the first section of the letter has many indications that the new status is not something essentially external to the believer, that receptive faith is not only receptive. Man only receives from the giving hand of God; but he does receive, and he works with what he has received. The faith created by the Gospel is a living power in man. Paul has spoken of the obedience of faith (1:5). That obedience is obedience to the Lord Jesus Christ, who is no idle Lord and keeps no idle servants. Paul has spoken of the faith of the Romans as having a working effect, felt "in all the world" (1:8); he expects that his faith and theirs will strike living sparks of mutual encouragement when he comes to them (1:12). Men justified by faith rejoice in sufferings, Paul has said; they are men of endurance, men of character who bear up manfully beneath the cruel pressures of this world (5:3). The men of faith are a stout and durable breed.

Paul has, moreover, read to the Romans the verdict of God on the high and workless theology of the Jew

105

(who makes the knowledge of the Law his boast), and he has made it plain that no sacramental wrappings, such as circumcision, can shield man from the fires of God's wrath (2:17-29). That God will judge the world (3:6) remains an axiom for Paul the apostle, as it had been for Saul the Pharisee; his Gospel proclaims that God will judge the secrets of men by Christ Jesus and will render to each man according to his works (2:6, 16). The living God, whose Gospel Paul proclaims, wants living men who work.

Paul's own portrayal of himself has been a witness to his faith as to a faith that works. It could be a working faith only because it was, first, a receiving faith; when Paul spoke of the God who justifies the ungodly (4:5), he thought first of himself, the persecutor of the church of God (1 Cor. 15:9; Gal. 1:13, 23; 1 Tim. 1:13). But as surely as his faith received, it worked; the acquitting verdict of God that reached him through the calling Christ made of him a slave, an apostle (1:1), a man who owed a ministry to all the world and eagerly fulfilled it (1:14-15). He could therefore assert that he upheld the Law when he bade men believe (3:31), and he rejected as a blasphemous distortion of his Gospel the charge that his preaching of a free acquittal by the grace of God through faith gave men the liberty to say: "Let us do evil that good may come of it, let us sin on to the greater glory of God." (Cf. 3:8)

It is thoroughly characteristic of Paul, as it is of the whole New Testament, that he first proclaims salvation as the sole work of God and speaks of "faith alone" as the only possible correlative of grace. He is echoing the preaching of Jesus, who spoke His first beatitude upon the poor, the beggars who can but accept the largesse of the King who comes to them (Matt. 5:3), and pro-

106

nounced His blessing on those who hungered and thirsted for righteousness (Matt. 5:6). It is equally characteristic of Paul that he goes on to echo his Lord's beatitudes upon the merciful (Matt. 5:7) and on those whose lives so run against the grain of this unrighteous world that they are persecuted for righteousness' sake (Matt. 5:10); Paul, like his Lord, goes from the beggary of faith in the face of the Gospel to the transforming power of the Gospel of God, to the new and noble life that it creates in man, to faith that works through love (cf. Gal. 5:6). "We are His workmanship," the product of our God's creative word, "created in Christ Jesus for good works" (Eph. 2:10). The same act of God that gave man his new status, namely the death and resurrection of God's Son, gave man his new life; it liberated him from the power of sin (Ch. 6; note especially 6:3-4, 11), from the Law (Ch. 7; note especially 7:4-6), and from death. (Ch. 8; note especially 8:3-4, 10-11)

Man Is Freed from Sin   6

Freed from Sin by Sharing in Christ's Death
and Resurrection Through Baptism   *6:1-14*

¹ **What shall we say then? Are we to continue in sin that grace may abound? ² By no means! How can we who died to sin still live in it? ³ Do you not know that all of us who have been baptized into Christ Jesus were baptized into his death? ⁴ We were buried therefore with him by baptism into death, so that as Christ was raised from the dead by the glory of the Father, we too might walk in newness of life.**

⁵ For if we have been united with him in a death like his, we shall certainly be united with him in a resurrection like his. ⁶ We know that our old self was

crucified with him so that the sinful body might be destroyed, and we might no longer be enslaved to sin. [7] For he who has died is freed from sin. [8] But if we have died with Christ, we believe that we shall also live with him. [9] For we know that Christ being raised from the dead will never die again; death no longer has dominion over him. [10] The death he died he died to sin, once for all, but the life he lives he lives to God. [11] So you also must consider yourselves dead to sin and alive to God in Christ Jesus.

[12] Let not sin therefore reign in your mortal bodies, to make you obey their passions. [13] Do not yield your members to sin as instruments of wickedness, but yield yourselves to God as men who have been brought from death to life, and your members to God as instruments of righteousness. [14] For sin will have no dominion over you, since you are not under law but under grace.

1 There is a certain logic in the opening question: "Since the increase of sin leads to the abounding of grace (5:20), shall we persist in sin in order that grace may abound?" But it is cool, Satanic logic; there is in it the Satanic suggestion that we should exploit God, make His grace serve our selfish will, use His gifts to support us in our rebellion against God. It is the logic which the Tempter used on Jesus: "If You are the Son of God and enjoy a Father's favor, then get some good out of it; eat, insure Your risks with His providence, compromise and reign—anything but obey!" (cf. Matt. 4:1-11). 2 Paul rejects this logic as impious logic (the phrase rendered as "By no means!" has overtones of religious horror). His answer to the blasphemous ques-

tion shows how completely the new life is the creation of God, how deeply it is rooted in the Gospel. Paul answers the question not with an appeal or a command but with a statement. This statement speaks not of something we have done but of something that was done to us: "We . . . died to sin." What happened to us makes any further connection with sin impossible. Sin *cannot* be our life-element any longer; it cannot be the compelling impulse of our wills and the controlling bent of our desires as it once was (cf. Col. 3:7), for dead men have no wills and no desires.

3 When did this all-decisive event of death take place? How did we die? Every Christian knows that, for every Christian has been baptized. We know that we were baptized "into Christ." Our baptism effectually committed us to Him, clothed us in Him (Gal. 3:27), incorporated us all in Him (1 Cor. 12:12-13). One baptism gave us all one Lord (Eph. 4:5). He is Lord of all in the power of His divine love; that love made His death a death for all (2 Cor. 5:14-15). Therefore baptism "into Him" is a baptism into His death. **4** His death was a real, human death. His burial makes that plain; all the evangelists are at pains to emphasize the reality of Jesus' death by recording, in considerable detail, His burial. Our participation in His death is also full reality; we share His burial through our baptism into His death. Jesus laid down His life freely that He might "take it again" (John 10:17); whenever He predicted His passion and death, He predicted also His resurrection (e. g., Matt. 16:21; 17:22-23; 20:18-19). The life which He laid down in obedience to His Father's will the Father restored to Him. He was raised up "by the *glory* of the Father" — there, in that triumph over death, God glorified His name (John 12:28), there the full weight of the

109

Godhead was manifested mightily, there God revealed Himself as the Creator who gives life to the dead (4:17).

If the death and burial of Christ involve us who are baptized in His name, His resurrection from the dead involves us too; we, too, shall rise from death (cf. v. 8). Paul's first concern here, however, is not our future resurrection; he is intent on bringing home to us the fact that through our baptism we share in Christ's resurrection *now*. Christ was raised from the dead "that . . . we too might walk in newness of life." The new life, the life beyond the reach and dominion of death, the life of the world to come which Christ inaugurated by His resurrection is a present reality, present and at work in the Word and sacrament of the Gospel. It is a powerful, dynamic reality. We do not merely exist in it. We "walk" in it. "Walking" is a Jewish expression for conduct and activity frequent in Paul's letters. (Cf. Rom. 8:4; 13:13; here the same Greek word is translated "conduct ourselves" by the Revised Standard Version, which renders the same word as "behaving" in 1 Cor. 3:3 and as "lead the life" in 1 Cor. 7:17.)

5-10 Paul expands the statement he has made. All that follows in vv. 5-10 serves to underscore and illuminate the two basic thoughts of vv. 3-4, namely (1) the reality of our union, through Baptism, with Christ in His death and resurrection and (2) the wholly new quality of that resurrection-life in Christ.

(1) *The Reality of Our Union with Christ*

Three times Paul asserts the reality of our union with the dying and resurrected Christ (vv. 5, 6, 8). First, we have been united with Him "in a death like his" and "shall certainly be united with him in a resurrection like his" (v. 5). Here Paul uses the strongest possible

110

expression for our union with Christ in His death and resurrection; he says, literally, that we have "grown together" with Him. He therefore uses the expression "like his" of our death and resurrection, to safeguard the uniqueness of that one Man's death and resurrection. The very real reality of what happened to us in Baptism depends wholly on the reality of the death and the new life of the Christ. Second, "our old self was *crucified* with him" (v. 6). The death Christ died on the cross was a criminal's death, the death of the accursed (Gal. 3:13). In that death our old criminal self was included; there our old criminal self was judged and destroyed. This makes the newness of the resurrection-life possible. Third, "we have died with Christ," and we "believe that we shall also live with him" (v. 8). The reality of Christ's death and resurrection determines our whole existence; the controlling reality of our life now is the fact that we *shall* live. Our present life gets its character, direction, and purpose from the fact that we shall live with Him who lives a life beyond death, a life lived wholly to God, now that He has died an atoning death, once for all, to sin. (Vv. 9-10)

(2) *The Wholly New Quality of the Resurrection-Life*

The life that follows upon our death in Baptism is a life of a new kind. Since our old criminal self, the self native to us as sons of Adam, has been condemned and executed, our "sinful body" has been destroyed (v. 6). This manner of speaking about the body is strange to us. To understand Paul's language here we must recall that Paul, and the men of the Bible generally, look upon the body as an essential part of a man's self, as the expressive instrument of man's will. They can therefore speak of the one part of the body particularly involved

111

in an action as representing the whole person. Jesus' command to pluck out the offending eye and to cut off the offending hand is a familiar example of this mode of thought and speech (Matt. 5:29-30). Hamlet's reference to his hands as "these pickers and stealers" is a modern echo of this Biblical way of speaking.

The "sinful body" is, then, the body as expressive of our old self and its will—the throat breathing forth corruption like an opened grave, the deceiving tongue, the mouth full of curses and bitterness, the feet swift to shed blood, the eyes that will not look upon the fearful majesty of God (3:13-18). *This* body has been put out of action; we are no longer slaves of sin, with no will but the will of sin to control our lives. Death puts an end to all claims and cuts all ties. The sin that lorded it over us all our lives has no further claim on us; the dead slave is free at last (v. 7). That liberation from sin is possible only because the death we died was the death of Christ, in whom is our redemption. It is His new life that we can live henceforth (v. 8). The life of the risen Christ is a life beyond dying, beyond the dominion of death. When He was raised from the dead, He did not return to the life "in the likeness of sinful flesh" which had been His from birth, the life with the mark of death upon it. "He died to sin, once for all." On the cross He reached the end of a life determined wholly by the sin of man, a life in which He became the very embodiment of human sin under the judgment of God (2 Cor. 5:21; Gal. 3:13). Now He lives to God and sets us free for a life lived to God, a life in which our body is no longer a "sinful body" but can be presented to God as a living sacrifice. The body has become the expressive instrument of our will to worship God and do His will. (12:1-2)

11 "So you also must consider yourselves dead to

sin and alive to God in Christ Jesus." "You . . . must" —
this is the first imperative in the Letter to the Romans.
The revelation conveyed in the apostolic Gospel addresses our will; in revelation God enters our life and
determines it. He must enter our lives, for we cannot
bring Him down to us. Revelation is therefore, first of
all, declarative; it reports and conveys what God has
wrought. But revelation is also imperative; the Gospel
of God addresses the imprisoned will of man and sets
it free. Man under the Gospel-revelation of God is set
free to respond to His revelation. "You have died; you
are alive" — that is the declaration brought to man and
enacted upon man in his baptism. "Consider yourselves
dead; consider yourselves men raised from the dead" —
that is the imperative addressed to man in his baptism.
"Appropriate God's revelation of Himself, spell out
your new freedom in your thinking, your willing, your
action. Accept and declare the fact that God has set
you free."

Paul has prepared his readers for this imperative
by three references to their "knowing" in the preceding
verses: they know that they have been baptized into
the death of Christ Jesus (v. 3); they know that their
old self was crucified with Christ, so that their slavery
to sin is over (v. 6); they know that the risen Christ lives
a life over which death has no dominion (v. 9). This
"knowing" cannot and dare not remain a *mere* knowing.
It must result in action, for to know Christ is to know
Him (and serve Him) as Lord. Therefore the call to
action which follows the statement is based on Christ
and His death and resurrection: "Consider yourselves
dead to sin and alive to God *in Christ Jesus*." To make
a *mere* knowing of this knowing would be to "suppress
the truth" (1:18) all over again.

113

12 The reign of sin has been broken (v. 7); the body as a "sinful body" has been destroyed (v. 6). Therefore the imperative can follow and must follow: "Let not sin reign in your bodies." To know Christ is to be under this command; to know Christ is to have the power to obey it. And we need this power from Him. The body is still a *mortal* body; the final redemption of the body, which shall make the body a perfect instrument of our obedience, is still to come (8:23). This body therefore still has on it the mark of this age, the age in which sin reigns in death; it is perpetually threatened by the instinctive stirrings of sin that may again commit it to death. Its desires are still the desires of this world, not those of the world to come. To make this body the expressive instrument of our new life therefore calls for a continual exercise of the liberated will, a constant, resolute denial of the passions of the body. 13 If the reign of sin is overcome, that signifies something positive and specific in the life of man. The imperative is therefore not merely the negative command, to cease from wickedness; it is the positive command to serve God in the newness of our resurrection-life. And the imperative is specific; we are to yield *our members* to God as instruments of righteousness for concrete, bodily actions that embody and proclaim our newly-given life.

14 Before the imperative there stood the statement of what God has done; after the imperative there stands His promise. The imperative is bracketed by the experienced fact of God's creative grace and by the assurance of the continued working of that grace. We who were once under the power of sin (3:9) are now under the power of God's grace. The inward and renewing power of grace, not the external compulsion of the Law, is the power that enables us to live to God.

Liberated from Sin and Enslaved
to Righteousness Through the Word   6:15-23

¹⁵ What then? Are we to sin because we are not under law but under grace? By no means! ¹⁶ Do you not know that if you yield yourselves to any one as obedient slaves, you are slaves of the one whom you obey, either of sin, which leads to death, or of obedience, which leads to righteousness? ¹⁷ But thanks be to God, that you who were once slaves of sin have become obedient from the heart to the standard of teaching to which you were committed, ¹⁸ and, having been set free from sin, have become slaves of righteousness. ¹⁹ I am speaking in human terms, because of your natural limitations. For just as you once yielded your members to impurity and to greater and greater iniquity, so now yield your members to righteousness for sanctification.

²⁰ When you were slaves of sin, you were free in regard to righteousness. ²¹ But then what return did you get from the things of which you are now ashamed? The end of those things is death. ²² But now that you have been set free from sin and have become slaves of God, the return you get is sanctification and its end, eternal life. ²³ For the wages of sin is death, but the free gift of God is eternal life in Christ Jesus our Lord.

15 The language of the promise in v. 14, "since you are not under law but under grace," once more raises the question with which Paul began the chapter. If we are no longer hedged in by the command and the threat of God's law, are we not set free for a career of sin? Paul rejects the implications of this question as vehemently as he had rejected those of the original question;

115

and he answers the question in much the same way
as he has answered it in 6:1-14. The second half of the
chapter is a restatement of the basic idea of the first
half. We should remember that the apostolic letters were
intended for the ear, being read to the assembled
churches in their worship services (Col. 4:16; 1 Thess.
5:27; cf. Rev. 1:3); the ear needs more repetition than
the eye, which can go back at will to refresh the memory.
But the restatement is made with a difference. While
the first statement is an unfolding of Jesus' command
to make disciples of all nations by "baptizing them"
(Matt. 28:19) and speaks of the new life created in man
in terms of death and resurrection, the restatement is
an unfolding of Jesus' command to make disciples by
"teaching them" (Matt. 28:20) and speaks of the new
life created in man in terms of a liberation from the
slavery to sin and a reenslavement to righteousness.
The restatement also contains an enrichment of the
theme, a warning reference to the uncanny enslaving
power of sin, which still threatens the new life in man,
and a portrayal of the eternal consequences of the choice
which the liberated will of man must make between
the dominion of sin and the reign of God. (Vv. 16, 20-23)

16 "Do you not know. . . ?" Again, as in vv. 3, 6,
and 9, Paul appeals to his readers' knowledge; he writes
his whole letter, he says, "by way of reminder" (15:15).
The whole rich theology of the Letter to the Romans
is not an embroidering on the basic Gospel but simply
the unfolding of all that is implicit in the Gospel that
the Roman Christians, like all Christians everywhere,
already know. What the Christian knows, but is always
tempted to forget, is the hard fact that we cannot take
sin or leave it. Once we take sin, sin has taken us; for
sinning is always at bottom rebellion against God and

116

removes us from Him. Removed from Him, we return inevitably to the domination of sin. Paul's word is an echo of Jesus' saying: "Every one who commits sin is a slave to sin" (John 8:34). Freedom to sin is therefore merely a passport to slavery and a consignment to death.

The alternative to this slavery is a slavery too. Paul calls it, rather strangely, a slavery to obedience. This "obedience" is the religious act which Paul has previously called "the obedience of faith" and of which he will speak again in the next verse. It is the basic surrender of man's liberated will to the call and claim of God, the source of all concrete acts of obedience to His will; it "leads to righteousness" and therefore to life (cf. 1:17; 6:23). We cannot take or leave this alternative either; we cannot sample this obedience. Man is committed by it as exclusively as he is by his obedience to sin. Another saying of Jesus is the background to this statement: "No one can serve two masters" (Matt. 6:24). Both Jesus and Paul had the ancient slave in mind, who was the servant wholly and exclusively of the one master who owned him. He was at his master's disposal seven days a week and 24 hours a day.

17 Thus there is really only the choice between two servitudes, not between servitude and autonomous freedom. And for the Christians the choice has been made. It was their choice; they became obedient "from the heart." "Heart" in the language of the Bible means the whole inner life of man, his thinking, willing, and feeling. Yet their choice was of God's working, and Paul thanks God for it. They did not of themselves freely choose the "standard of teaching" that liberated them from sin. They "*were* committed" to it. The passive voice here, as so often in the New Testament, indicates an action by God; He committed them, He confiscated

117

them with His call. The Word of God is here called "standard of teaching," for here the transforming and formative effect of the Word is to be emphasized, an effect as decisive as that of Baptism.

18 This "standard of teaching" freed them from sin and made them slaves of righteousness. **19** And yet "slavery" is not wholly adequate to describe the gracious working of the call of God, that divine laying-claim to men's lives for which Paul has given thanks. That confiscation gives man the only genuine freedom that human history knows, the freedom for communion with his God, the liberty to live in the free obedience of a son of God (Rom. 8:14-16; Gal. 4:6-7). Paul has described the alternative in terms of human slavery "because of your (the Roman Christians') natural limitations" (literally, "because of the weakness of your flesh"). The man in whom the flesh and the spirit are still at war with each other (cf. Rom. 8:12-14; Gal. 5:17), the man who still recognizes in his heart the will of disobedient Adam, the man who still must fight off the claim of sin upon his mortal body—he needs to be told that sonship means obedience for all sons of God. For this aspect of sonship there is no better or stronger term than "slavery." And so Paul, after he has qualified his use of the image of the slave, speaks the slave-imperative: Be good slaves now to righteousness, as singly and as totally devoted to your master as when you were slaves to sin. You devoted your members, all your powers of action, to that service; render that same full-time, whole-man service now to righteousness. That former service was one which defiled you, and it exhausted itself in opposition to God ("iniquity"); it was dominated by the Satanic will of sin, which is stupid, monstrous, pure negation of all that is divine. Your service now is "for sanctification"; that

118

means that your action is caught up in God's action, for it is God alone who sanctifies. Your members all unite to confess in deed that God has consecrated you to be His own, that His "teaching" molds and governs all you do.

20-23 In closing Paul asserts once more how false a freedom the freedom to sin is and how true a freedom the enslavement to God is. He does so by pointing to the immediate and the everlasting consequences of the dominion of sin and of the reign of God.

20 The enslavement to sin had in it a sort of freedom. The slaves of sin were free "in respect to righteousness"; they could and did ignore the will of God. **21** But what a freedom it was! Men claimed by God and freed from sin look back upon the fruits of that freedom with shame, and they know where that freedom was doomed to end, in death. **22** But the slaves of God reap a rich harvest; they are caught up now into the motion of the God who sanctifies them and makes them doers of His will. They are caught up in God's motion and are swept toward God's eternal goal. God is the Creator, and He will have life, eternal life. **23** Sin is a tyrant who pays the stipulated soldiers' pay, no more, no less; the wages sin pays is death. But God is the Giver of the free and unearned gift, the Dealer-out of blessings to His undeserving own. He gives eternal life, and this life is "in Christ Jesus our Lord," in Him who is for us the very Righteousness of God.

Man Is Freed from the Law   7

Paul has drawn a hard line of division between the Gospel and the Law. The saving revelation of the righteousness of God is a revelation "apart from law" (3:21); a man is justified by the faith which the Gospel

119

creates in him "apart from works of law" (3:28; cf. 3:20). The Law is not, as Paul's Jewish contemporaries believed and asserted, a power for salvation; its working and effect is negative and destructive, the very opposite of the working and effect of the Gospel. The Law, far from saving the Jew, indicts him; it stops all mouths and makes all men accountable to God (3:19). Through the Law sin becomes an experienced, full reality in the life of man (3:20). The Law therefore "brings wrath" (4:15). The Law cannot stop the trespass of Adam, which flood-like sweeps all acres of mankind; rather, the Law only increases the trespass (5:20). Every statement Paul makes concerning the actual working of the Law, its effect on the life and fate of man, is a negative one.

This no to the Law comes to a climax in Ch. 6: "Sin will have no dominion over you, since you are not under *law* . . ." (6:14). Here liberation from sin and liberation from the Law are put into the closest possible relationship; the one is not possible without the other. Now, the statement that a life lived to God in full and unbroken devotion is possible only if the dominion of sin over man be overcome is clear and understandable; there is an evident religious logic in it. But liberation from the Law seems to be quite another matter. Why must a man be liberated from the Law in order to become a new creature who does the will of God? For the Law has, for Paul, too, a high and positive content and a profound significance. Paul was not being ironic when he said that the Jew had in the Law "the embodiment of knowledge and truth" (2:20). According to Paul, the Jew is doomed because he has sinned "under the law" (2:12), and the Gentile is accountable before God because God has inscribed upon his heart "what the law requires" (2:15). "Doers of the law" will be justified on that Day when God judges the secrets of men (2:13, 16). The Law is a word of the living God, the revelation of His will. It therefore bears witness in its own way to the righteousness of God now manifested in Christ (3:21); and the proclaimers of the Gospel can say, "We uphold the law" (3:31). To the original question — "Why must man be liberated from the Law?" — there is added the second question — "How can man be liberated from the Law, the express and uttered will of God? Who dares to set the Law aside?" Paul deals with these two questions in Ch. 7.

How Can Man Be Liberated from the Law?   *7:1-6*

¹ Do you not know, brethren — for I am speaking to those who know the law — that the law is binding on a person only during his life? ² Thus a married woman is bound by law to her husband as long as he lives; but if her husband dies she is discharged from the law concerning the husband. ³ Accordingly, she will be called an adulteress if she lives with another man while her husband is alive. But if her husband dies she is free from that law, and if she marries another man she is not an adulteress.

⁴ Likewise, my brethren, you have died to the law through the body of Christ, so that you may belong to another, to him who has been raised from the dead in order that we may bear fruit for God. ⁵ While we were living in the flesh, our sinful passions, aroused by the law, were at work in our members to bear fruit for death. ⁶ But now we are discharged from the law, dead to that which held us captive,

so that we serve not under the old written code but in the new life of the Spirit.

1 Paul answers the question "How can man be liberated from the Law?" by pointing to the Law itself. Law demands works, but with death all working ends. Death therefore ends all claims of the Law. 2 Paul illustrates this limitation of the Law from the law of marriage. A woman is bound to her husband by law as long as the husband lives. Once the husband dies, however, she is free, legally free, free on the law's own terms. 3 While her husband lived, to live with another man was a crime that stigmatized her publicly. The same action is now perfectly legal and wholly innocent. So radical is the difference brought about by death. 4 Applied to Christians, this means: In their case, too, death has made the mighty difference. They, too, were liberated from the Law by death. They too are legally free, free on the Law's own terms.

More than that, they were set free by God's own act; they owe their freedom not to any act of theirs, not to a new theology brought in by Paul, but to God Himself. They "died to the law through the body of Christ." When Christ's body hung upon the cross, when God spared not His own Son but gave Him up for us all (8:32), when Christ took on Himself for all of us the curse of the Law that struck us all (Gal. 3:13), then we died to the Law. The Law had done its utmost and was done with us, for we were all included in the body of the Crucified; His love, God's love, has made His death the death of all (2 Cor. 5:14). The same act of God that delivered us from the dominion of sin has freed us from the dominion of the Law, and for the same purpose: that we might live to Him who died and rose

122

for us and thus bear fruit for God, the fruit of a life drawn from His life and lived to His glory.

5 No such life is possible under the Law, for the Law cannot transform our "flesh." The Law cannot make sons of God out of sons of Adam. In the sons of Adam the Law can only arouse those sinful passions that work in man's members to make them "instruments of wickedness." In the face of the Law the rebellious will of man becomes incarnate in the sinful act. And with each sinful act that removes man from his God, the Fountainhead of life, the reign of death is strengthened and enriched. Men in their revolt against God "bear fruit for death." 6 But our death in Christ has changed all that. Death has released us from the old order under which we could only revolt and die. The old order of the written code of the Law, which could command but could not give us power to obey, has given way to the new order, the order of the Spirit promised for the world's last days (cf. Acts 2:17). The Spirit is the Lord and Giver of life, and in the new life which He creatively bestows we can become the people of God, His sons set free to serve Him. (Cf. Ex. 4:23)

This is the first mention of the Spirit in this section (Chs. 6–8); in vv. 5-6 Paul has set up fingerposts which point, not only to the rest of Ch. 7 but beyond that to the theme of Ch. 8, "the law of the Spirit of life in Christ Jesus." (8:2)

Why Must Man Be Liberated from the Law?   7:7-25

Paul has drawn a close parallel between sin and the Law. Everything that can be said of our relationship to sin can also be said of our relationship to the Law: We died to sin, and we died to the Law (6:2; 7:4);

if the result of our death to sin was "that . . . we . . . might walk in newness of life" (6:4), the result of our death to the Law was that we "serve . . . in the new life of the Spirit" (7:6); if death set us free from the claim of sin (6:7), it is also by death that "we are discharged from the law" (7:6). The alliance between the Law and sin seems so close and so unbreakable that the question "Shall we say that the law is sin?" seems inevitable and the answer to it almost obvious. But the obvious answer would be the answer of fatalism, not the answer of faith. Paul disclaims the obvious answer and goes on to make clear the connection between the Law and sin, first by recalling his own experience with the Law before Christ came to him (vv. 7-13) and then by vividly portraying the agonizing inner struggle that the Law provokes even in the new man Paul (vv. 14-25). In doing so he makes fully clear why man must be liberated from the Law if he is to walk in newness of life.

PAUL'S EXPERIENCE WITH THE LAW
BEFORE HIS CONVERSION   7:7-13

⁷ What then shall we say? That the law is sin? By no means! Yet, if it had not been for the law, I should not have known sin. I should not have known what it is to covet if the law had not said, "You shall not covet." ⁸ But sin, finding opportunity in the commandment, wrought in me all kinds of covetousness. Apart from the law sin lies dead. ⁹ I was once alive apart from the law, but when the commandment came, sin revived and I died; ¹⁰ the very commandment which promised life proved to be death to me. ¹¹ For sin, finding opportunity in the commandment, deceived me and by it killed me. ¹² So the law is holy, and the commandment is holy and just and good.

13 Did that which is good, then, bring death to me? By no means! It was sin, working death in me through what is good, in order that sin might be shown to be sin, and through the commandment might become sinful beyond measure.

7 The Law and sin are utterly disparate; and yet there is an uncannily close connection between the two. Paul came to "know" sin, to experience it as a powerful reality in his life, when he was confronted by the Law. It was the Law, with its "You shall not covet" that was the occasion of his coveting. The prohibition set the object of his coveting sharp and clear and bright before the window of his soul. He then looked full upon forbidden fruit and saw that it was good; then he was led to pit the contorted self-seeking of his desire against the will of God. 8 Yet it was not the Law itself but sin, that power which came into the world and reigned since Adam's fall, that wrought in him concupiscence and taught him

> . . . the black art to dispense
> A several sin to every sense.

Sin was the cause, the Law was but the occasion, of his coveting; sin found its opportunity "in the *command-ment*," in the Law which addressed him in the singular, personally, with an inescapable thou. "Apart from the law sin lies dead"—the Law is the footstep of God upon the grass that rouses the serpent sleeping there to life.

Paul speaks of the "commandment" here and in the following verses; "commandment" occurs five times in vv. 8-13 and only once elsewhere in the Letter to the Romans (13:9). This confirms what the use of the past tense in this section suggests, that Paul is speaking

125

of his Jewish past in these verses. The Jew tended to think of the Law as a series of separate commands and prohibitions; the Christian thinks of the Law as one unbroken whole, one great twin command of love, as Jesus did (Matt. 22:37-40). The latter view is reflected in vv. 14-25, where only the term "law" occurs.

9 "I was once alive apart from the law," Paul says; he is looking back to his youth perhaps. A Jewish boy was not held to an independent keeping of the Law until he was 13 years and one day old. Looking back to those sheltered years, Paul sees in them the time when the unselfconscious personality (not yet driven by sex, ambition, avarice, and the fear of death) has not yet grown up into full and conscious contradiction to the will of God. But the unmarred vitality of those years ended when the commandment confronted him personally. Then sin sprang into life and exercised its dominion over him; then he came to know the reign of sin in his life as a reign "in death" (cf. 5:21). **10** The commandment promised life, but only to the doer: by *doing* the statutes and ordinances of the Lord a man shall live (Lev. 18:5). The alternative to the promise of life is: "Cursed be he who does not confirm the words of this law by doing them" (Deut. 27:26), and the curse means death. **11** It was the Satanic power of sin, not the Law itself, that invoked the deadly curse on Paul. That black day when the serpent used the command of God to alienate man from his God (Gen. 3:1-5) was repeated in the life of Paul; sin exploited the commandment to deceive him and so killed him. The prospect of transgression conjures up the vision of the free, the full, the unfettered life; only when we have taken the unretraceable step down the road of transgression do we come to know that we are on the road of death.

126

12 So the Law itself remains holy, whatever unholy uses sin may put it to; it is God's own word and expresses His will. The claim it makes on man in the commandment is God's own claim, a holy claim; it is the claim of the Creator on His creature, a just claim. The commandment is good—its promise of life is a true promise. 13 That which is "good" in the supreme sense of that much-worn word, that which is clothed with the qualities of God Himself, cannot be the cause of death. When sin uses this good to work death in man, sin is unmasked as what sin really is, as total opposition to the goodness of God, as utter negation of all that is divine, as the Satanically monstrous will that wills to ruin the creation of God, that very good creation which moved the morning stars to sing together and made the sons of God all shout for joy. (Job 38:7)

Man under the Law is man exposed to this monstrous will of sin; he is impotent to resist it and cannot overcome it. He must be liberated from the Law if he is to be a doer of the will of God, and only the new life of the Spirit can create the new heart of the servant and son of God. The Law can take man to that ultimate dead end where he must turn and hear the word of God which gives him life; but the Law itself has not the power to make alive. (Gal. 3:21)

PAUL'S EXPERIENCE WITH THE LAW
AS A CHRISTIAN   7:14-25

14 We know that the law is spiritual; but I am carnal, sold under sin. 15 I do not understand my own actions. For I do not do what I want, but I do the very thing I hate. 16 Now if I do what I do not want, I agree that the law is good. 17 So then it is no

127

longer I that do it, but sin which dwells within me. [18] For I know that nothing good dwells within me, that is, in my flesh. I can will what is right, but I cannot do it. [19] For I do not do the good I want, but the evil I do not want is what I do. [20] Now if I do what I do not want, it is no longer I that do it, but sin which dwells within me.

[21] So I find it to be a law that when I want to do right, evil lies close at hand. [22] For I delight in the law of God, in my inmost self, [23] but I see in my members another law at war with the law of my mind and making me captive to the law of sin which dwells in my members. [24] Wretched man that I am! Who will deliver me from this body of death? [25] Thanks be to God through Jesus Christ our Lord! So then, I of myself serve the law of God with my mind, but with my flesh I serve the law of sin.

SOLD UNDER SIN

14 In vv. 7-13 Paul spoke in the past tense; he now speaks in the present tense and continues to speak in the present tense to the end of the chapter. He is, it would seem, speaking of his current Christian experience with the Law. He sets himself over against the Law: The Law is "spiritual," that is, it has on it the mark of its divine origin, and it makes a claim as sweeping and as profound as only God Himself, the Creator, can make; it says, "Give me your heart." Paul, when confronted by the Law, is everything that the Law is not; he is "carnal," a creature of flesh and blood confronted by God, who is Spirit (John 4:24). Another power lays claim to him and unnaturally divides his loyalty. He is "sold under sin." Such a description, applied to a man in Christ, is a startling one. It should be noted, however,

that Paul does not use the term he has used of man outside Christ in his relationship to sin; he does not say of himself in the present what he said of the Romans in their pagan past. He does not call himself a "slave" of sin. Slavery involves a total undivided devotion which shuts out every other claim and makes impossible any other tie (cf. 6:20). In the present case, the relationship of the "I" to sin is not simply that of slave to Lord.

The following verses (15-17) make clear that the tie described by "sold under sin" is not an absolute tie and that the claim of sin is offset by an anterior, competing, and superior claim. 15 Paul does not "understand" his own actions. The word translated "understand" is the same word which is usually rendered as "know" and often has, in Biblical usage, a peculiarly strong and personal meaning. For example, when Jesus "on that day" shall say to those who called Him Lord but did not do His Father's will, "I never *knew* you" (Matt. 7:23), the meaning of His words will be: "There never was a personal communion between you and Me, I do not know you as My own, you cannot rightly call Me Lord." There are many examples of this kind of "knowing" in the Bible, a knowing which involves a communion between the will and heart of the knower and the thing or person known (for Paul, cf. 1 Cor. 8:3; Gal. 4:9; Phil. 3:10). What Paul is saying of his sinful actions is, then: "These deeds are not properly *mine;* I do not recognize them as children of my will." Note also that the idea of "not understand" is repeated and intensified in the words "not . . . want" and "hate."

16 There is an inner dissonance in Paul's life, a disharmony between his essential will, which assents to the Law, and his actions, which contradict that will. 17 Paul's expression for this inner dissonance is even

stronger here; he describes it as a clash between his "I," his very self, and "sin which dwells within" him. This clash is elaborated in the following verses. (Vv. 17-20)

"I" AND "INDWELLING SIN"

18 Paul "knows"; sin, though it still dwells in him, can no longer deceive him (cf. v. 11). He is conscious of his impotence for good as he never was before — in his "flesh," in his coveting human self, which still seeks to withdraw itself from God, no good dwells; no goodness has its permanent abode in him; he has no righteousness that he can call "his" (cf. Phil. 3:9; Rom. 10:3). He cannot live on the illusion that God will count the will for the deed, for God's law says, "Do!" The willed good that remains undone is no good at all. **19** More than that, there is for Paul no intermediate state between good and evil. Paul cannot paint any deed of his in neutral hues. He wills what is good; he does what is *bad*. V. 19 goes beyond v. 15 in that it expressly calls the will good and the deed bad. **20** And so Paul repeats his previous verdict (v. 17) upon himself; there is an apparently hopeless cleavage, or contradiction, between his essential "I" and "indwelling sin."

THE BATTLE OF THE "LAWS"

21 This is a difficult verse, one in which Paul writes his own peculiar kind of shorthand. The rendering of the Revised Standard Version is the one adopted by the majority of scholars, and it makes good sense, namely: This clash between the "I" and "indwelling sin" is a "law"; it is recurrent, regular, unfailing, like the operation of the law of gravity. But it is doubtful whether in all the varieties of meaning in which Paul uses "law" (e. g., 3:27, translated "principle"; 7:23; 8:2)

there is an exact parallel to this one, which seems so
natural to us of the scientific Western world. Moreover,
Paul did not write "*a* law"; he wrote "*the* Law," and
"*the* Law" has all along meant "the law of God." A very
literal translation of his words would read thus: "So
then I find the Law: When I desire to do what is good,
what is evil lies ready to my hand." It seems best to
take "the Law" in the usual sense. One can then reproduce the apostle's meaning thus: "This is what my
experience with the Law comes to: When I desire to
do the good which it enjoins, the evil which the Law
forbids lies always ready to my hand." The verse, then,
serves to recall the main theme of the section, the necessity of liberation from the Law, and to introduce the
following description of the battle of the laws within
believing man. (Vv. 22-23)

22-23 In these verses the description of the dissonance between the ready will of man as confronted
by the Law, on the one hand, and the impotence of
man to achieve righteousness by way of the Law, on
the other hand, reaches its climax. Paul caps his previous statement, "I agree that the law is good" (v. 16),
with the stronger statement, "I *delight* in the law of
God"; and he explicitly attributes that delight to his
"inmost self" (literally, "the inner man"). This "inner
man" would correspond to the essential "I" of vv. 17
and 20, the "I" opposed to "indwelling sin." In the two
other passages where Paul uses "inner man" (2 Cor.
4:16; Eph. 3:16), "inner man" signifies the man in Christ,
the new creature, the man who is already tasting the
powers of the world to come.

It is the new man Paul who gives his glad assent
to the law of God; but he "sees" (again, that new clarity
of vision, that unshrinking honesty in observation which

the power of sin cannot overcome with its deceit) – he sees himself, his bodily existence, as a battlefield on which conflicting forces meet to join battle. There are four forces: The law of God, the other law, the law of the mind, the law of sin in the members. Two of them are major forces: The law of God, in which Paul delights, and the other law, which wages a war of conquest in Paul's members. This other law is, it would seem, that power of sin which came into the world with Adam's sin and seeks continually to extend, or to reestablish, its reign. Each of the major forces has its own ally within Paul, fifth-column forces as it were. The law of the mind is the ally of the law of God; it is the "I" that calls the Law good, the "inner man" who delights in the Law. The law of sin in the members is the ally of the other law; this is the power of sin which lives in man and strives to commit him to the other law, which is in opposition to the law of God. If the other law would win, it must overcome the law of the mind; it seeks to do so by utilizing the law of sin in the members. (The phrase, "making me captive *to* the law of sin" might perhaps be better rendered as "making me a captive *by means of, with the help of,* the law of sin which dwells in my members.")

24 The battle is a desperate one; the unceasing encroachment of sin threatens ever and again to make the body a "sinful body" (6:6) and thus to doom it to death. Paul cries out for deliverance; it here becomes plain that the sharp distinction which he has drawn between his "I" and "indwelling sin" is not an attempt to excuse his sinning. His sinning is his guilt, and Paul fears the death which is the penalty of sin. Paul cries out for deliverance from "*this* body of death," *this* body as beset by powers too strong for him. He is not crying out for a state of disembodied bliss; we need read no further than 8:23 to learn that Paul hopes and prays for "the redemption of our bodies." He longs for the re-deemed body, the body which shall be the perfectly expressive instrument of his will to love and serve his Lord.

25a The man sold under sin, the desperate and wretched man, even he, does not cry out in vain. Paul's prayer, he knows, is heard; and he gives thanks to God "through Jesus Christ our Lord." Through Him we have peace with God and have access to the grace in which we stand (5:1-2). Through Him we have received reconciliation and shall be saved through Him from the wrath to come (5:9, 11). Through Him we shall reign in life, for through His righteous deed and His obedi-ence we shall be justified (5:17-19). Through His body we have died to the Law (7:4). In the midst of our strug-gle and failures He remains our Lord; through Him we desperate and embattled men can still give thanks to God. The lowering sky above our battlefield has sud-denly grown bright.

25b The brighter vistas opened up by Ch. 8 are now in view. "Indwelling sin" is not the whole and certainly not the decisive reality in the Christian life, real and terrible as it is; *the* decisive reality is the in-dwelling Spirit (8:11). Paul can once more sum up, calmly now, the theme that has been dominant since v. 14. The essential I, dominated by the law of the mind, is a de-voted slave to the law of God; but the devotion is real and becomes a living reality only in a constant struggle against the law of sin, to which the flesh is loyal—just as the liberation from sin (6:6-7) is an actuality only in the Christian's constant, active no to sin (6:12-13). No one who takes this apostolic word seriously can any

133

longer doubt that if the righteous is to live he cannot become righteous and live by way of the Law; he must be liberated from the Law.

THE "WRETCHED MAN"

To many, Paul's acute consciousness of the sin that dogs the Christian even in his new, free life seems over-wrought, and his picture of the perpetual failure of the new man in his confrontation with the law of God seems overdrawn. Is there not something morbid about this hypersensitivity to sin, this grim introspection, this un-sparing castigation of oneself? But it is not Paul who is morbid. It is the 20th-century man who is diseased with a sickly secularity. Modern man calls "natural" that which a healthy judgment, made whole by the Spirit of God, can only call in the highest degree unnatural, namely, withdrawal from God, revolt against God, a turning-away from the life of God to death. That is how Jesus looked on sin. Sin is, for Jesus, the son leaving the father's house, going away to live like a pig and, finally, with the pigs (Luke 15:11-16). What healthy judgment can call that normal, natural, or venial? That is how Paul looks on sin. Paul's view of sin is not ori-ented in some ethical code; it is oriented in God, God as now revealed in Christ. He called man's primal sin ungodliness; man's exuberant and varied acts of wick-edness are but the corollary to the fact that man has refused the invitation of God. "Whatever does not pro-ceed from faith is sin," Paul says (14:23). Whatever removes the Lord Jesus Christ from His Lordship over any portion of man's life, however "indifferent" it may be in itself, is sin in Paul's eyes. We need not imagine unknown lurid chapters in the life of Paul as back-ground to his words "I do the very thing I hate" (7:15).

134

These words come true in every thought or act that does not spring from man's communion with his Lord.

Paul's portrait of the stumbling, struggling saint in 7:14-25 is therefore of inestimable value. It keeps Christianity Christian, in the full sense of the word. It is the authentic commentary on Jesus' words concerning the vine and the branches, "Apart from me you can do nothing" (John 15:5). It cuts off the delusion that the disciple of Jesus can ever cease to be a disciple, that he can become autonomous, with a righteousness that he can call his own. Paul's words also put an end to the delusion that the Christian life can ever be a static life. The Christian life is of necessity a life to be lived on the forgiveness of God. Such a life will be that straining forward to lay hold of the Christ who has laid hold of man (Phil. 3:12-13). The new clarity of vision that comes to man in Christ is agony; the new man sees sin in himself where he did not see it before. But it is an integral part of the new life; the new man never leaves it wholly behind him in this world, but the new man again and again rises above it and finds help and peace where he did not find it before, through Jesus Christ, his Lord. There is no way to the victorious confidence of Romans 8 but the unshrinking self-appraisal of Romans 7. It is over the waters of man's ruined manhood that the Spirit broods and works.

To many others the picture that Paul draws in 7:14-25 seems not only overdrawn; it seems to them inconceivable as a picture of the same Christian who is pictured in Ch. 6 as liberated from sin and in Ch. 8 as triumphing over death. They therefore take the whole section 7:7-25 as a portrait of man simply (*not* man in Christ) as confronted by the Law. This man, they concede, is viewed with the eyes of faith, for no man apart from Christ could diagnose the deep disease of man so surely. But it is man in general, not man in Christ, who is pictured here by Paul. Thus the problem created by such strong expressions as "sold under sin" and "this body of death" is solved. But is the solution a real solution? The following points should be noted:

1) Chs. 6, 7, and 8 constitute a unit. In each of them the new life created in man by the Gospel is described. In each of them this new life is a reality just in its conflict with the old. Man liberated from sin is called upon to struggle against sin (Ch. 6). Man freed from the law of sin and death and endued with the Spirit of sonship is still longing for full sonship and redemption of the body and is called upon to assert the new life of the Spirit in battle against the old (8:2, 15, 23). Into this scheme of things Ch. 7, as interpreted above, fits perfectly; the new, decisive reality, that of liberation from the Law, is a reality which is present and actual in conflict and struggle.

2) Paul changes from the past tense to the present tense at v. 14. It is hard to explain why, if he is not turning from the pre-Christian past to the Christian present.

3) If we take 7:14-25 to refer to the new man, we remain in harmony with Paul's thought elsewhere. Gal. 5:17, addressed to Christians and speaking of the Christian life, speaks in equally drastic terms of the conflict between the Spirit and the flesh: "These are opposed to each other, to prevent you from doing what you would." If we refer 7:14-25 to man outside Christ, we find Paul here attributing to the natural human "mind" an assent to, and a harmony with, the law of God which he expressly denies elsewhere, in the very next chapter of the Letter to the Romans in fact. (8:7)

136

Other arguments might be advanced, but these are the essential ones. The passage is a difficult one and leaves us with unsolved problems on any interpretation. But it is hardly wisdom to purchase a solution of some of the problems at the cost of creating new ones.

Man Is Freed from Death:
The Law of the Spirit of Life in Christ Jesus   8

The Establishment of the Law of the Spirit of Life   8:1-8

¹ There is therefore now no condemnation for those who are in Christ Jesus. ² For the law of the Spirit of life in Christ Jesus has set me free from the law of sin and death. ³ For God has done what the law, weakened by the flesh, could not do: sending his own Son in the likeness of sinful flesh and for sin,ⁱ he condemned sin in the flesh, ⁴ in order that the just requirement of the law might be fulfilled in us, who walk not according to the flesh but according to the Spirit. ⁵ For those who live according to the flesh set their minds on the things of the flesh, but those who live according to the Spirit set their minds on the things of the Spirit. ⁶ To set the mind on the flesh is death, but to set the mind on the Spirit is life and peace. ⁷ For the mind that is set on the flesh is hostile to God; it does not submit to God's law, indeed it cannot; ⁸ and those who are in the flesh cannot please God.

ⁱ Or *and as a sin offering*

1 "Not under the old written code but in the new life of the Spirit" (7:6); the new life, if it is to be *life*, cannot be a return to the Law. The new life is wholly

137

and exclusively life in Christ. "Therefore" — since Christ is the answer to our every need, since He is the righteousness of God for us in the beggary of our own unrighteousness — "therefore," the logic of faith asserts, if the Law condemns us, we are free from condemnation in Christ, free forever in the great "now" of the manifestation of righteousness of God (cf. 3:21).

2 Where sin reigns, there is death (6:16, 21, 23); where the Law holds, there is death (7:5, 10, 11, 13, 24). Where Jesus Christ is Lord, sin is overcome and the Law no longer controls and condemns. Where Jesus Christ is Lord, there is a new "law," a new powerful and compelling order of things which sets men free from every other order. Christ's order is the order of righteousness and life, before which the old order of sin and death goes down in defeat forever. Forever, for this life is genuine life, life given by "the Spirit of life."

THE HOLY SPIRIT

Our English use of "spirit" and "spiritual" has cast a gray veil over the meaning of "Spirit of life"; the Spirit of God has become for us a pale and unsubstantial member of the Holy Trinity. We need to recall what a mighty and creative power the Spirit, in the language of the Bible, is, active in the creation of the world (Gen. 1:2), active in the mighty deeds of Israel's judges, those deliverers whom God raised up for His people when all seemed lost (Judg. 3:10; 6:34; 11:29); active in Israel's anointed kings (1 Sam. 16:13), in the history of Israel among the nations (Is. 31:3), in the Word of God that came to Israel's prophets (e. g., Ezek. 3:12, 14; 11:5; Zech. 7:12); active in the Messiah destined to restore God's righteous order and the peace of paradise on

138

earth (Is. 11:2) and in the Servant of the Lord destined to bring God's people back to God and to shed God's redeeming light on all the peoples of the earth (Is. 42:1, 6); active in the promised re-creation of the people of God (Ezek. 37:14; Is. 4:2-4; 44:3; Joel 2:28-32) and of the world (Is. 32:15 ff.); active in the Christ who came, who was conceived by the Spirit (Matt. 1:18, 20; Luke 1:35), endued with Spirit at His baptism (Matt. 3:16), led and empowered by the Spirit in His victory over Satan (Matt. 4:1-11; 12:28), who performed His mighty deeds in the power of the Spirit (Luke 4:14; Acts 10:38); active in the apostolate (Acts 1:8). Everywhere where man's possibilities are at an end and the free and sovereign creative possibilities of God begin, we find the presence and the working of the Spirit of God.

For the writings of Paul the first statement in this section concerning the Spirit is characteristic; the Spirit is the author of "new life" (7:6), that new divine life which breaks into a world under the reign of death and ushers in the new world of God, the world to come. The kingdom of God with its ultimate gifts of righteousness, peace, and joy, is present "in the Holy Spirit" (14:17). The apostles, the messengers of Christ, are Spirit-filled, Spirit-guided and Spirit-empowered men; their ministry is a ministry of the new covenant, a ministry in the Spirit (2 Cor. 3:6, 8; cf. Rom. 15:19; 1 Cor. 2:4, 13; 7:40; 2 Cor. 4:13; 1 Thess. 1:5). To the Spirit they owe the revelation given them (1 Cor. 2:10; Eph. 3:5; 1 Tim. 4:1) and their inspiration (1 Cor. 2:13; 12:8); their word is a word filled with the power of the Spirit (1 Cor. 2:4). Their word calls into being a new people of God "sanctified by the Holy Spirit" (Rom. 15:16). The characteristic token of this people is that the Spirit dwells in them, in all of them. (Rom. 8:9; 1 Cor. 3:16; 6:19; 2 Tim. 1:14; cf. Gal. 6:1)

139

This Spirit-filled people live upon the threshold of the world to come, they breathe the air of the new world of God. The present working of the Spirit is the first fruits, the beginning of the greater harvest of the world to come (Rom. 8:23), the guarantee to God's people that they shall enter into the promised inheritance (2 Cor. 1:22; 5:5; Eph. 1:13-14). With the gift of the Spirit, God has set His seal upon His people, has marked them as His own forever, destined them for new, unending life with Him (Eph. 1:13; 4:30). What Jesus promised for the end of days, that His disciples should be called the sons of God (Matt. 5:9) is a reality already inaugurated in this people, inaugurated by the Spirit (Rom. 8:14-16; Gal. 4:6) and therefore sure to be completed and consummated (Rom. 8:23). By the Spirit life belongs to the members of this people, new life, eternal life, the life of God (Rom. 8:6, 10, 11; 2 Cor. 3:6; Gal. 6:8). The glory of the world to come shines on them now, and day by day they grow more like the Lord of glory, whose they are. (2 Cor. 3:18)

By the Spirit they taste the powers of the world to come, and these powers of the Spirit are powers that move men to obedience and enable them to walk according to the will of God. Men do not "enjoy" the Spirit or luxuriate in Him; they are *led* by Him and walk by Him (Rom. 8:14; Gal. 5:16, 18, 25). It is by the Spirit that men learn to call Jesus Lord and learn to serve, to use the Spirit's gift for ministry to all (1 Cor. 12:3 ff.). The Spirit is the Spirit of wisdom and revelation (Eph. 1:17), operative in the Word they hear (Eph. 6:17), in Baptism and in the Supper of the Lord (Titus 3:5-6; 1 Cor. 12:13). The Spirit guides their prayers (Rom. 8:26; Eph. 6:18) and shapes their worship (Phil. 3:3). The Spirit is the power in their daily lives of hope (Rom.

15:13; Eph. 3:16); He puts upon those lives the impress of meekness (Gal. 6:1), of fidelity to one's trust (2 Tim. 1:14), and of love (Rom. 15:30; Col. 1:8; cf. 1 Cor. 13, which comes under the heading, "Concerning spiritual gifts," 1 Cor. 12:1); and He inspires in men the will to unity. (1 Cor. 12:13; Eph. 4:3, 4; Phil. 1:27)

The Spirit makes men's lives to be healthy, divinely normal lives; these lives know peace (Rom. 8:6; 14:17). This peace is not the grim and quiet piety which sings psalms in a doleful dump and through its nose. Men who through the Spirit know this peace have access to the Father. Their lives are lives of liberty (Rom. 8:21; 2 Cor. 3:17), of sure hope (Rom. 5:5), lives that glow (Rom. 12:11), lives of joy (Rom. 14:17; 1 Thess. 1:6), lives with a high intoxication which breaks into song. (Eph. 5:18)

All that the Christ is for His own is present and at work in the Spirit. Paul can even, on occasion, simply equate the Spirit and his Lord (2 Cor. 3:17; cf. 1 Cor. 6:11, 17; 15:45). The life of the Spirit is "life in Christ Jesus." (Rom. 8:2)

3 It is only natural to hear, then, that the law of the Spirit of life, this bright new order, was inaugurated and established by the sending of the Christ, the Son of God. Over against the order of sin and death the Law was impotent; "the law, weakened by the flesh, could not"—these words recall what Paul has said of the Law in Ch. 7 and at the close of Ch. 5. The Law cannot bring life to men in the flesh, to sons of Adam, because the Law cannot overcome the "law of sin and death." The Law can only bring out into the open, intensify, and increase the trespass of Adam, and it makes of man's body a "body of death." What the Law could not do God has done; again it is the death of

141

Christ, the Cross, that is the supreme revelation of God. There, in the Cross, the Son of God appeared wholly identified with man; there He was fully and openly "in the likeness of sinful flesh." It was a full likeness, a complete identification; and yet it was a "likeness" only, for here One "who knew no sin" was made "for our sake . . . to be sin" (2 Cor. 5:21). Flesh was not native to Him, and sin was alien to Him. Therefore He could be what no other man in the flesh could be "for sin," a pure sacrifice for the sin of others, One whose blood could make atonement for men's souls (Lev. 17:11).

His death was a sacrificial death; and it was a penal death, a death under the judgment of God. In the incarnate Son, in His flesh, God "condemned" sin. In the divine judgment there is no gap between the pronouncement of judgment and the execution of it; verdict and execution are one. "Condemnation" therefore means that sin was executed, its power broken, as the following verse makes plain. 4 In the life of Jesus the Spirit invaded mankind; by the death of Jesus the Spirit was released for man, the creature of flesh. The new law of the Spirit of life in Christ Jesus is now operative. And so the purpose and result of the death of the Son of God is that "the just requirement of the law is fulfilled in us." Paul speaks of the *"just requirement"* of the Law, not of the Law itself or of the commandment; he is not reverting to the Law, and he is not making the Law the measure of man's righteousness. But he is saying what he has said before, that the Law is the revelation of the will of God. Therefore the Spirit wills what the "spiritual" Law wills; and that spiritual will is now created *in* man, man who now walks by the power of the Spirit. No fulfillment of the will of God is ever a fulfillment *"by* us"; Ch. 7 has made that plain.

It is fulfilled "*in* us," in men whose life is no longer determined by the flesh, in men who are no longer inheritors of the will of Adam; it is fulfilled by men in whom the Spirit dwells and creates a new will.

5 Nothing less than this new, creative action of God will do; the situation is too radically desperate for anything less. For "flesh" is not only something about man that hinders him; "flesh" is the whole bent and set of his mind, the whole impetus of his life. Likewise the Spirit is not something added to man, an auxiliary force or an enabling plus; the indwelling of the Spirit means the creative renewal of the whole man which gives a wholly new bent and set of mind. 6 And these two bents, or impulses, are an absolute antithesis; one means death, the other life and health ("peace"). 7 The bent of the flesh is an impetus toward death, for it is hostility to God, and its essence is an instinctive resistance to God. 8 Men in the flesh cannot "please" God; they can render Him no free and willing service.

The Present Life of the Christian Under the
New Law   8:9-17

⁹ But you are not in the flesh, you are in the Spirit, if the Spirit of God really dwells in you. Any one who does not have the Spirit of Christ does not belong to him. ¹⁰ But if Christ is in you, although your bodies are dead because of sin, your spirits are alive because of righteousness. ¹¹ If the Spirit of him who raised Jesus from the dead dwells in you, he who raised Christ Jesus from the dead will give life to your mortal bodies also through his Spirit which dwells in you.

¹² So then, brethren, we are debtors, not to the

143

flesh, to live according to the flesh — [13] for if you live according to the flesh you will die, but if by the Spirit you put to death the deeds of the body you will live. [14] For all who are led by the Spirit of God are sons of God. [15] For you did not receive the spirit of slavery to fall back into fear, but you have received the spirit of sonship. When we cry, "Abba! Father!" [16] it is the Spirit himself bearing witness with our spirit that we are children of God, [17] and if children, then heirs, heirs of God and fellow heirs with Christ, provided we suffer with him in order that we may also be glorified with him.

9 The Christian is no longer "in the flesh" in the sense of 7:5, in the sense, namely, that the flesh wholly dominates his life and dictates his actions; he is "in the Spirit." That is the dominant and decisive reality of his existence. There still is indwelling sin, but it is the indwelling Spirit that is the characteristic mark of the Christian, of every Christian. Unless the Spirit of God and of Christ dwells in him, he does not belong to Christ, he is not a member of the new people of God. 10 This fact determines the present life of the Christian. Though the body be still "this body of death" (7:24) because of indwelling sin and though the body still awaits its redemption in the world to come (8:23), the law of the Spirit of life is in force "because of righteousness," that is, because of Christ. He is the given righteousness of God in Person, and the new life is "in Him." The believer is clothed in that righteousness, and he shall therefore live.

The translation "*Your spirits* are alive because of righteousness" is possible, but the rendering "*The Spirit is life* because of righteousness" sticks closer to the words of Paul and is supported by the following verse, which speaks of "mortal bodies" and of "the Spirit" and of the contrast and the connection between the two.

11 If the indwelling of the Spirit determines the present, it determines the future too. In fact, it determines the present just because it determines the future, for the Christian lives on his prospects (cf. v. 13). The indwelling Spirit is the Spirit of God who raised Christ Jesus from the dead. God raised Him who identified Himself wholly with our sinful flesh and bore the whole guilt and condemnation of our sinful flesh. If He was raised, that involves us, for we are by Baptism incorporated in Him. Through the creative Spirit the God who does wonders will "give life to" our mortal bodies. Our bodies will not be raised to live the old life over again; they will be wholly freed from the reign of death. They will no longer be bodies of death but live bodies whose members are instruments of righteousness, redeemed for everlasting service to our God.

12 That is the present reality; any faithful picture of it must be a picture of the future too, just as a true description of an heir (cf. v. 17) must include a description of the wealth he will one day call his own. If it is a present, divine reality, it is therefore also a present obligation, a divine claim laid upon us: "We are debtors." We owe it to our Creator and Deliverer to *live* the life which He has given us. We dare not go the way of the flesh again, for that would be to nullify His work in us. **13-14** For that way means death. The Spirit is not only a blessing to be enjoyed but a power which must work in us. The Spirit does not destroy our will but makes us capable of willing and of doing; through Him we can put to death, that is, make cease, those "deeds of the body" which make the body "this body of death."

145

So we shall please God and fulfill the just requirements of His law; so we shall live. The Spirit of the Son has made us sons (cf. v. 9b). The Son lived a life of pure obedience to His God (Matt. 4:1-11); He was "led by the Spirit" into conflict and to victory. Sons of God are sons in action, or they are not sons at all; they are *led* by the Spirit.

15 We are sons, free sons; the new life with its new obligation is not a reenslavement to the Law, in failure and fear. Our prayers testify to that. We have access to God in the Spirit (cf. Eph. 2:18); we call Him Father; we can even use Jesus' own Aramaic word "Abba" when we speak to Him. God has drawn so close to us in His Son, and in His Spirit is so near to us, that we can make bold to use the impertinent familiarity of that children's word to call on Him. **16** No man of flesh, no man of the Law could be so free with God; the Spirit alone is Author of such liberty. And so our Abba-prayers are the Spirit's own witness to our new and free estate as children of God. **17** In this new life of freedom the wall between the present and the future has become as thin as air; one can no longer speak truly of the present without speaking of the future too. Our lives are now the festive evening before the feast. Children are heirs; if the Son by His Spirit makes us sons, He also makes us heirs. We are fellow heirs with Christ, heirs to all that God our Father has. Being one with Him will set our feet on paths of suffering in this world. We speak the no which He has spoken to this world and its desires; the reproaches of those who reproached God fell on Him (15:3), and they must fall on us. But just as surely as His way has led Him to the throne of God, so surely shall our paths of suffering lead there too.

146

The Future Life of the Christian Under the New Law 8:18-39

THE GREATNÉSS OF THE GLORY OF
OUR INHERITANCE 8:18-27

[18] I consider that the sufferings of this present time are not worth comparing with the glory that is to be revealed to us. [19] For the creation waits with eager longing for the revealing of the sons of God; [20] for the creation was subjected to futility, not of its own will but by the will of Him who subjected it in hope; [21] because the creation itself will be set free from its bondage to decay and obtain the glorious liberty of the children of God. [22] We know that the whole creation has been groaning in travail together until now; [23] and not only the creation, but we ourselves, who have the firstfruits of the Spirit, groan inwardly as we wait for adoption as sons, the redemption of our bodies. [24] For in this hope we were saved. Now hope that is seen is not hope. For who hopes for what he sees? [25] But if we hope for what we do not see, we wait for it with patience.

[26] Likewise the Spirit helps us in our weakness; for we do not know how to pray as we ought, but the Spirit himself intercedes for us with sighs too deep for words. [27] And he who searches the hearts of men knows what is the mind of the Spirit, because [j] the Spirit intercedes for the saints according to the will of God.

[j] Or *that*

"Glorified with Him"—with that we stand before the unutterable. No one in the New Testament really attempts to explain what the new world will be like. Paul does not attempt it either; he is content to hint

147

at the greatness of the glory that awaits us. He does so by contrasting it to our present suffering (v. 18) and by picturing the longing which the prospect of it evokes, not only in ourselves (23-25) but also in the whole created world (19-22) and in the Spirit Himself, the Inspirer of our petitions that God's kingdom come. (26-27)

18 What is it like, that future splendor that we shall inherit with Christ? There is no "like" that man can use; he can only say, in the assured conviction of his faith, that all the present sufferings of the church (and both Paul and the Roman church knew what suffering meant, 8:35-36; cf. Heb. 10:32-34) cannot weigh in the scale over against that weight of glory (cf. 2 Cor. 4:17), the glory which will come into our lives. **19** Paul can point to the eager yearning for that glory which runs through all creation. He ascribes to "creation," to man's world and all that is therein, an intense longing for the day on which the children of God will emerge from their hiddenness, their shame and suffering, and will stand revealed as what they are, as justified men who need not shrink from Him who judges the secrets of men, sons of God who see Him face to face. (Col. 3:4; 1 John 3:2; Matt. 5:8)

20 Creation yearns for release from the sorry sway of the "law of sin and death"; for creation, too, has come under that sway. It was not by an act of its own will that creation was doomed; that will was another's, man's. Again Paul harks back, as in 5:12 and 7:11 (cf. also 16:20), to the account of Gen. 3. The beasts and birds and creeping things did not revolt against the God who made them; only man, made in God's image for answerable converse with his God, did that. But the rent which man made between himself and God ran through all creation; after man's willed, fatal trespass

148

nothing was as it had been before. The ground was cursed for Adam's sake. Sin entered the *world* (5:12); man's doom, his alienation from God, was inscribed upon man's world. Paul calls that doom "futility" here. A little later (v. 21) he calls it "bondage to decay." The world we know, Paul is saying, goes but lamely on the paths appointed for it by God. If "Aristotle was but the rubbish of an Adam," the present world is but the rubbish of that brave new world which came to be at God's creative word. "All things are full of weariness; a man cannot utter it," the Preacher said (Eccl. 1:8). This agonized and dying world longs for surcease.

How Paul came to know this cosmic longing and to write this poetry which is truer than the truest prose — that is his secret, and the Spirit's. But this much we can know: The secret of the insight is in Christ; unless a man comes to know Jesus Christ, he cannot know the heaven under which He lived and died or the earth on which He walked the way to the cross as Reconciler of all things in heaven and earth to God (Col. 1:20; Eph. 1:10; Phil. 2:10-11). But there was hope, hope for man's world as well as hope for man, even on that black day when man willed to revolt and sin and death began their reign. The promise of the woman's Seed (Gen. 3:15) was given before the ground was cursed because of man. (Gen. 3:17)

21 Creation itself will be set free. The day that sees the sons of God set free in glory will see the liberation of all creatures from their "bondage to decay," their futile round of blind perpetual death. **22** Meanwhile all creation groans. But since Christ came and God pronounced anew His benediction on the creature man and on man's creature world, the world's agony is the agony of travail; there is in it the promise of a glad new

149

birth. What Jesus said of history, pocked with wars and shaken by catastrophes, that it is an agony of child-birth, with a terminus and a prospect (Matt. 24:8), Paul here says of the world. "We know," Paul says. We who under the law of the Spirit know redemption also know the weight of sin; we know that all the cosmic agony we see is guilt of ours. No creature dumbly dies without our being struck by it.

Paul teaches us to hope for a re-creation of the world. He does so more explicitly, perhaps, than any other writer in the New Testament. But his is not a solitary voice. The whole Bible rings with glad praise of the Creator; the incarnation of the Son of God is God's yes, in spite of all that sin has done, to His creation. He would not have sent His Son into the world if He were minded to take us out of this substantial world, as disembodied spirits, into some vague and insubstantial heaven of His own. The ministry of Jesus was God's yes to His creation spelled out in act; Jesus dealt with the body and the bodily "dis-ease" of man. He fed and healed men, and He raised them bodily from death. He bade the sea which threatened man be still. His resurrection was a bodily resurrection; the Jesus who spoke and ate with His disciples was no ghost. The promise of our resurrection is a promise of the resurrection of the body. We wait for a heaven and an earth that shall be a wondrously and unimaginably *new* heaven and earth. But the same continuity that makes the body of the future one with our present body connects the new unsullied world of God with the world we know, the world whose frustrate beauty makes us marvel still, whose futile workings still can testify to Him who once said "Very good!" and will again say "Very good!" to all His hands have made.

150

23 Creation dumbly yearns, and we, who in the Spirit have a foretaste and a guarantee of God's new world, yearn too; we groan inwardly as we wait. No mean part of the Spirit's work is to implant in us a deep nostalgia for our true and everlasting home. He is the Spirit of sonship, and He makes us long for the fullness of our adoption as sons, just because in Him that sonship is a foreshadowed reality. He dwells in us; our bodies are His temple (1 Cor. 6:19). Therefore we long for the redemption of our bodies, the transfigured bodies which shall be the Spirit's fit abode and perfect instruments for His most lively work. **24** We were saved in this hope; Baptism has united us with Him who was marked out as "Son of God according to the Spirit of holiness by his resurrection from the dead" (1:4). Our lives since Baptism have been tensed toward greater things to come. The teaching to which we were committed (6:17) filled the present with good things, but it gave us, with our faith, a hope. We hold to things unseen, we live by things not yet. **25** We walk toward that unseen but certain world with the resilient steps of men whose future is so sure and great that the present burden of our secular knapsacks seems no weight at all. That is what Paul means by "patience," this waiting for God's time with the athletic stamina of certain hope.

26 Creation groans, and we groan inwardly. And yet, our prayers rise up too feebly. The weariness of all things in this world (Eccl. 1:8) infects us too. "We do not know how to pray as we ought"; the strength of our prayers is not in proportion to the glory that we pray for. But the law of the Spirit of life is no mere general atmosphere in which we live; it is the personal presence of the Spirit, who helps us in our weakness. He knows the world of God and how men ought to pray

151

for it. He puts His power into our praying of "Thy kingdom come," a power which breaks the limits of our human speech and makes us cry "with sighs too deep for words." He intercedes for us; He is our Paraclete, our Counselor. 27 These Spirit-prompted prayers may be inarticulate, but they do not go unheard for all of that. God knows our hearts and understands our fumbling prayers. He has been waiting for such prayers as these and welcomes them. The Spirit's intercession for His poor, weak, unsaintly saints is prayer according to His will.

There can be no doubting the greatness of the future that evokes such sighs and prayers as these. The agonized creation, the men in whom the Spirit dwells, the Spirit Himself, all testify, each in his degree, to the fullness of the glory of that world toward which we move.

THE CERTAINTY OF THE FUTURE GLORY   8:28-30

28 We know that in everything God works for good *k* with those who love him, *l* who are called according to his purpose. 29 For those whom he foreknew he also predestined to be conformed to the image of his Son, in order that he might be the firstborn among many brethren. 30 And those whom he predestined he also called; and those whom he called he also justified; and those whom he justified he also glorified.

> *k* Other ancient authorities read *in everything he works for good,*
> or *everything works for good*
> *l* Greek *God*

The glory that is to be revealed to us is great beyond telling; it is also certain, sure to come. The law of the Spirit of life confers life with an authority that cannot be gainsaid. "We know" — we in whom the Spirit dwells, we who are led by the Spirit, we who have the Spirit of sonship and call God Abba with the brash and imperturbable confidence of children, we who in the Spirit have even now the firstfruits of the world to come, we who know the aiding intercession of the Spirit in our prayers — we know that we love God because He first loved us (cf. 5:8-11); we know that we came under the sound and power of His Gospel according to *His* purpose. Whoever may have been the vehicle of His call, a Peter or a Paul or one of those thousands of nobodies who carry on their apostolic work, it was *God's* call, not any man's, which reached us and made us lovers of Him. No accident of history made us His; therefore there are no "accidents" in our history anymore. He was in charge, and He is in charge; all the "accidents" of history are His working for our good.

29 It was His will, His purpose, that counted in our lives, independently of any doing or deserving of ours. If it was His purpose, it was solely His, and so it was from everlasting. He *fore*knew, and He *pre*destined. He "foreknew," not that something would happen but in order that it might happen. God foreknew us in order that we might be His own and serve Him. Here again we have to do with that dynamic sense of "knowing" which has occurred before (7:7, 15; cf. 2 Cor. 5:21). This knowing means personal communion between the knower and the known; it becomes a power in the life of the person who is known. Thus Paul can say that if a man loves God, it is because God has known him (1 Cor. 8:3). The Old Testament uses "know" to express God's election of Israel to be His people ("You only have I known of all the families of the earth," Amos 3:2) and of God's loving care for His own. The Lord "knows the way of the righteous" (Ps. 1:6) means: the Lord has laid a blessing on his life (cf. Ps. 1:3). The contrast to this "knowing" of God's is: "the way of the wicked will perish" (Ps. 1:6). Hosea can sum up all the Lord's loving care for His people in their years of wandering with the words: "It was I who knew you in the wilderness" (Hos. 13:5). Paul echoes this Old Testament usage in 11:2 when he calls the true Israel "the people whom He foreknew." "Foreknow," then, expresses not primarily the omniscience of God but a motion of the heart of God; when faith says, "He foreknew me," faith says, "He has chosen me."

God's foreknowing therefore has a purpose and a goal; His choosing love is a predestinating love. The purpose and the goal is nothing less than that men may be His sons. They shall be conformed to, made like, the image of the Son. All that characterized the history of the Son on earth and all that marks Him as the Son at God's right hand, all this is destined to be theirs: the perfect manhood of the Son, the free and complete obedience of the Son led by the Spirit of God, the full communion with the Father which the Son enjoyed, the high enthronement at the right hand of the Father, and the joy of free obeisance to the Father, that God, all enemies cast down, may now eternally be all in all (1 Cor. 15:28). *The* Son retains His primary place and preeminence; it is the sheer condescension of the First-born that makes us brothers of the Only-born, that makes us share a glory which is, rightly, His alone. But it does make us share His glory. The royal reign of God in Christ sets beggars on His throne (cf. Matt. 5:3). God's will for His beloved Son is that the Son be glorified by having many brothers, redeemed and glorious brothers, at His side.

30 The purposes of God make history; when our God wills a thing, He comes and walks upon our earth. His predestinating purpose took form and became substance in His call. His Son called sinners to His table and His fellowship under the bright sky of the forgiveness won for them on the cross. The Son's messengers proclaimed the Gospel of God, and God's call made alive the dead and called into being things that were not; it created righteous men. It justified the ungodly and bade them live. "And those whom He justified, He also glorified." The thing is done; all that Paul has said about the certainty of future glory is crystalized in this past tense of "glorified." "There is . . . now no condemnation for those who are in Christ Jesus" — as surely as Christ Jesus is glorified, those who are in Him now are also glorified.

DIVINE ELECTION

Rom. 8:28-30 is one of the classic passages on election and predestination. Heads and hearts have been broken over that doctrine. But it cannot fairly be said that Paul, or anyone else in the New Testament, is responsible for the breakage. When the New Testament speaks of election, it speaks as Paul does here, in terms of adoration and doxology. The New Testament speaks of it personally and concretely ("we know"), not in general and theoretically. The New Testament therefore holds absolutely to the revelation of God's elective will in Christ (v. 29), the will that took concrete, historical, knowable form when the Father sent His Son in the likeness of sinful flesh (8:3). There man can see spelled out the will of Him who tells His children, "I have chosen you." To speak of election is to confess that God alone is Author of our salvation; to speak of eternal election is simply an intensified expression of that same

155

certainty: "He has loved me with an everlasting love." If we stay with the New Testament, the intellectual puzzles and the agonizing uncertainties which so often attend an abstract consideration of election need not arise. Questions like: "What of the others, those not elected?" "Why some and not others?" "How can this particular and personal elective will of God be brought into harmony with the fact that He would have all men to be saved?" "How can I be sure that He has chosen me?"—questions like these are gray and sightless creatures born to live in darkness. They simply cannot live in the air and light of the New Testament. When the New Testament speaks of election, it is speaking a personal and heartening word to the called saints of God about their sainthood. It is not in search of a theory to explain the fact that the Word of God is a fragrance of death to some and a fragrance of life to others.

TRIUMPHANT CERTITUDE   8:31-39

^{31} **What then shall we say to this? If God is for us, who is against us?** ^{32} **He who did not spare his own Son but gave him up for us all, will he not also give us all things with him?** ^{33} **Who shall bring any charge against God's elect? It is God who justifies;** ^{34} **who is to condemn? Is it Christ Jesus, who died, yes, who was raised from the dead, who is at the right hand of God, who indeed intercedes for us?** ^{m} ^{35} **Who shall separate us from the love of Christ? Shall tribulation, or distress, or persecution, or famine, or nakedness, or peril, or sword?** ^{36} **As it is written,**
> **"For thy sake we are being killed all the**
>   **day long;**
> **we are regarded as sheep to be slaughtered."**

^{m} Or *It is Christ Jesus . . . for us*

³⁷ No, in all these things we are more than conquerors through him who loved us. ³⁸ For I am sure that neither death, nor life, nor angels, nor principalities, nor things present, nor things to come, nor powers, ³⁹ nor height, nor depth, nor anything else in all creation, will be able to separate us from the love of God in Christ Jesus our Lord.

31 "What then shall we say to this?" Paul's answer makes fools of his interpreters; how is one to comment on this outburst? If ever a man was set free by the law of the Spirit of life in Christ Jesus, Paul was that man. If ever words were given man to utter by the Spirit of life in Christ Jesus, these words were. Paul answers his opening question with another question, one full of high defiant faith: "If God is for us, who is against us?" "God for us" is a three-word summary of redemptive history, that history of God's free, elective love that culminated in the sending of His Servant and Son, called "Emmanuel, God with us" (Matt. 1:23). With these words in his heart a man can put down enemies and tread down assailants (cf. Ps. 118:6-7). 32 When God in these last days said once more and said climactically to His people and to all mankind, "I will be your God," He wrote those words in blood. He did not spare His Son. The Judge of mankind gave up (for the judicial tone of the expression, cf. 1:24, 26, 28; Luke 24:20) His Son into a death in which He bore the penalty for man's sin (cf. 4:25; Is. 53:4, 5, 6, 8, 12) and by His blood atoned for it (for the sacrificial coloring of "gave up," cf. Eph. 5:2, 25). Our guilt is dealt with; He has trodden our iniquities under foot and cast our sins into the depths

157

of the sea (Micah 7:19). There is no dead center in God's dealings with mankind; if He is not against us as the Judge of our transgressions, He is for us, wholly and forever for us. If He has given us His Son, He has given us all that is the Son's, for we are fellow heirs with Christ (8:17). All time, all space, all history, all the world are ours (4:13; cf. 1 Cor. 3:21), all things in heaven and earth which Christ has by His reconciling death brought home to God. (Col. 1:20)

33-35a Paul used no punctuation marks; the drift of his meaning had to give his readers the guidance which we give by periods or question marks. There is therefore often room for difference of opinion in details as to the meaning, and scholars differ in their punctuation of the present passage. The reading given by the Revised Standard Version in the margin, which makes v. 34b a statement rather than a question seems preferable. For one thing, the idea that Christ might rise to accuse us and dispute the justifying verdict of God seems, in this context, somewhat farfetched, even as a rhetorical question. For another, God's justifying verdict and the death of Christ are for Paul two aspects of one reality, two sides of one coin (cf. 3:24-25). We have, then, one defiant question, "Who shall bring any charge?" To this Paul opposes two answers: (a) the God who justifies, and (b) the Christ who died. Each of these answers is in turn followed by a question designed to make clear how final and definitive the answer given is.

    Who shall bring any charge?
        a) It is God who justifies. If this Judge acquits, who shall condemn?

b) It is Jesus Christ who died, rose, sits enthroned, and intercedes for us. His love has overcome all that might condemn us, — who shall separate us from that love?

33 The case is closed; who can reopen it? The acquitted are the *elect* of God; their innocence and inviolability is grounded in the eternal and unchangeable designs of God. He has foreknown them, predestined them for sonship, justified them through the redemption which is in Christ Jesus. He has in His Son already glorified them. What power in heaven or earth can successfully intervene? **34** Who dares dispute the verdict of *this* Judge, who is both the Judge and the Deliverer of the men whom He has chosen? Beside the Judge is He who shares His throne, the Christ, the anointed King; He still bears the name that binds Him to the guilty history of our race, Jesus, the name which marks Him as the Savior (Matt. 1:21), who died to set men free. He is no dead martyr but our living Lord; the law of the Spirit of life is His law, which He executes in power on the throne of God. The voice of Him who loved us and gave Himself for us speaks always for us; "we have an advocate with the Father," as John puts it (1 John 2:1). Even when we sin and fail, His love still holds us.

35 Who shall separate us from that love? Perhaps it is not too fanciful to see in the seven nouns which follow the compressed history of a Christian martyrdom. There is, first, "tribulation" (literally, "pressure"), the constant pressure of a pagan society against whose culture, religion, and morals the Christian life is a perpetual witness. Then comes "distress" (literally, "narrowness"); the pressure mounts to enmity, and the

159

place in which the Christian dwells has no room for him. He flees and is pursued ("persecution"). His pursuers press him hard ("peril"), and he is overtaken. At the end, the "sword" of the Roman executioner awaits him (cf. 13:4). However that may be, all the adversities enumerated (except, of course, the "sword") can be paralleled from Paul's references to his own sufferings in his Letters to the Corinthians, written just before the Letter to the Romans (1 Cor. 4:11; 2 Cor. 11: 23-33), and the sword of the executioner eventually struck Paul too.

36 The new people of God is tried by suffering and tempted to despair, as Israel was; they can make the psalmist's words their own (Ps. 44:22) when he cries out that his people, defeated, made prisoners, deported, mocked by neighboring nations, are "regarded as sheep to be slaughtered" because they are the Lord's and have been faithful to His covenant (cf. Ps. 44:17). **37** But the new people of God can also renew their strength at those same wells of life from which the psalmist drew, the wells of the "steadfast love of God" (Ps. 44:26; cf. 44:3). God has written the record of His steadfast love into the history of His ancient people (Ps. 44:1-8). He has shown forth that same love in Christ, who loved us, in an act of love for those who loved Him not, an act that dwarfs all revelations of the past and makes the future one great certainty. (5:8-11)

38 "I am sure," Paul says. The overwhelming act of God in Christ has put into his heart a certitude which all his sufferings in the past have left unshaken and unshakeable: "We are more than conquerors" *in* all these things, in the midst of this life in the shambles under the shadow of death. Each suffering undergone has made our hope more sure. Our troubled life, our certain death, these hard realities that go to make the open history of this age, these cannot separate us from the love of God in Christ Jesus our Lord, for Jesus Christ is "Lord both of the dead and the living" and we are His in life and death (14:8-9). The mysterious powers at work beneath the troubled surface of our history, powers which we cannot know and cannot hope to control, the "angels and principalities," do not escape the rule of Him who makes all things work for good to His elect; they are under the Lordship of our Lord Jesus Christ (cf. Eph. 1:20-22). The hidden realities of our existence are still mysterious, but they are no longer terrible. The revelation of God's love in Christ spans even that gap which all our human wisdom cannot span, the gap between the present and the future. We cannot pierce the wall that separates tomorrow from today, but God can. He has pierced it, and light falls from the future into the present. The Christ who came will come to us again; the law of the Spirit of life will hold and work forever. "In this hope we were saved." (8:24)

39 Perhaps "height" and "depth" are meant to explain the broad term "powers" (v. 38). We cannot make out certainly just what shade of meaning Paul and his readers would associate with these terms. Some scholars catch an allusion here to astrology; the Romans were to think of their pagan past when they sought to read their fortunes from the skies and trembled, or took courage, as they noted the position of the stars whose influence shaped their fortunes. From these dark superstitions they have been removed; no baleful star can make them tremble now. But the terms in which Paul speaks are not specific enough to make this interpretation a certainty. Perhaps it is best to leave the meaning more general, referring "height" and "depth" to the

161

geographical framework of our lives. Then the meaning would be: no power from on high has power to destroy us; the sun shall not smite us by day nor the moon by night (Ps. 121:6). No power from below has power to harm us really; the earth which spews forth lava or quakes and opens up beneath our feet is no terror to us now, nor are the depths of the sea. This interpretation would provide an easy transition to the last member of the series, "nor anything else in all creation." Since it is *in creation*, it cannot harm us, for the Creator, who called into being all those powers and dimensions of the universe that seem to dwarf us into insignificance, is *our* God. He is for us; these powers all serve His love, the love which we have come to know in Christ Jesus our Lord.

THE GOSPEL CREATES A NEW ISRAEL OUT OF JEW AND GENTILE   9:1 — 11:36

The Gospel, the revelation of the righteousness of God and His power for salvation, is going through the world "bearing fruit and growing" (Col. 1:6) as it goes. It creates a new status for men, and it brings forth men who stand before their God as righteous and shall live. It creates new life in justified men. Freed from the tyranny of sin, freed from the Law, freed from the dark dominion of death, set free by the law of the Spirit of life, these men are empowered by the Spirit to bear fruit for God. They are "the vineyard of the Lord . . . His pleasant planting" (Is. 5:7); they are what Israel and Judah had been, in God's intention, of old. The Gospel creates a new people of God to live before Him. The Gospel of God is now in these last days doing, in ultimate fullness and universality, what God's promise

162

did for Israel of old. The promise of God gave Abraham a blessing, a future, and a son; it created for Abraham descendants innumerable as the stars, a people called by God to be a blessing to all the families of the earth (9:8-9). The promise created Israel.

Paul has, throughout the first eight chapters, emphasized the continuity, the wholeness and oneness, of the creative working of the Word of God in past and present history. He has acknowledged that his Gospel has its roots deep in the promise given to Israel. He has used the Old Testament Scriptures in a way that leaves no doubt that they are for him, as for the Jews, the voice of God. He has called the Law a witness to the righteousness of God revealed in Christ, a spiritual word, and he has praised the Law's commandment as "holy, just, and good" (7:12). He can even use the hallowed term "law" of the new order of things inaugurated by Christ and revealed in the Gospel (3:27). He sees in circumcision the mark of God's covenant with Israel, "a sign or seal of righteousness" (4:11). He has acknowledged the Jew's place of priority in redemptive history, for the Gospel comes "to the Jew first" (1:16). The titles which Paul gives to the new people of God again and again mark the continuity of the new people of God, created by the Gospel, with ancient Israel, created by the promise: "called," "saints," "children of Abraham," "servants," "sons of God," "those that love God," "the elect of God" — these can all be paralleled from the Old Testament. And Paul applies an Old Testament word concerning the sufferings of the people of God directly to himself and the saints of the New Testament. (8:36; Ps. 44:22)

But there is discontinuity as well as continuity. There is a cleavage which Paul also emphasizes. The

163

great "now" of the manifestation of the righteousness of God is not merely the continuation of God's previous revelation; it is the culmination, and it brings a revolutionary change. The promise retains its value and validity and is taken up into the fulfillment; but the Law, while it retains its value as a witness to the righteousness of God and stands as the expression of the holy will of God, is removed from that centrally mediating position which it had occupied in the life of God's people from Sinai to Calvary. The Law plays no positive part in the creation of the new status for man. The revelation of the righteousness of God is given "apart from law" (3:21), and man is justified "apart from works of law" (3:28). The Law plays no part in the creation of new life in man. On the contrary, man must be liberated from the Law if the new life is to be his to live (6:14; 7:1-6). The impotence of the Law as a power for salvation stands revealed now as never before. (8:3)

And what of the ancient people of God, the people separated from the nations by the Law? The old line drawn by the Law between Jew and Gentile is gone. Though it is true that the Gospel is the power of God for salvation "to the Jew first," the decisive truth is that the Gospel is a power for salvation "to *every one* who has faith . . . also to the Greek" (1:16). The Gospel goes, as Jesus had commanded, "to all nations," and Israel is but one among the nations now. The guilt of the Jew is as manifest as the guilt of the Gentile, now that the wrath of God is revealed from heaven on all ungodliness and all unrighteousness; his mouth, too, is stopped, and he receives the righteousness of God on the same terms as the Gentile, giftwise, by the *forgiving* verdict of God. The Jew comes into the new Israel in the beggary of Abraham's faith, or he does not come in at all.

164

Here is where the problem raised by this discontinuity becomes agonizingly acute for Paul and the church. As a nation Israel did not come into the new Israel at all. When Paul wrote to the Romans, the great mass of the sons of Abraham were not walking in the footsteps of believing Abraham and were not destined to inherit the world with him. There was an Israel which could not join in the exultant joy of 8:31-39, an Israel which turned in bitter hate on those who brought the Gospel to the Jew first (1 Thess. 2:14-16), an Israel for whom Paul mourned. This was so obvious and so well-known a fact that Paul did not have to speak of it in so many words at all. When he spoke of his sorrow for his "kinsmen by race" – the Jews – everyone in the church knew why he sorrowed.

But Paul is not preparing to write a three-chapter elegy on the Jew. He is writing to the church, for the church, in the interests of the onward movement of the Gospel of God. The unbelief of Israel raises the critical religious question: "How can it be that the promise given to Israel should fail so signally in its fulfillment just in Israel? Can the fulfillment of the promise to Israel come to this, that it means death for Israel? For surely Israel is doomed if Israel in opposing the Gospel 'be found opposing God,' as Gamaliel once said (Acts 5:39). Is this to be the end of that long history of grace which began with father Abraham?" The alternate question, the one that moved the church most deeply, would be: "Can the Gospel which has failed just in its appeal to Israel, to the people prepared for it by the promise of God, really be the Gospel *of God*, as the apostles proclaimed and the church believed? Has Jesus, the Christ proclaimed by Paul, really confirmed the promises given to the patriarchs (15:8)? Do all the prom-

165

ises of God 'find their yes in Him'?" If the Gospel is not the Gospel of God, then the church which it has called into being is not the church of God; it cannot claim to be the Israel of God in these last days. Then the "called saints" have not been called by God and are not saints; they are deluded enthusiasts. They have no right to call Jesus Lord, no right to exist alongside the synagog, which calls Jesus accursed, no right to speed Paul on his way to Spain to preach the Gospel there. (15:24)

The question was a life-or-death question for the church A. D. 56. It is wholly understandable that when Paul came to speak of the new people of God created by the Gospel he should speak of the old Israel and the new, the real Israel, the "Israel of God." (Gal. 6:16)

God's Freedom to Create His Israel
as He Wills   9:1-29

Paul Mourns for Israel   9:1-5

[1] **I am speaking the truth in Christ, I am not lying; my conscience bears me witness in the Holy Spirit [2] that I have great sorrow and unceasing anguish in my heart. [3] For I could wish that I myself were accursed and cut off from Christ for the sake of my brethren, my kinsmen by race. [4] They are Israelites, and to them belong the sonship, the glory, the covenants, the giving of the law, the worship, and the promises; [5] to them belong the patriarchs, and of their race, according to the flesh, is the Christ. God, who is over all, be blessed forever.[n] Amen.**

[n] *Or Christ, who is God over all, blessed forever*

1 Paul's conscience, enlightened by the Holy Spirit, bears witness to the fact that he speaks the truth "in

Christ," for those who have received the Spirit of God have "the mind of Christ" (1 Cor. 2:12, 16). 2 And so Paul can speak of Israel as Christ spoke, in sorrow and in anguish of heart (cf. Matt. 23:37-39; Luke 19:41-42), but without rancor, although he bears on his body the marks of Israel's malice (2 Cor. 11:24) and would soon be exposed once more to the fanatical hatred of "the unbelievers in Judea" (15:31; cf. Acts 21:27-36; 22:22; 23:12-15). 3 He speaks, not with the soured malice of a renegade who gloats over the doom of the people which has cast him out, but in love. He speaks with the love of a Moses, who was willing to be blotted from the book of God for his apostate people's sake when the Lord's wrath burned hot against the men who had bowed down before the golden calf. (Ex. 32:32)

He speaks with the love of a Jesus, who interceded for His enemies and gave His life for them. "I *could* wish," Paul says when he utters the wish that he might be accursed, cut off from Christ and life, for his Jewish kinsmen's sake, for a people apostate now as it had been in Moses' day. He knows that his wish cannot be fulfilled; he knows that only one man's life, the life of "the man Christ Jesus" could be a ransom for the lost lives of men (1 Tim. 2:6):

> . . . no man can ransom his brother,
> or give to God the price of his life. (Ps. 49:7)

4 Not Israel's former greatness but the greatness of God's gifts to Israel, squandered now by Israel's disobedience, makes Paul mourn for Israel. Paul calls the roll of all that made this nation a holy nation, God's peculiar people, the prototype of the church. They are "Israelites," they bear the sacred name that marks them as the favored and elect recipients of the revelation,

167

the grace, and the promise of God (cf. Eph. 2:12). They are God's sons, called into being and placed into history by God's will and word. "Israel is my first-born son," the Lord said to Pharaoh, " . . . Let my son go that he may serve me" (Ex. 4:22-23; cf. Deut. 14:1; 32:6; Jer. 31:9; Hos. 11:1). To them, as to no other nation on the earth, the Lord their God disclosed His glory, the weight and splendor of His manifested Godhead. His "glory" appeared to them (e. g., Ex. 16:7, 10; 24:16) and dwelt among them in the tabernacle (Ex. 40:34-35) and in the temple (1 Kings 8:10-11). To them belonged the covenants; to them God said, "I will be your God." He put His grace upon them and laid His claim to them as His peculiar people in covenants with Abraham (Gen. 15:18), with the nation at Mount Sinai (Ex. 24), and with David. (2 Sam. 23:5)

The claim of the covenant was spelled out for Israel in the "giving of the law." In the Law the Lord demanded of each member of His people a whole love for Himself and a whole love for his neighbor. The Law ordained and regulated the worship of Israel. That worship, with its assurance of the presence of a gracious God, was in itself a promise, a shadowing-forth of good things yet to come (Col. 2:17). The worshiping Israelite breathed an air charged with future blessings. What was implicit in the worship, "the promises" spoke out. The promises of God again and again opened up the future when Israel's unfaithfulness had slammed and bolted shut the door to future blessings. The promises bade the Israelites look beyond the ruinous judgment of God upon their sins to that great day when God their King should send His Servant and Anointed to restore all that man's sin had ruined and should thus take up His power and reign. 5 The promises began with the fathers. It was the God who dealt faithfully with Abraham, Isaac, and Jacob who led His people out of the house of bondage in Egypt and gave them a land. It was the God of Abraham, Isaac, and Jacob, the God of the fathers, who fulfilled all promises in *the* Seed of Abraham, *the* Son called out of Egypt, *the* Son of David, in the Christ. The Christ is of the race of Israel "according to the flesh," in fulfillment of the promises. But that does not yet describe His glory, for it does not express His infinitely gracious condescension to His people. David's son is David's Lord (cf. Matt. 22:45). He is "God over all, blessed forever."

The reading given in the footnote of the Revised Standard Version seems preferable to that given in the text, which puts a period after "Christ" and makes the rest of the verse a doxology to God, not to Christ. As in 1:3, the phrase "according to the flesh" calls for a counterpart; that counterpart is there given in the phrase "according to the Spirit of holiness" (1:4) and is given here in the words "God over all, blessed forever." A Christ who is *only* "according to the flesh" is not the Christ of Paul. Moreover, the phrase fits in naturally as a doxology to Christ, whereas a doxology to God comes in awkwardly here. The situation is quite different from that of 1:25, where the doxology to the Creator comes in with inevitable naturalness.

The difficulty that weighs most heavily with many scholars and leads them to adopt the reading given in the text is the fact that Paul, for all his deep veneration for the Christ, does not elsewhere call Him "God." A verse like Titus 2:13, where Paul speaks of "our great God and Savior Jesus Christ," is not accepted as evidence by them, since they generally do not accept the Pastoral Letters as genuine letters of Paul's. But quite

169

apart from the question of the authenticity of the Letter to Titus (which cannot be argued here), is this so great a difficulty that it can determine the reading? If Paul can speak of Christ as existing, before His incarnation, "in the form of God" and on terms of equality with God (Phil. 2:6), so that He "emptied Himself" in becoming man (Phil. 2:7); if Paul distinguishes Jesus from all other sons of God by calling Him God's "*own* Son" (8:32); if he sees the risen Christ "at the right hand of God" (8:34); if he can call Jesus "Lord" and himself His "slave," using the very terms which he as an Israelite had used to mark his relationship to the Lord his God; if Paul can speak thus of Jesus, why can he not call Him "God," should the occasion demand it?

The present context *is* one which would provoke the use of this high term for Jesus. "God over all," applied to Christ, marks the line of cleavage between Paul and Israel, between the church and Israel. The scribes thought Jesus a blasphemer because He claimed for Himself an authority that belonged to God alone, the authority to forgive sins (Mark 2:7). The Jews sought to kill Jesus because He "called God His Father, making Himself equal with God" (John 5:18; cf. 8:18). They took up stones to stone Him because "being a man He made Himself God" (John 10:33). And they had Him executed for blasphemy (Matt. 26:65-66). "God over all," applied to Jesus, was an abomination for Jewish ears; that is why Paul mourned for Israel. Israel had cast out and slain the Son; they had forfeited the Kingdom because they would not bow before this final Messenger of God, the Son of God. (Matt. 21:37-43)

The Word of God Has Not Failed   9:6-13

⁶ But it is not as though the word of God had

170

failed. **For not all who are descended from Israel belong to Israel, ⁷ and not all are children of Abraham because they are his descendants; but, "Your descendants will be reckoned through Isaac." ⁸ This means that it is not the children of the flesh who are the children of God, but the children of the promise are reckoned as descendants. ⁹ For this is what the promise said, "About this time I will return and Sarah shall have a son." ¹⁰ And not only so, but also Rebecca had conceived children by one man, our forefather Isaac, ¹¹ though they were not yet born and had done nothing either good or bad, in order that God's purpose of election might continue, not because of works but because of his call, ¹² she was told, "The elder will serve the younger." ¹³ As it is written, "Jacob I loved, but Esau I hated."**

6 If the Israelites are cause for mourning, does that mean that the Word of God which came to them has failed? Has it proved an ineffectual Word? This is what makes the enigma of the non-Christian Israelite so serious and so critical for the church, for he will not call Christ his Lord, even though He is "God over all." If the Word of God can fail, the church has no grounds for faith and hope. For the Word of God, only the Word of God, has called the church into being; and the church lives and dies in the power of the Word. Paul looks into the history which the Word of God has made and sees there the revelation of God's will that will solve the enigma of Israel: "Not all who are descended from Israel belong to Israel." 7-8 If physical descent from Abraham makes man a true son of Abraham and an inheritor of the promise given to Abraham, then Ishmael, "the child of the flesh," was Abraham's son and heir, and the

171

future of God's people hung on him. But the Word of God fixed on Isaac and made him son and heir. In fact, the Word of God, God's promise, called Isaac into being. The Word of God, then, creates the people of God and defines the people of God. **9** The *Lord* spoke, and His will was done; He said, "I will return and Sarah shall have a son." What Paul is saying is this: "If you would know where Israel is, look where the promise is at work creating Israel, not at Abraham and Hagar and Ishmael, that tawdry story of the flesh of man at work. The Word of God in sovereign freedom overrules the fleshly will of man; God creates His Israel as He wills."

10 The same sovereign freedom of the Word is apparent also, and more fully, in the story of the sons of Isaac. Rebecca was no slave concubine but the free wife of Isaac, and both of her twin sons were free. **11-12** But here, too, the Word of the promise determined everything; independent of any will or work of man, it made the choice between Esau and Jacob before the boys were born. It overrode the hallowed right of primogeniture, ordaining that the firstborn should be servant to the younger son. Here God's purpose, God's free choice, God's call were wholly sovereign, independent of the will of man. **13** The history of the nations descended from the sons of Isaac confirmed what God's Word had said of the nations Israel and Edom. Centuries later, God through Malachi could say, "Jacob I loved, but Esau I hated" (Mal. 1:2-3). Men and nations do not live by bread alone, nor by being begotten and being born alone, but by every word that proceeds from the mouth of God. (Matt. 4:4; Deut. 8:3)

Paul speaks of "God's purpose of election" here (v. 11), but he is speaking of that purpose as it works in the history of men. He is not speaking here, as he spoke in 8:28-30, of the eternal predestination of God's elect to righteousness and glory; he is not now uttering the doxology of the redeemed. Rather, he is showing how God freely chose Isaac and Jacob for the furthering of His purpose, to bless all the families of the earth, in order to make clear that all depends on Him and on His Word alone. His choice of Isaac does not of itself doom Ishmael to perdition; Ishmael, too, received a blessing from God (Gen. 17:20; 21:13), and Ishmael, too, comes under the blessing promised to all the families of the earth in Abraham's seed. God's purpose of election does not mean that all Ishmaelites and Edomites were to be damned, no more than it means that all descendants of Isaac and Jacob should be saved. Even the words from Malachi, "Esau I hated," must be understood in the light of their setting and in accordance with the Hebrew mode of speech. Malachi is speaking of the fate of Jacob and Esau as nations, not of their eternal weal or woe. And to "hate" in Hebrew usage often means little more than the opposite of "prefer" or "choose." In Gen. 29:31, for instance, the words, "Leah was *hated*," simply restate what was said in Gen. 29:30: "He *loved* Rachel *more* than Leah." This mode of speech is found in the New Testament too; to "hate" one's life, mother, wife, children, etc. means to surrender them, to love them less than Christ. (Luke 14:26; cf. Matt. 10:37-39)

Still, Paul, in emphasizing the fact that the unbelief of physical Israel does not call in question the power of God's Word to Israel, has spoken boldly, to the point of ambiguity. The question can arise: "Is God, then, unjust? Is not this freedom of His mere arbitrariness, a tyrannous assertion of His will because it is His will?" Paul anticipates that question.

God Has Not Been Unjust 9:14-29

¹⁴ What shall we say then? Is there injustice on God's part? By no means! ¹⁵ For he says to Moses, "I will have mercy on whom I have mercy, and I will have compassion on whom I have compassion." ¹⁶ So it depends not upon man's will or exertion, but upon God's mercy. ¹⁷ For the scripture says to Pharaoh, "I have raised you up for the very purpose of showing my power in you, so that my name may be proclaimed in all the earth." ¹⁸ So then he has mercy upon whomever he wills, and he hardens the heart of whomever he wills.

¹⁹ You will say to me then, "Why does he still find fault? For who can resist his will?" ²⁰ But, who are you, a man, to answer back to God? Will what is molded say to its molder, "Why have you made me thus?" ²¹ Has the potter no right over the clay, to make out of the same lump one vessel for beauty and another for menial use? ²² What if God, desiring to show his wrath and to make known his power, has endured with much patience the vessels of wrath made for destruction, ²³ in order to make known the riches of his glory for the vessels of mercy, which he has prepared beforehand for glory, ²⁴ even us whom he has called, not from the Jews only but also from the Gentiles?

²⁵ As indeed he says in Hosea,
"Those who were not my people
I will call 'my people,'
and her who was not beloved
I will call 'my beloved.' "
²⁶ "And in the very place where it was said to them,
'You are not my people,'
they will be called 'sons of the living God.' "

²⁷ And Isaiah cries out concerning Israel: "Though the number of the sons of Israel be as the sand of the sea, only a remnant of them will be saved; ²⁸ for the Lord will execute his sentence upon the earth with rigor and dispatch." ²⁹ And as Isaiah predicted, "If the Lord of hosts had not left us children, we would have fared like Sodom and been made like Gomorrah."

14 Paul rejects the question "Is there injustice on God's part?" as verging on the blasphemous. But he deals with the doubt underlying the question (a) by pointing to God's revelation of Himself in the Old Testament (vv. 15-18); (b) by asserting the absolute authority over man which God possesses as man's Creator and by showing how God has used His authority in the service of His mercy (vv. 19-24); (c) by citing the words of Hosea and Isaiah which prefigured and foretold the history of God's undeserved compassion on the Gentiles and His rejection of the mass of the Israelites. (Vv. 25-29)

15 Paul is tracing the course of Israel's history. After the history of the patriarchs (vv. 7-13) comes the history in which Moses plays the leading role as servant of the Lord, the history of the Exodus and the wanderings in the wilderness. The history of those years shaped Israel's faith as no other period of history did; on those events the faith of Israel again and again looked back and found there strength for the present and confidence for the future. A word which recalled God's speaking and acting then, when He laid bare His glorious arm to set His people free, would speak with special warmth and urgency to every Israelite. As his previous citations from Genesis make plain (vv. 7, 9), Paul is quoting Old Testament words with a full

175

consciousness of their original setting and with the intention that their original setting be recalled. The words, "I will have mercy on whom I have mercy," are no detached oracle of God; these words were spoken in the wilderness when the children of Israel had made gods for themselves of gold, when *their* "will and exertion" (v. 16) was a blow in the face of the gracious majesty of God and merited His wrath. In that setting Moses said, "I pray Thee, show me Thy glory," and the Lord replied, "I will make all my *goodness* pass before you," and proclaimed His name to Moses, a name which meant this: "I will be gracious to whom I will be gracious, and will show mercy on whom I will show mercy" (Ex. 33:18-19). Even Moses, whose innocence the Lord Himself attested (Ex. 32:33), could stand before Him and live only on terms of His free mercy. Because God is a God who will have mercy, the Israelites have the gifts with whose enumeration Paul began: the sonship, the glory, the covenants, and the rest; because God is a God of mercy, the Christ has sprung from Israel according to the flesh. **16** What room is there for any talk of injustice in the face of that mysteriously free mercy? Man's will and man's exertion impose no obligation on God. He is not compelled by man; His grace is free.

17 His total freedom is apparent in His judgments too, in His withholding of His mercy. Pharaoh did what Pharaoh willed to do; he opposed the Word of God that Moses brought to him. Yet Scripture speaks to Pharaoh still (again the voice of Scripture is the voice of God) and tells him: "In your rebellion you did not once escape the hand of God; your history of obdurate refusal was the free disposing of the will of the Lord and had to serve the revelation of His power and grace;

176

you made His name to be proclaimed in all the earth. *God* held you fast in your resistance and locked you up in the sin that was your will."

18 "So then he has mercy on whomever he wills, and he hardens the heart of whomever he wills." Thus Paul sums up his survey of God's dealings with men in history. He does not say that God has from eternity determined to harden the hearts of some. He does say that Pharaoh was "raised up" by God, given his power and his place in history, in order to fulfill God's purposes; he does not say, however, that God created Pharaoh to destroy him. Paul is, for the time being, dwelling with strict exclusiveness on the sovereignty of God; that more can be said and must be said about the responsibility of man when God deals with him, that is clear from what has gone before in previous chapters and from what follows in Ch. 10.

Paul's argument in this section is convincing only for those who share with him two convictions: (1) the conviction that the Old Testament is the Word of God, an adequate disclosure of God's being and will; (2) that God Himself, as disclosed in His Word, is the standard of righteousness. Paul is not *proving* that God is righteous by applying to His deeds an abstract standard of righteousness; he is illustrating the righteousness of God by pointing to God's words and deeds of old. If the great mass of the men of Israel now stand in Pharaoh's place, hardened like him (cf. 11:7, 25), held fast and locked up in their rebellion by God, and are thus compelled to make His name to be proclaimed in all the earth as the Gospel of God turns from them and goes out to the Gentiles, that is a monstrous and tragic interchange of roles. But Israel cannot say, and the church need not fear, that the Word of God has failed;

177

now as then, the Word of God is working in the free fulfillment of the will of God, who manifests Himself, now as then, as the God in whom there is no unrighteousness.

19 In grace or in judgment, it is God who is in control; it is inevitable that the question that arose at 3:5-8 should arise again: If God is so omnipotently sovereign, even in the handling of human disobedience, what becomes of human responsibility? Is there really such a thing as guilt if man is, apparently, a helpless puppet in the hands of God? "For who can resist his *will?*" Pharaoh resisted God's Word, but he could not ultimately resist His will; God's will was done in spite of Pharaoh, through Pharaoh. God's will is being done through obdurate Israel. If the law holds that God hardens the heart of whomever He wills, can God hold Pharaoh and Israel responsible? Thus the question "Is there injustice on God's part?" recurs in a new form. **20** Such fatalistic talk is, in the last analysis, an accusation leveled at God; man is in effect saying to his God: "Thou art the Author of my sin." Paul therefore answers the question by first pointing up the impiety of the question: "Who are you, a *man,* a creature, to answer back to your Creator?" There are religious (or, irreligious) questions which dare not be answered objectively; we cannot talk "about" God, as if He were not Witness to our every word. The pride that prompts such questions must be exposed and judged.

Paul then proceeds to picture once more in the strongest terms, in the image of the potter and the clay, the sovereign freedom of God, a freedom no creature dare challenge. Paul's use of the image of the potter is an echo of the Old Testament. The image occurs in three passages in Isaiah (Is. 29:16; 45:9; 64:8) and once

178

in Jeremiah (Jer. 18:6). Various applications are made of the potter-vessel relationship; it can depict man's accountability to his Maker (Is. 29:16), or the impiety of man in questioning the ways of God (Is. 45:9), or the humility of an appeal made by a sinful people to the mercy of the God who created them (Is. 64:8), or God's freedom to visit wrath or mercy on a nation according to His will, even if the nation is His chosen people (Jer. 18:6). Basic to all is the idea of God's unquestionable authority over the history of His creature, man. 21 That is the idea expressed in Paul's use of the image: God has authority; His word counts; He assigns the roles, and man is responsible to God in the role which He has assigned, whether the role happens to be a splendid one or the reverse. Man dare not say, "Why have you made me thus?" His portion is to bow and to obey.

22 When man has bowed before the revelation of the Scriptures (vv. 14-18) and has submitted in responsible obedience to his Creator (vv. 19-21), then it is given him to look into God's ways with other eyes and see in them the logic of God's mercy. He is then given eyes to see the vast forbearance of the God who must, as God, be minded to manifest His wrath and power; he can see how wrath and judgment always are the work of God's left hand, how He endures with long patience the disobedience of men and nations who are ripe for the visitation of His wrath. (The translation "made for destruction" can be misleading. Paul does not here use the word which he used for "make" in vv. 20 and 21. The word which he uses means, rather, "finished," "fitted," "due," or "ripe," for destruction. Paul never uses this word for God's creative "making," although the author of the Letter to the Hebrews does, Heb. 11:3.) God's longsuffering is His mercy in the midst

179

of wrath (cf. Rom. 2:4). Because of His longsuffering, Jerusalem, whose destruction Jesus had foretold, has not fallen yet, and a door is open still to Israel.

23 God is patient with the vessels of wrath, and He makes these vessels of wrath serve the work of His right hand, His work of mercy. He uses them to make known the riches of His glory; they serve the fulfill-ment of His elective purpose, to shed His gracious glory on those whom He has before prepared for just this end. Thus he once dealt with Pharaoh—how many chances that hard despot had and lost!—and thus He deals with Israel now. Israel's rejection of the Gospel has sent the Gospel out into the Gentile world, that His glory might be manifested there; "by their trespass salvation has come to the Gentiles" (11:11). 24 Paul and the Romans have been witnesses to that; the potter's free authority has been documented in their lives. "He has called *us*," Paul says, "not from the Jews only but also from the Gentiles." In the light of these twin facts, God's forbearance conjoined with God's inexplicable mercy, how can there be any talk of injustice?

25 God's freedom to constitute His people as He wills, as the potter shapes the clay, has been set forth by Israel's own prophets. Hosea had pronounced the wrath of the Lord upon the people which had committed harlotry in forsaking the Lord (Hos. 1:2). 26 But the same Lord was ready to receive again this people which had lapsed into paganism and to call the unloved child His beloved once more; to call this people, which had forfeited all right to be His people, His people again, His sons, alive with the life of the living God (Hos. 1:10; 2:23). If such is the free majesty and boundless reach of His love, it is but a small step to the inclusion of the Gentiles, to the point where pagan men in Corinth or in

Rome are called "sons of the living God." **27-28** And as for the children of Israel's proud dream that God was bound to them, that they somehow *possessed* the Lord, Isaiah had already shattered that illusion. He had cried out concerning Israel that God would smite this "godless nation," this "people of His wrath" (Is. 10:6), and that of all the fruitful families in Israel only a remnant would be saved; the rigorous sentence of the Lord would be executed speedily on them. **29** And the salvation of the remnant would be the doing of the Lord of hosts, His alone. (Is. 1:9)

God's Justice in Rejecting Ancient Israel   9:30 — 10:21

"Be still and know that I am God" (Ps. 46:10) — that has been the tenor of Paul's proclamation in 9:1-29. God is free to call His people into being and to form it as He wills. If Israel has now become a vessel of His wrath and if Gentiles now praise Him for His mercy (15:9), no one can say His Word has failed or that His strangely hidden ways have not been just:

> "The Rock, his work is perfect;
>   for all his ways are justice.
> A God of faithfulness and without iniquity,
>   just and right is he." (Deut. 32:4)

But Paul, for all his boldness in asserting the high and sovereign majesty of God, has not said that God *creates* men to be vessels of His wrath, that He dooms men to wrath from everlasting. There is another, equally important aspect to the fall of Israel, and to it Paul now turns. God's wrath is not a primal motion of His will, in eternal equilibrium with His love; wrath is God's reaction to the guilt of men. If Israel were guiltless, God's wrath against Israel would not be the divine righteous-

181

ness at work but the blind working of an arbitrary power. Paul can say, "Be still before your God," but he must also bring home to Israel Israel's guilt and say, "If you will not believe, surely you shall not be established." (Is. 7:9)

³⁰ What shall we say, then? That Gentiles who did not pursue righteousness have attained it, that is, righteousness through faith; ³¹ but that Israel who pursued the righteousness which is based on law did not succeed in fulfilling that law. ³² Why? Because they did not pursue it through faith, but as if it were based on works. They have stumbled over the stumbling stone, ³³ as it is written,

> **"Behold, I am laying in Zion a Stone that will make men stumble,**
> **a rock that will make them fall;**
> **and he who believes in him will not be put to shame."**

The section 9:30-33 forms a transition from the first theme to the second. It looks back to 9:1-29 in its emphasis on God's sovereignty: *He* lays the Stone in Zion; man may stumble over It or be saved by It, but man can neither lay the Stone nor question Him who lays It. And the section looks forward to 10:1-21 in its emphasis on the necessity of faith and the guilt of unbelief.

30 Paul's theme is not simply the fate of ancient Israel; he is speaking of the church, the Israel of God in the world's last days, of the saints of God called from among Jews and Gentiles (9:24), with Gentiles in preponderance. The picture presented by the church is an ethically offensive one, a scandal to right-thinking moral men. Those who did not run at all are winners in the race; Gentiles, who ignored the revelation of the power and deity of God, who in their futile thinking exchanged the immortal God for images of man and beast (1:21-23), these Gentiles have attained righteousness, by faith alone. **31** Those who ran hardest in the race have won no prize at all. The men of Israel who served God earnestly by day and night (Acts 26:7) as they awaited the fulfillment of His promises, who ate and drank the Law and sought to incise its every jot and tittle on their hearts, these men of Israel "did not succeed in fulfilling that law."

32 Paul's thesis, "It depends not upon man's will or exertion (literally, 'running') but upon God's mercy" (9:16), is, to be sure, borne out by this history, the history of the church created by the Gospel. But is this the revelation of the righteousness of God, and can this church be called the Israel of God? This is the question which the Jews might well ask. Paul answers them out of their own Bible. Theirs was the sin of Israel in Isaiah's day; they went the self-chosen way of their own exertions and not the way of faith in the Lord of hosts. **33** Paul's Old Testament quotation is a fusion of two passages from Isaiah (Is. 8:14; 28:16). Both passages speak of a stone, or rock; in both passages the stone represents the saving way which the Lord is in His freedom taking; in both passages the stone stands in contrast to the self-willed, feverish exertions of men who seek to save themselves by making an alliance with one of the world powers, Assyria (Is. 8) or Egypt (Is. 28). In Is. 8 the Lord of hosts is Himself the Stone; the same Lord who will prove a Sanctuary, a Refuge and Defense to those who regard Him as holy and fear Him (Is. 8:13-14a) will become "a stone of offence and a rock of stumbling" on which the fluttering politicians who disregard

183

the prophet's call to faith (cf. Is. 7:9) "shall fall and be broken; they shall be snared and taken" (Is. 8:14b-15). In Is. 28 the Lord lays the Stone in Zion, the citadel of His anointed King; the Lord alone opens up the way to the future and the future's Messianic King; no alliance with Egypt, no treaties and no trickery, can save a man from the "overwhelming scourge" which the Lord will let sweep through the land (Is. 28:14-18); only faith in Him, the "sure foundation," gives a man a future and a hope: He who believes in Him will not be put to shame. —Is. 28:16 does not speak of the coming Messiah in so many words. But Isaiah is particularly rich in references to the great anointed King who shall establish God's eternal reign (Is. 7:10 ff.; 9:1-6; 11:1-10; 16:4-5), and so the reference to the Foundation Stone laid in the royal citadel of Zion is quite naturally taken to refer to the Messiah by both Peter (1 Peter 2:4-6) and Paul, as well as by the teachers of the Jews.

¹ Brethren, my heart's desire and prayer to God for them is that they may be saved. ² I bear them witness that they have a zeal for God, but it is not enlightened. ³ For, being ignorant of the righteousness that comes from God, and seeking to establish their own, they did not submit to God's righteousness. ⁴ For Christ is the end of the law, that everyone who has faith may be justified.

⁵ Moses writes that the man who practices the righteousness which is based on the law shall live by it. ⁶ But the righteousness based on faith says, Do not say in your heart, "Who will ascend into heaven?" (that is, to bring Christ down) ⁷ or "Who will descend into the abyss?" (that is, to bring Christ up from the dead). ⁸ But what does it say? The word is near you,

on your lips and in your heart (that is, the word of faith which we preach); [9] because, if you confess with your lips that Jesus is Lord and believe in your heart that God raised him from the dead, you will be saved.

[10] For man believes with his heart and so is justified, and he confesses with his lips and so is saved. [11] The scripture says, "No one who believes in him will be put to shame." [12] For there is no distinction between Jew and Greek; the same Lord is Lord of all and bestows his riches upon all who call upon him. [13] For, "everyone who calls upon the name of the Lord will be saved."

[14] But how are men to call upon him in whom they have not believed? And how are they to believe in him of whom they have never heard? And how are they to hear without a preacher? [15] And how can men preach unless they are sent? As it is written, "How beautiful are the feet of those who preach good news!" [16] But they have not all heeded the gospel; for Isaiah says, "Lord, who has believed what he has heard from us?" [17] So faith comes from what is heard, and what is heard comes by the preaching of Christ.

[18] But I ask, have they not heard? Indeed they have; for

"Their voice has gone out to all the earth,
and their words to the ends of the world."

[19] Again I ask, did Israel not understand? First Moses says,

"I will make you jealous of those who are not a
nation;
with a foolish nation I will make you angry."

[20] Then Isaiah is so bold as to say,

"I have been found by those who did not seek me;

185

I have shown myself to those who did not ask for
    me."
**²¹ But of Israel he says, "All day long I have held out
my hands to a disobedient and contrary people."**

1 Paul has already touched on the theme which is
to occupy him through 10:21, but before he states it
explicitly and develops it fully, he once more speaks of
his compassion for the people whose unbelief it is his
duty to expose. He is intercessor for them, not their
accuser. Jesus' warning, "Judge not" (Matt. 7:1), lives
in his servant's heart. The fact that Paul can still in-
tercede for these "vessels of wrath" and pray "that they
may be saved" confirms our understanding of his words
in Ch. 9. If these were men eternally foredoomed by
God to wrath, Paul could not pray for them. He would
then be invading the majesty of God the Judge.

2 "I bear them witness that they have a zeal for
God." The candor of this man of God is an amazing
thing; he does not paint the synagog a solid black in
order to make the church appear pure white. Paul paid
this tribute to Judaic zeal once again, some months
later, in Jerusalem, when he spoke to "men of Israel"
before the temple gate, to men who had been howling
for his blood and soon would howl again (Acts 22:3).
"But it is not enlightened"; it is not, literally, "according to knowledge." When zeal is not enlightened by
clear knowledge of its object and its goal, it centers in
man's self.

3 This murky religiosity could not exclude boasting; there still was room in this blind zeal for the self-
assertion of Judaic man. When the righteousness of God
was manifested, this zeal had no eyes for "the righteousness that comes from God." How could it have? These

186

men thought *their* thoughts and willed *their* will; the Law could not bring them to a knowledge of their sin, to a realization of their own impotence. They could not even face the Law full face. They worked out a theory that a man's good deeds could somehow compensate for the ill that he had done, a theory which was an insult to the God of justice. He who would judge impartially the Gentile's sins was asked to overlook the minor disobediences of the Jew. Thus they sought to "establish their own" righteousness, and therefore they did not submit to the righteousness of God. To submit to God's righteousness would have meant giving up their own, pleading guilty before God, admitting that the lost sheep of the house of Israel were really lost, that all had gone astray.

4 This was their sin; they disbelieved and disobeyed the supreme revelation given by their God in Christ. "Their" righteousness could flourish on the soil of law (cf. Phil. 3:9). When the Christ came, to do what the Law was impotent to do, to give them what the Law could not bestow, the righteousness of God, they crucified Him, for His coming meant the end of law. He was God's yes to all God's promises, God's nonetheless to the condemning verdict of the Law. But this Word of God their unenlightened zeal could not and would not hear.

Verses 3 and 4 state the theme of the whole chapter (cf. vv. 16 and 21). When Israel was confronted by the revelation of the righteousness of God in Christ, Israel was summoned to believe, find righteousness, and live. But Israel chose instead a righteousness of its own, based on the Law. That wrong choice was unbelief and therefore guilt. 5 For the choice had inevitably to be made, and the right choice could be made. The very terms of God's revelation made it clear that the revelation of the righteousness of God is "apart from law," that the revelation given in Christ transcends and supersedes the Law. The written code of Moses plainly says, "Practice righteousness and live" (Lev. 18:5). Here all depends on man's will and man's exertion. 6 But the voice of righteousness by faith speaks wholly otherwise; it bids man cease his willing and his running after righteousness. Man need not scale the heavens to bring Christ down; Christ has come down and that, too, in the likeness of our sinful flesh and as a sacrifice for sin (8:3). 7 Man need not go into the dark abyss of death, to bring Christ from the dead; He has been raised up from the dead by the glory of the Father, raised for our justification. (6:4; 4:25)

Paul's language concerning the Word of faith echoes that of Deut. 30:11-14, which speaks of the Law. This has created difficulties for some; they either find some sort of inner unity between the Law and the Gospel suggested here by Paul, or they conclude that Paul is quoting Old Testament words without regard for the meaning they had in their original setting. But there does not seem to be room for either idea. Paul is not "quoting" the Old Testament at all; there is here no formula of quotation such as "it is written," and Paul makes a clear distinction between what "Moses *writes*" (v. 5) and what "righteousness *says*" (v. 6). Moreover, the reproduction of the language of Deuteronomy is very free; the phrase "descend into the abyss," so important for Paul's thought, is not found in the Deuteronomy passage at all. The phrases "ascend into heaven" and "descend into the abyss" seem to have become proverbial for attempting the impossible; in Paul they get their color from the incarnation and the resurrection of the Lord. The most that one can fairly say is that Paul's language is here, as so often, tinctured by that of the Old Testament.

8 The voice of righteousness by faith says not "Do!" but "It is done!" God's justifying deed is *there*, available to man, in the Word which comes to him ("which we preach"); man need not discover it or devise it. He need but believe it; it is a "word of faith," a Word which asks for faith and creates it (cf. 1:17). This Word is near him, creating faith in his heart and evoking a confession from his lips. **9** Thus this "word of faith," this Gospel, is a power for salvation. For if a man confesses with his lips that Jesus is Lord, he has Jesus for his Lord, he has peace with God through his Lord and can rejoice in God through Jesus Christ, his Lord (5:1, 11). If he believes that God has raised Him from the dead, without *his* willing or exertion, he shares the resurrection-life and resurrection-glory of his Lord. (Cf. 6:4, 8)

10 With the heart a man believes. In the language of the Bible, "heart" covers the whole inner man, his mind no less than his emotions and his will. An unenlightened Christian zeal is no better than the blind zeal of Jewry. He believes, and so he is cleared of guilt; he comes under the justifying verdict which God has spoken in the death and resurrection of His son, and righteousness is his. He *confesses* and is saved. Faith and confession are two aspects of one reality; they constitute one life before God under the lordship of Jesus Christ. Man does not come to faith in solitude; when those who preach the Word of faith to him say, "Believe in the Lord Jesus, and you will be saved," he replies with the confession, "I believe in Him." No man who has the Lord Jesus for his Lord remains a silent servant of his Lord, ashamed to acknowledge Him before men (Mark 8:38), but he confesses Him before men. And his

189

Lord will confess him at the judgment before His Father. So he shall be saved. (Matt. 10:32; Luke 12:8)

11 The Old Testament had already pointed Israel down this road of faith and had given to Israel the promise that no faith in the Lord would be put to shame. Paul cites Is. 28:16 again, as in 9:33. However, there are two slight but significant differences here. One is this: in the Old Testament the object of faith is the Lord, the covenant God of Israel; here in Paul "Lord" must mean the Lord Jesus Christ. This is one of many instances in the New Testament where Old Testament passages that refer to the Lord, the God of Israel, are unhesitatingly applied to Jesus (cf. 10:13). This speaks eloquently of the place which Jesus occupied in the faith of the apostles and the apostolic church; they believe in Him as God and Lord. The other difference is this: Paul emphasizes the universality of the promise made in Isaiah; "he who" becomes "every one who" (rendered as "no one who" by the Revised Standard Version in the interest of style). This universality is suggested in the original, though it is not stated explicitly; for if access to the Lord and His salvation is by faith, then the Lord is accessible to all, both those under the Law and those without the Law. (Cf. 3:22-24; 28-30)

12 No one who has faith will be put to shame. All, Jew and Gentile, have sinned (3:23); all are justified through faith. Faith gathers all men, Jew and Greek, beneath the lordship of one Lord, a Lord who has riches that suffice for all, riches of mercy for all who call on Him. 13 The universality which is implicit in Isaiah's word is explicit in the word of Joel (Joel 2:32). Through Joel God had promised that at the coming of "the great and terrible day of the Lord" *everyone* who called upon the name of the Lord should be delivered. Peter had

spoken this word of Joel's at Pentecost when he called on all Israel to repent and call on Him whom God had made both Lord and Christ for their deliverance (Acts 2:21, 36, 40). Paul speaks it now with broader reference still, with reference to all men, Jew and Greek alike.

If Israel ignored the righteousness of God revealed in Christ and sought a righteousness based on the Law, which man can call his own, Israel is guilty. For the revelation itself made plain that a choice had to be made. The choice was inevitable, and the choice was easy. The beggar's hand of faith, any beggar's hand, could receive this gift of righteousness.

14 Man needs only to call upon the name of the Lord, this Savior of men, and the Lord is to be found. But to call upon His name is an act of faith, and faith is created only by the Word of God. Man does not hatch out faith by thinking hard about his need for it; man comes to faith in the Lord when he has heard news of Him or has heard His voice (the Greek admits of either rendering). **15** No man can, of himself, bring news of God; the Gospel is the Gospel of *God*, and only "preachers," heralds authorized to speak for God, can utter it. God does send forth His heralds now as He did of old. When God took up His royal power and freed His people from the Babylonian captivity, His heralds brought the good news of deliverance to desolate Jerusalem. To Jerusalem there was no sight so beautiful as the racing feet of those messengers who announced: "Your God has taken up His power and reigns" (cf. Is. 52:7). God has not changed; His heralds, now as then, go forth to bring to captive men the good news of His reign.

16 But men have disbelieved; they have not all heeded the Gospel. Paul sums up the response of men to the apostolic heralding in the same words from Isaiah

191

which John uses to sum up Israel's response to Christ Himself: "Who has believed what he has heard from us?" (John 12:38; Is. 53:1). Isaiah spoke of his prediction of the Servant of the Lord, whom the Lord had chosen

> to raise up the tribes of Jacob
> and to restore the preserved of Israel (Is. 49:6),

the Servant given by the Lord "as a light to the nations" that the salvation of the Lord might reach to the end of the earth (Is. 49:6). The Servant was to go the way of full obedience into suffering and death, to bear the sins of many, to be smitten and afflicted by the Lord and thus make many to be accounted righteous. This revelation of the Lord in servant's form seemed to the men of Israel a preposterous thing. Who could see in this unlovely man of sorrows the arm of the Lord laid bare in its redeeming power? The ministry of the Servant-Christ and the Gospel of the Servant-Christ have met the same response in men as did the prophecy of the Servant-Christ. "Who has believed what he has heard from us?" is not Isaiah's question only. John and Paul must ask it too.

17 But the unbelief of man does not make void the Word of God. If men have "not *all* heeded the Gospel," some have heeded it; and for them the arm of the Lord, the power of God, has been revealed through it. The golden chain which binds men to the Lord in faith has been fully forged; every link is there, from "sending" to "believing" and to "calling on His name." Christ has preached, in word and deed, His messengers have gone forth and have borne abroad His name, and men have come to faith and called upon His name for their salvation.

18 "Have they not heard?" "They," the men for whom Paul intercedes, the men of Israel, the men of unenlightened zeal for God, have *they* not heard? Has no enlightenment been offered them? The tone of Paul's question is incredulous, and his answer is brief. It is a strange sort of answer; Paul quotes the fourth verse of Ps. 19. This psalm speaks of the heavens that tell the glory of God, of the firmament which proclaims His handiwork, of the ordered times of day and night which give men knowledge of the God who ordered them. Paul's answer is an allusive one, an indirect reply to his question. But the allusion is not too difficult to catch: When God, the almighty Creator, wants to be heard, He will be heard. He has all power in heaven and earth at His command. He can raise up men to preach His Gospel. That Gospel has been "fully preached" and that, too, "from Jerusalem" (15:19). The men of Israel have heard, no doubt of that.

19 Yet one more question, and the guilt of Israel is proved beyond all contradictions: "Did Israel not understand?" Paul asks, again in a tone of incredulity. His answer is taken from the Law and the Prophets. The song of Moses had forewarned the men of Israel that the Lord would punish their infidelity by hiding His face from them and provoke them to jealousy with "a foolish nation" (Deut. 32:21) by revealing Himself to this foolish nation. In other words, Paul's answer is: The Gentiles have understood, have come to faith, have called upon the saving name, have come to be the "Israel of God." How could Israel fail to understand if these untutored tribes without the Law have understood? **20** Isaiah, too, has witnessed to a God whose will and word are so compelling and so clear that even men who do not seek Him somehow stumble on His grace (Is. 65:1), as the Gentiles did, who almost unawares have found in the Lord Jesus Christ a righteousness which they had not pursued (9:30). 21 Isaiah calls the sin of Israel by its proper name; not ignorance is their fault, but disobedience (Is. 65:2). The Lord has all these years been holding out His hands to them, inviting them to come by faith into the riches of their Lord. But they have not believed and they have not obeyed. They have not with their lips confessed their Lord; they have contradicted Him (the word translated "contrary" means, literally, "contradicting").

God's Wisdom in the Creation of His New Israel 11:1-36

God is free, and Israel is guilty. This should suffice "to justify the ways of God to man." Chs. 9 and 10 would by themselves provide a neat theodicy, a vindication of God. If Paul were a religious philosopher, he might well stop here. But Paul is not a philosopher; he is an apostle of Jesus Christ. Jesus knew of no limits to the creative possibilities of God; He knew that all things are possible with God (Matt. 19:26). He saw in the hopeless spectacle of the harassed and helpless lost sheep of Israel the harvest-field of God (Matt. 9:36-37). Paul serves Him, for Paul has the mind of Christ.

Paul has been set apart for the Gospel of God. He serves the Creator God, whose Word has never failed (9:6). God's Word says, "Let light shine out of darkness" (2 Cor. 4:6; Gen. 1:3; cf. Is. 9:2). His Word can make light shine even out of Israel's darkness; His Word has uses for the dead branches cut from the tree of Israel (11:17), for Israel hardened in obdurate resistance to God (11:25). For God's almighty Love is in His Word.

The Present State of Israel   *11:1-10*

¹ **I ask, then, has God rejected his people? By no**

194

means! I myself am an Israelite, a descendant of Abraham, a member of the tribe of Benjamin. ² God has not rejected his people whom he foreknew. Do you not know what the scripture says of Elijah, how he pleads with God against Israel? ³ "Lord, they have killed thy prophets, they have demolished thy altars, and I alone am left, and they seek my life." ⁴ But what is God's reply to him? "I have kept for myself seven thousand men who have not bowed the knee to Baal." ⁵ So too at the present time there is a remnant, chosen by grace. ⁶ But if it is by grace, it is no longer on the basis of works; otherwise grace would no longer be grace.

⁷ What then? Israel failed to obtain what it sought. The elect obtained it, but the rest were hardened, ⁸ as it is written,

"God gave them a spirit of stupor,
eyes that should not see and ears that should not
hear, down to this very day."
⁹ And David says,
"Let their feast become a snare and a trap,
a pitfall and a retribution for them;
¹⁰ let their eyes be darkened so that they cannot see,
and bend their backs forever."

1 God's Word has not failed. Therefore "a disobedient and a contrary people" (10:21) cannot be the end and goal of all God's ways with Israel. God has not rejected His people. Paul himself is living proof of that. There he stands, an Israelite, a son of Abraham in every sense, a member of the tribe of Benjamin. There he stands, with God's favor on him, a monument to God's fidelity to Israel. There he stands, and there he works. God is using him to carry out the purpose for which He

first called Israel's father, Abraham, and elected Israel: to bless all the families of the earth (Gen. 12:3). 2 No, God has not rejected the Israel whom He foreknew, Israel the bearer of His promise and His blessing, the Israel which never was simply identical with the full number of the physical descendants of Abraham. Israel exists in order to carry out God's purposes; Israel is a functional quantity. While one Israelite fulfills Israel's function, Israel is *there*; Israel is not rejected. But Paul does not stand utterly alone in the midst of an apostate people, no more than Elijah once stood utterly alone.

3 Elijah thought he did and had good cause to think so as he sat under the broom tree and wished that he were dead (1 Kings 19:4). He saw the prophets of the Lord cut down, the altars of the Lord demolished, and he feared for his own life. He could not see that God's Word had *not* failed, that God in hiddenness and secrecy had reached the hearts of 7,000 men with that "still small voice" of His, that there were 7,000 left who had not bowed the knee to Baal (1 Kings 19:18). 5 Elijah found that he was not alone; and Paul, who knows the deadly enmity of Israel as Elijah did and has looked full upon the tragic wreckage of his people, broken on the Stone of stumbling, Paul, too, knows that he is not alone. He knows that out of Israel God's elective grace has now called forth men who do not disobey and contradict God but call Jesus Lord and believe that God has raised Him from the dead. These men have gone the way that all who go into the new Israel of God must go; they have gone the way of grace and faith, not trying to establish a righteousness of their own but renouncing their own righteousness and submitting freely to the given righteousness of God. 6 These men were chosen by grace, just as the Gentiles were. They found a gra-

cious God by faith alone, just as the Gentiles did. There is no such thing in God as a diluted grace, a partial grace. If grace is not the free and round and whole and undivided love of God, the same to all, pure gold in every hand that holds it, then it is not grace. Where God's grace works, there simply is no room for works of men, for human merit and acquired reward.

7 What then? What is the present state of Israel? In 9:30-31 Paul drew a line between the nation Israel and the Gentiles. These Gentiles attained righteousness by faith; the nation Israel did not. Now Paul draws the same line within Israel, between the nation Israel and the elect in Israel. The elect have obtained what was offered to all, the righteousness of God, salvation. They constitute the remnant in Israel, the "remnant chosen by grace" (cf. v. 5). The rest were hardened; God petrified them in their stony resistance to the truth. God hardened them, but He hardened them because of their unbelief. He did not harden them from everlasting, to prevent them from believing. Still, God is not mocked; His judgment on the proud rejectors of His Word is fearful to behold. If men will not have the light created by His Word, they shall have the darkness which *they* have chosen as His doom upon them.

8 Paul reads the judgment of God on hardened Israel in the words which Isaiah once spoke to Jerusalem (Is. 29:10), when God marshaled the armies of Sennacherib against the city that would not hear His Word and made blind the city that willed to be blind to God's threats and promises (Is. 29:9, 11-12). Paul quotes freely, perhaps from memory, and adds touches from similar passages (Deut. 29:4; Is. 6:9-10). His words recall Jesus' indictment of His unbelieving contemporaries (Matt. 13:11-15). 9 Beside the pronouncement of God's judg-

197

ment stands the invocation of God's judgment from Ps. 69 (22-23), which calls down the wrath of God on the enemies of the man who is consumed with zeal for the house of God (Ps. 69:9), whose cause is the cause of God (Ps. 69:6-7), who has no one to look to but God (Ps. 69:8). His enemies have given him poison for food and vinegar to drink. (The New Testament sees in the sufferer of Ps. 69 a prefiguration of our Lord in His suffering.) The enemies of the righteous have triumphed; now they feast richly in security, while the servant of God perishes. He calls on God to vindicate him: their table, symbol of their triumphant security, is to be their doom. 10 The eyes of those who have looked without pity on him whom God has smitten (Ps. 69:26) shall be blind eyes, and the proud backs of the oppressors shall be forever bent beneath the yoke of slavery. Israel's guilt is like theirs; their fate threatens Israel.

God's Uses for Israel   11:11-16

¹¹ So I ask, have they stumbled so as to fall? By no means! But through their trespass salvation has come to the Gentiles, so as to make Israel jealous. ¹² Now if their trespass means riches for the world, and if their failure means riches for the Gentiles, how much more will their full inclusion mean!

¹³ Now I am speaking to you Gentiles. Inasmuch then as I am an apostle to the Gentiles, I magnify my ministry ¹⁴ in order to make my fellow Jews jealous, and thus save some of them. ¹⁵ For if their rejection means the reconciliation of the world, what will their acceptance mean but life from the dead? ¹⁶ If the dough offered as firstfruits is holy, so is the whole lump; and if the root is holy, so are the branches.

11 Is this the end: a remnant saved as a brand from the burning, and the mass of Israel forever doomed? Is this the total fruitage of the history that began with Abraham, a history in which the Word of God again and again opened up new vistas of salvation to the eyes of faith? Has hardened Israel stumbled so as to fall, to lie prostrate forever? The history which God has governed and shaped says no. The Spirit of God enables Paul to read God's purpose in that history. Paul has seen with his own eyes how the "trespass" of the synagog, the Jews' rejection of the Word of God, had sent the Word of life out to the Gentiles. (Acts 13:45-47; 18:5-6)

Paul knows from the Old Testament that the remnant in Israel is no mere fixed and inert residue; it is a "holy seed" (Is. 6:13), a productive core. Isaiah in his day knew that he, the prophet, and his disciples stood in Israel as the remnant's beating heart, as "signs and portents . . . . from the Lord of hosts" (Is. 8:18), even while the Lord was hiding His face from the house of Jacob (Is. 8:17). While his people went their blind and blinded way, Isaiah could still say, "I will wait for the Lord . . . and I will hope in Him" (Is. 8:17), for he knew that into Israel's darkness the light of God's new day would shine and usher in the birth of God's anointed King (Is. 9:2-7), that from the judged and cut-down house of David, from the "stump of Jesse" a Shoot would spring up to give to Israel a reign of righteousness and peace (Is. 11:1-10) — "in that day the Lord will extend his hand yet a second time to recover the remnant which is left of his people." (Is. 11:11)

Paul stands in the succession of the prophets, the bearers of the Word of God; he, too, is the beating heart of the remnant of Israel in his day. And so Paul knows

199

that the coming of salvation to the Gentiles, in which his own ministry played so large a part, serves to further God's purpose for Israel too. It serves "to make Israel jealous" (cf. 10:19). Even hardened Israel is a weapon of light in God's hand, and hardened Israel is not left untouched by the use to which God puts this weapon. Israel is provoked to longing jealousy by what God's Word creates among the nations round about. 12 What has happened to Israel has in it a promise for Israel. If God can reap such a harvest with Israel's "trespass" and "failure" (the Israelites' rejection of the Word of life); if God enriched the world and blessed the nations by using just *this* people in their unbelief, is there not a hidden purpose here, a nonapparent hope? What will not God do when Israel becomes a willing weapon in His hand, alert to do His will?

The words translated "their full inclusion" can also be translated "their fulfilling," namely, "of God's will." This is the meaning adopted in the interpretation given above. If the rendering of the Revised Standard Version is retained, one may think of the possibilities created by the increased number of converted Israelites, who would become what Paul is now, the means by which God carries out His gracious purpose for mankind. On either interpretation it is clear that the hardening of Israel took place "in hope," like the subjection of creation to futility. (8:20)

13 Gentile Christians may not simply write off Israel; they may not conclude that the Lord has done with Israel. For them to do so would be sinful pride on their part (cf. 11:18, 20, 25). More than that, it would frustrate Paul's mission to his fellow Jews. Paul cannot reach his fellow Jews directly; they break into anathemas at the sight of him. He must seek them roundabout,

200

through the Gentiles; the Gentile Christians *are* Paul's mission to the Jews. Therefore Paul "magnifies" his ministry; he boasts of the new Israel gathered by his Gospel **14** to make his fellow Jews jealous and thus save some of them. Paul indulges in no idle, unkempt hope. He knows that he will not bring all the flock of Israel back into God's fold; he will save only some. He does not quarrel with the ways of God but goes his way in meekness, just as Jesus did (Matt. 11:29; 21:5), grateful for the men God gave Him for His own. (Matt. 11:25)

15 Even God's negative dealings with the Jews meant reconciliation for the world. When they crucified the Son and persecuted His messengers, God worked the stubborn stuff of their rebellion into the fabric of His gracious plan. What shall come to be when God receives into His new people these "some," these Israelites whom Paul will convert and save through his work among the Gentiles — what will that act of God be called? This will be the miracle of the dry bones restored to life, revived by the Spirit of God, of which Ezekiel wrote (Ezek. 37:1-14); this will be "life from the dead" indeed, God's proper work (cf. 4:17) made clearly evident. **16** And this will happen. The eyes of man can see in Israel, as Israel now stands, only a hopeless case. But the eyes of faith, opened to God's revelation, see differently. They look back to Israel's beginnings and see there the imperishable work of God. There, at the beginning, is the calling of Israel's forefathers (cf. 11:28), the election of Israel.

Paul uses two figures to bring home the enduring significance of this fundamental fact. The first, that of the firstfruits of the dough, is taken from the worship life of ancient Israel. The offering of dough made from the first grain of the harvest consecrated the whole harvest to the Lord, the Giver of the harvest. The consecration of the part effects the consecration of the whole. What happened to the forefathers remains significant for their descendants. God has laid His hallowing hand on them and claims them for His use. This first figure argues from the part to the whole. The second figure, that of the root and the branches, argues from the source to the product. What grows from the root gets its character from the root. The promise to the forefathers is the root from which all the subsequent life of Israel springs; from it the nation gets its character and its history.

Paul speaks of the root and the *branches*, not of the root and the *tree*. This is due partly to the fact that Paul already has the subsequent development of the image in mind, in which branches are essential (vv. 17-24). But it has its reason also in the nature of the case. The consecration of the root consecrates the tree as a whole, sets it apart for God; but still each branch on the tree has its individual life and its peculiar fate, as the past and present history of Israel make clear. Paul is not saying that the hallowing of the root automatically assures the salvation of the tree or of every individual branch. God remains free to hack out fruitless branches and to graft in new branches. He still is free to create His Israel as He wills.

The Tree and the Branches   11:17-24

¹⁷ **But if some of the branches were broken off, and you, a wild olive shoot, were grafted in their place to share the richness °of the olive tree, ¹⁸ do not boast over the branches. If you do boast, remember it is not you that support the root, but the root that**

°Other ancient authorities read *rich root*

202

supports you. [19] You will say, "Branches were broken off so that I might be grafted in." [20] That is true. They were broken off because of their unbelief, but you stand fast only through faith. So do not become proud, but stand in awe. [21] For if God did not spare the natural branches, neither will he spare you. [22] Note then the kindness and the severity of God: severity toward those who have fallen, but God's kindness to you, provided you continue in his kindness; otherwise you too will be cut off. [23] And even the others, if they do not persist in their unbelief, will be grafted in, for God has the power to graft them in again. [24] For if you have been cut from what is by nature a wild olive tree, and grafted, contrary to nature, into a cultivated olive tree, how much more will these natural branches be grafted back into their own olive tree.

17 Paul has been speaking, since v. 13, to the Gentile Christians. He has reminded them that they are not the first and not the only ones to whom the Word of God has come. Again it is apparent that Paul's topic is not only the Jews, his kinsmen by race, but the church, the Israel of God; he is speaking of ancient Israel's place in that people created by the Gospel. Now Paul confronts an individual Gentile Christian, just as he confronted an individual Jew in 2:17, in order to quell in the Gentile a pride that could be as fatal to him as Jewish pride has been to the Jew. He develops further the image of the tree and branches. God has broken branches from His olive tree; that is the same thought as "the rest were hardened" in v. 7. The Gentile is tempted to look with dangerous complacency upon these ruined branches and to think: "*I* have replaced the Jew." Paul's comment

203

is designed to humble him. Paul tells the Gentile that *he* has done nothing; *God* has engrafted him (the passive voice here, as so often, indicates an activity of God), and that too in defiance of the rules of husbandry, as a wild olive branch on a cultivated olive tree. This action makes no horticultural sense; it certainly indicates no merit in the Gentile and is no ground for Gentile pride. It is a miracle of sheer, incomprehensible grace.

18 The Gentile cannot and dare not boast against the dead branches; he cannot boast at all, for he is a branch only, not the root. He has his place in a tree of God's planting and draws his life from the life with which God has endowed the root. The root supports him; he is, in a very real sense, indebted to Israel.

19 The Gentile in his pride can be as argumentative as the Jew (cf. 3:1-9). He can reply: "Well, yes; but still, God broke off branches to make room for *me*." **20** Paul's "That is true" is not without irony, as the rest of his answer shows. He now breaks through the image and calls things by their proper names, "unbelief" and "faith." *All* branches on the tree are there because God's mercy put them there; all have *received* from God their place and their connection with the root which now sustains their life. The severed, withered branches perished because they did what no other branch on earth can do: they have refused to take their life from the giving hand of God. The hardened Jew has perished by his unbelief; the Gentile has his place and life by faith. Where faith is, boasting "is excluded" (3:27). Faith cannot "become proud" at the sight of God's judgment upon unbelief. When faith sees broken branches lying withered on the ground, faith is filled with fear and says: "There but for the grace of God lie I."

21 If God's judgment did not halt before the disobe-

204

dience of Israel, God's firstborn son, if His judgmental hand broke off the "natural branches" of the tree which He Himself had planted, how can Gentile pride suppose that He will spare the engrafted branch, that He will not visit judgment on the disobedience of His late-born sons? **22** Holy fear is a natural and necessary component in the life of faith. Therefore fear is the beginning of wisdom. In reverent awe believing man can "note" the kindness and severity of God, His unplumbed mercy and His inscrutable judgment, and can come to know his own place and function under the overarching sway of the wisdom of God; he learns the "meekness of wisdom" (James 3:13). He learns that he dare not usurp God's judgment (cf. v. 20) and that he must live all his life in whole dependence on God's mercy. He cannot claim that mercy as his due; he can only "continue" in it, desperately, with the alternative of judgment always before his eyes.

23 The meek wisdom from on high knows, too, that no one may set limits to the creative power of God's mercy. The wise man learns to say with the prophet, "O Lord God, *Thou* knowest," when God asks, "Can these bones live?" (Ezek. 37:3). The unbelief of hardened Israel no *man* can break, but God has power to engraft the branches He has broken away. **24** If God could take the Gentile from his hopelessly abandoned wild-olive state and make him grow on the tree of Israel, who shall say that He has not the power to engraft the hewn-out branches in their native tree?

The Mystery   *11:25-27*

²⁵ **Lest you be wise in your own conceits, I want you to understand this mystery, brethren: a hardening has come upon part of Israel, until the full number**

of the Gentiles come in, ²⁶ and so all Israel will be
saved; as it is written,
   "The Deliverer will come from Zion,
   he will banish ungodliness from Jacob";
²⁷ "and this will be my covenant with them
   when I take away their sins."

25-26 "Lest you be wise in your own conceits" —
lest their wisdom be the false wisdom of man, com-
placent and critical, in order that their wisdom may be
the true wisdom from on high, rooted in the holy fear
that trembles at the Word of God and meekly goes the
way God would have it go, Paul states in another form
what he has already said in the figure of the tree and the
branches. He calls this form a "mystery." His words now
are a prophetic utterance concerning God's hidden
counsels, which only God can reveal and does reveal
now in the world's last days, His plan for governing and
guiding history for the realization of His redemptive
purposes. (Cf. Dan. 2:28; Rom. 16:25)

There is a particularly measured solemnity to this
utterance. Its oracular form makes this mystery, taken
by itself, somewhat obscure, but what precedes and
follows makes its chief intention clear enough. There
are three elements in this mystery: (1) The hardening
which has befallen Israel is only partial, and there is
still a time of grace for Israel; (2) this time of grace will
endure "until the full number of the Gentiles come in,"
that is, until the end of this age, when history ends
and judgment comes (the history of Israel's salvation
is linked organically with that of the Gentiles: until the
end of the age, the coming-in of the Gentiles will continue to provoke Israel to jealousy and call Israel to

206

repentance); (3) "and so" – by God's wise governance of the history of the Gentile and the Jew – "all Israel" (the whole of God's people from among the Gentiles and the Jews) "will be saved." There will be men of Israel, too, in that "all Israel" at the end of days, for God's ancient promise to Israel holds.

What the image of the tree and branches opened up as something *possible* with God, the mystery asserts as an action of God. What God can do He will do. He will engraft fallen branches into their native tree. The promised Deliverer, who comes from Zion, the citadel of David, the Messiah, will "banish ungodliness from Jacob." 27 God will through His Anointed establish a new covenant with Israel, under which Israel will repent and be forgiven. Paul's quotation of the promise from the Old Testament is extremely free; it might almost be called variations on a theme from Isaiah (Is. 59:20-21). The basic thought is from Is. 59, that mighty liturgy of repentance and absolution, an absolution spoken by the Lord, who Himself restores righteousness and brings salvation, so that all the world in East and West must fear His name. But there are added touches from the Psalms (Ps. 14:7; 53:6), and the picture of the promised covenant is colored by reminiscences of Jeremiah. (Jer. 31:33-34)

The promise that "all Israel will be saved" is taken by many, perhaps most, interpreters to mean that Israel *as a nation* will be saved. This mass conversion of Israel is often thought of as taking place at the very end of days, after the conversion of the full number of the Gentiles, as if Paul had written "and *then*" and not "and *so*." This seems to be making Paul say more than he actually does say concerning Israel's future, and it brings Paul into contradiction with himself. The mean-

ing of "all Israel" and the scope of the prophecy will
be further discussed after v. 32.

Enemies and Beloved   *11:28-32*

²⁸ As regards the gospel they are enemies of God,
for your sake; but as regards election they are beloved for the sake of their forefathers. ²⁹ For the gifts
and the call of God are irrevocable. ³⁰ Just as you were
once disobedient to God but now have received mercy
because of their disobedience, ³¹ so they have now
been disobedient in order that by the mercy shown
to you they also may ᵖ receive mercy. ³² For God has
consigned all men to disobedience, that he may have
mercy upon all.

ᵖ Other ancient authorities add *now*

28 Yet once more Paul confronts the Gentile with
the curiously enigmatic features of historical Israel. The
men of Israel are both "enemies" and "beloved," just
as they are both dead branches and at the same time
branches which the mighty grace of God can once more
engraft upon their tree, and just as they are both "hardened" and under the power of the promise of the Deliverer from Zion. Israel as a nation has turned a deaf
ear to the Gospel which proffered them the free gift
of the righteousness of God; that has made them enemies of God. The wrath of God, invoked upon them
by their own sacred Scriptures (vv. 8-10), is their present
lot. Paul tells the Gentiles: "They are enemies of God,
for your sake." As surely as God lifts up His countenance
upon His Gentile people who call Jesus Lord, so surely
is His face set against the men who persecute His church
and say that Jesus is accursed. And yet, no simple
scheme of wrath and retribution is sufficient to enclose

208

the inexhaustible workings of the Word of God. That Word once said to Israel, "I have chosen you," and swore fidelity to Abraham and his seed (Gen. 22:15-18). The men of Israel are not only enemies but also beloved. **29** God is God and not a man. His gifts and His call have their cause and origin in Him alone; they are not generated by the goodness of man, and they do not evaporate before the badness of man. His gifts and call are "irrevocable," so far as His will to give and to call are concerned. "God's love," Luther says, "does not find the object it can love; God's love creates it."

30 God's love *must* create the object God can love, for the history of man is a history of his disobedience to God. Paul once more puts down the pride of the Gentile Christians: The history of their past, he tells them, is one long chronicle of disobedience. God's gifts and call came to them in their disobedience "now," in this present time of grace. The disobedience of the Jew was the occasion of the mercy shown to them (the Gentiles), but they did not, on their part, merit mercy by any previous obedience of their own. **31** Now Israel in turn has proved disobedient in the face of the Gospel, which fulfilled the promise made to Israel. But Israel's dead end is not the end of the road for God; in the very act of showing mercy to the Gentiles He has been intent on mercy for His Israel too. The light that falls upon the Gentiles in the church is reflected back on Israel in order that Israel may be provoked and may find mercy too "now," in these days when the righteousness of God has been manifested. (The reading given in the footnote, which adds "now" after "they also may," is to be preferred, being well attested in the ancient manuscripts and consistent with the sense of the passage.) **32** "God has consigned all men to disobedience." In His wisdom He has by strange ways brought all men, both Israelite and Gentile, into that blind alley where disobedient man must turn about and face the wrath of God, where man must cease to "boast," must cease to offer pleas in his defense, and must throw himself completely on the mercy of his God, acknowledging his disobedience. The Hound of Heaven hunts men down, that He, the passionate Pursuer of His enemies, may at the last have mercy on them all.

"ALL ISRAEL"

These three sections (vv. 17-24; 25-27; 28-32) are markedly parallel. Each section contains an explicit or implicit warning against the Gentile pride that tended to despise and to dismiss from history the nation Israel. Each connects the history of rebellious Israel intimately with the history of the obedient, believing Gentiles. Each presents Israel in a curiously double aspect. In the first section, the Israelite is a dead branch cut off from the tree, but at the same time there is over him the possibility and the hope that God can restore him to his native tree and to life. In the second, there is a judgment of hardening on Israel, and yet there is hope for Israel; the hardening is partial, and the history of Israel and the Gentiles runs together toward its redemptive close. There is over hardened Israel the promise of a Redeemer out of Zion and of a new covenant of forgiveness and restoration. In the third section, the Israelite has become an enemy of God for the Gospel's sake, and yet there hovers over him a cloud which is big with blessing, the cloud of the irrevocable gifts and call of God. Furthermore, each section closes with a universal prospect of salvation. In the first, the tree of God's planting stands before Him in full-branched splendor,

210

the ancient root providing life for native branches, for engrafted wild-olive branches, and even for hewn-out branches miraculously restored to their place. In the third section, God's locking-up of all men in their disobedience has the goal "that He may have mercy on *all*." In the second section, the parallel to the completed tree of God and to the "all" who receive God's mercy is this: "All Israel shall be saved." This parallelism confirms the interpretation given for "all Israel" above, namely, that "all Israel" signifies the whole redeemed people of God from among Jews and Gentiles. This interpretation gives to the second member of the series the same broad outlook that is characteristic of the other two.

It should be noted also that this is the only place in all the letters of Paul where the expression "*all* Israel" occurs, although he speaks of "Israel" more than a dozen times. The exceptional expression, "*all* Israel," as here used by Paul, expresses in two words the whole idea of continuity-discontinuity that runs through Paul's presentation of the church in Chs. 9 – 11. "All Israel" corresponds to the "all" of Gal. 3:26-29; in this "all" there is neither Jew nor Greek in the old sense of "Jew" and "Greek," for all are now one in Christ Jesus, all are Christ's, all are Abraham's offspring and heirs according to the promise. "All Israel" is the same sort of imagery as the 144,000 "out of every tribe of the sons of Israel" in Rev. 7:4. And, finally, the fact that "all Israel" occurs as the content of the "mystery" speaks for taking the term in this comprehensive sense, for the "mystery" has from Daniel onward (cf. Dan. 2:28 ff.) associations of comprehensiveness and universality. (Cf. Rom. 16: 25-26; 1 Cor. 15:51; Eph. 1:9-10; 3:3-6, 8-10; Col. 1:26-28; 1 Tim. 3:16)

211

If "all Israel" is made to refer to the nation Israel, Paul's words are being pressed to make Paul say more than Paul plainly says concerning Israel. And if the conversion of "all Israel" is referred to a time *after* the conversion of the Gentiles, Paul is being made to say something that he does not say at all. Paul says "and *so*," not "and *then*," in 11:26; and the threefold "now" of vv. 30-31 (there seems to be no valid reason for removing the third "now" from the text) keeps the history of Israel's hope within the time span of the Gentile's time of grace. And if Paul is understood to mean that the whole nation Israel will at last be saved, he is understood as contradicting himself; for he has opened his whole discussion with the basic statement that "not all who are descended from Israel belong to Israel" (9:6), that "it is not the children of the flesh who are the children of God, but the children of the promise are reckoned as descendants" (9:8). If "all Israel" means "children of the flesh," this basic distinction has been abandoned. As interpreted above, the beginning and the end of the section (Chs. 9 — 11) correspond to each other, both in their emphasis on God's freedom (cf. also 11:35) and in their use of the name "Israel"; the "all Israel" of 11:26 is then Israel in the sense given by 9:6-8, "the children of the promise."

Doxology   *11:33-36*

[33] O the depth of the riches and wisdom and knowledge of God! How unsearchable are his judgments and how inscrutable his ways!
[34] "For who has known the mind of the Lord, or who has been His counselor?"
[35] "Or who has given a gift to him that he might be repaid?"

³⁶ For from him and through him and to him are all things. To him be glory forever. Amen.

Paul breaks out into doxology. This may seem surprising if 11:25-27 does not, after all, predict salvation for the total nation Israel; what is so overwhelming about the prediction, as it stands, that the Israelites have a door opened to them still and shall go to make up, with the Gentiles, the final Israel of God? We must remember how flatly improbable Paul's inspired prediction must have sounded to Paul's hearers and to Paul himself. When men took in by faith, A. D. 56, what God had given Paul to say (that Israel's rebellion is not the end of Israel's history), they could not but join the apostle in his adoration. For they remembered Jesus' prediction of the fall of Jerusalem and the destruction of the temple, the abandoned house of God, and His command to His disciples that they should separate themselves from Judaism. They were witnesses to Israel's fanatical persistence in revolt against the Christ (cf. 1 Thess. 2:14-16); they saw Israel playing Pharaoh's role as hard and hardened enemy of the people of God (cf. 9:17-18). They read the verdict of God upon His apostate people in the Scriptures (11:8-10). There was nothing probable at all about a possible reversal in the feelings and fortunes of Israel when Paul wrote; even four decades later John was to speak of a Jewish house of prayer as "a synagog of Satan" (Rev. 2:9; 3:9). That there should be successors to the converted Israelite Paul, that the improbable, fantastic miracle of Paul's conversion should reoccur, and that, too, on a grander scale – this taxed the faith of Christians and was a high, exhilarating hope.

33 All men end up in beggary (11:32); only God is

213

rich, inexhaustibly rich, rich in kindness and forbearance (2:4), rich in glory (9:23), and the Lord whom He
gave to Jew and Greek is rich in His beneficence toward
all who call on Him (10:12). God cannot fail for lack of
means in compassing His ends. And God is wise. He
uses all His riches in a sure, astounding governance
of history that overawes and humbles men. When men
put their trust in chariots and horsemen, those old reliable makers of successful history,

> . . . he is wise and brings disaster. . . .
> When the Lord stretches out his hand,
>> the helper will stumble, and he who is helped
>> will fall,
> and they will all perish together. (Is. 31:1-3)

And when world empires fall (Is. 10) and Israel is judged
and ruined, royal house and all, He makes His Spirit
of wisdom rest on the Shoot that grows from Jesse's
stump (Is. 11:1-2) and through Him makes His earth
a land of righteousness, a paradise of peace (Is. 11:3-9).
Men quarrel with His ways; they carp at His prophet,
the Baptist crying in the wilderness, and at His Son,
the Son of man who eats and drinks with men, and
yet His "wisdom is justified by her deeds" (Matt. 11:
16-20). God knows, as no man knows; His knowing is
a knowing with a will and an effect. When He "fore-
knows" His people (11:2; 8:29), He has shaped His
people's history. As man's only riches worth the name
is to be enriched by Him, so man's only real knowledge
is to know that he is known by Him (2 Cor. 8:9; 1 Cor.
8:3). Man's only wisdom is to fear, to stand in awe of,
Him and to obey.

His judgments are unsearchable; out of them salvation springs (cf. 11:32):

Thy judgments are like the great deep;

man and beast thou savest, O Lord. (Ps. 36:6)

His ways through history are inscrutable; who could have predicted that the fulfillment of His promises to Israel would bring judgment on Israel? Or that the darkling Gentiles should reflect the light of God upon the Jew? **34** "Who has known His mind? Who has given Him advice?" Isaiah asked (Is. 40:13) — who ever spoke one syllable that told the Creator how He should create (Is. 40:12)? Who ever told this Governor of history how He should govern history? (Is. 40:15; cf. vv. 22-23). **35** No one has ever bent God's will with his advice; no man has ever made God his debtor with a gift. "Who has given to me, that I should repay him? Whatever is under the whole heaven is mine," the Lord told trembling Job (Job 41:13). That all His ways are ways of grace, grace to the Gentile and the Jew, lies in His will alone. **36** He stands at the beginning as the Creator of all, the Giver of all gifts. He holds the reins of all man's sorry history in His wise, almighty hands. He shall bring all His creation home, purged by His judgment, restored by His grace, that all may witness to His glory everlastingly. The apostle leads the church in a song that gives to Him His everlasting glory now, even now before the glorious end of all His ways has made His glory manifest.

The Gospel Creates a New Worship for the New People of God 12:1—15:13

All Life, in the Church and in the World, a Spiritual Worship *12:1—13:14*

The Gospel Basis *12:1-2*

[1] I appeal to you therefore, brethren, by the mercies of God, to present your bodies as a living sacrifice, holy and acceptable to God, which is your spiritual worship. [2] Do not be conformed to this world [q] but be transformed by the renewal of your mind, that you may prove what is the will of God, what is good and acceptable and perfect. [r]

[q] Greek *age*
[r] Or *what is the good and acceptable and perfect will of God*

1 The new people of God comprehends all nations. The new worship comprehends the whole life of the new man in a sense and in a depth in which the worship of an ancient Israel could not yet comprehend it. For the old worship was worship under the Law; "the giving of the law" and "the worship" of Israel belong together (9:4). The new worship is grounded in "the mercies of God." In that phrase Paul sums up the creative and transforming power of the Gospel of God as he has been proclaiming it in the first 11 chapters of his letter. The worship of old Israel was regulated; the new worship is inspired, not imposed *on* man but created *in* man by the God who gives life to the dead. By the mercies of God the members of the new Israel have risen with Christ to walk in newness of life (6:4), they have been "discharged from the Law" so as to "serve not under the old written code but in the new life of the Spirit"

(7:6), they have been liberated from the "law of sin and death" by the "law of the Spirit of life" (8:2) and have become children of God led by the Spirit (8:14). Therefore Paul can appeal to them to present their bodies to God. Their bodies, once bodies of sin (6:6), bodies of death (7:24), bodies that still await their redemption (8:23) can be an acceptable sacrifice, "holy," that is, consecrated to God.

They are to be a living sacrifice. With the hallowed term "sacrifice" Paul marks the continuity of the new worship with the old worship under the Law; with the modifier "living" he marks the discontinuity, the newness of the new worship. The worshiper no longer gives to God the life of another creature; he gives God his living self. Since all men have bodies, all can sacrifice, all have become priests. Since men are never without their bodies, worship is constant. Since bodies are visible, all worship becomes a witness and a proclamation, a lived doxology to God; God is glorified in His servant people (cf. Is. 49:3). This is "spiritual" worship. What the old system with its ritual prescriptions for sacrifice foreshadowed has become substance and reality. This is now worship in its truest and deepest sense. All previous worship has been but a parable to this reality.

2 The members of the new people of God are called upon to anticipate, in their bodily activity, the life of the world to come, to assert in action the reality of that world *now*. They are to be God's bridgehead in the alien and hostile territory of this world in this age. Consequently their worship is a constant and embattled no of nonconformity to this world, or age, which is an "evil age" (Gal. 1:4), a world whose "god" is Satan. (2 Cor. 4:4)

They can continue to be the strenuous minority

for God in this age only by being perpetually transformed by the mercies of God brought to them continually in the Gospel. The Gospel is their only power,
that "Word of God *at work* . . . in . . . believers" (1 Thess.
2:13). This is not a mystic's dream of being absorbed
into the life of God; it is conscious, waking, responsible
life in the presence and in the service of God. This trans-
formation therefore involves a perpetual renewal of
the *mind*, a making-new of the religious intellect for
the life in the new age. In every case, as each case may
arise, the child of God is called upon to "prove" the
will of God, that is, to weigh and ponder and decide
what the revealed will of his Father God is asking of
him now. The child knows that will; it asks of him that
what he says and does be "good," that it be a kindly,
gracious furthering of the welfare of the man whom
God has set beside him as his neighbor. It asks of him
that what he says and does be "well-pleasing," well-
pleasing to God, who is the measure of all things in the
transformed life of the renewed mind. No blind sentimental love, which ignores God's will and word and
in the last analysis works harm, can be a service done
to Him, a sacrifice with which He will be well pleased.
The Father's will asks of the child that what he says
and does be "perfect," that it go all the way and reach
its goal, like God's love for His enemies (Matt. 5:43-48),
regardless of the worth of the recipient, regardless of
the kind of answer it finds. (Cf. 12:14)

With that Paul has established a Gospel basis for
his admonitions. The long series of imperatives that
follows has a rather miscellaneous character, especially
in the latter half of Ch. 12. Paul's instruction for the
new worship is suggestive rather than exhaustive. He
gives examples of how the new man "proves" the will

of God; he does not prescribe in such detail that no man need do any "proving" for himself. The order of his admonitions seems to be suggested by his familiar triad (cf. 1 Cor. 13:13; Col. 1:4-5; 1 Thess. 1:3; 5:8) of faith, love, and hope.

The Renewed Life as a Life of Faith   12:3-8

³ For by the grace given to me I bid every one among you not to think of himself more highly than he ought to think, but to think with sober judgment, each according to the measure of faith which God has assigned him. ⁴ For as in one body we have many members, and all the members do not have the same function, ⁵ so we, though many, are one body in Christ, and individually members one of another. ⁶ Having gifts that differ according to the grace given to us, let us use them: if prophecy, in proportion to our faith; ⁷ if service, in our serving; he who teaches, in his teaching; ⁸ he who exhorts, in his exhortation; he who contributes, in liberality; he who gives aid, with zeal; he who does acts of mercy, with cheerfulness.

3 Faith is individual; God never created two beings alike. Paul therefore addresses the individual in this section. "Every one . . . himself," "each," "individually," "gifts that differ," "*he* who teaches," "*he* who exhorts" — such expressions point to the individuality of faith. Paul addresses the individual in order to overcome individualism, with its self-will and pride. For there is in the individuality of faith a temptation; the individual endowment given to the believer tempts him to "be conformed to this world," in which greatness consists in being greater than others, in exercising authority over

and lording it over others (cf. Matt. 20:25). The world's pride invades the church and its worship in Christian form, as pious pride, the nastiest kind of pride there is. Paul wrote these words from Corinth; he had seen how the life of the Corinthian church had been corrupted by this conformity to the world, how self-seeking individualism had misused the gifts given to believers for mutual ministry to exalt self and create divisions in the church. (Cf. 1 Cor. 12 – 14)

The apostle first removes all self-willed individualism from himself; he speaks "by the *grace given*" to him. He employs that grace in the service of the Lord who gave it; he therefore speaks to help and build up others in the obedience of faith, to glorify his Lord, not himself. Thus he can speak to each individual in the church at Rome and bid each man beat down his pride. "Every one" needs this word; there is no endowment so slight but that a man can build a tower of pride on it. All men are soloists by nature and inclination; they must learn the art of playing in God's orchestra. Each man must learn to "think with sober judgment" of himself; he must learn to see, with a vision not intoxicated by pride, the part that God would have him play. He must "prove" what is the will of God for him and learn to function in the ensemble of the church "according to the measure of faith which God has assigned *him*."

The expression, "measure of faith," occurs only here in the writings of Paul and has caused difficulty. Does not every faith receive all God's gifts, the Christ and the "all things" God gives with the gift of His Son (8:32)? There is only one answer to that question, of course. But Paul is here speaking of the functioning of faith, of the life of faith in ministry to others with the gifts received from God. Here there are differences, here there is variety according to the "measure" bestowed by God. Moreover, Paul is primarily concerned with the rich variety of gifts, not with any difference in value or prestige that may attach to individual gifts. His warning against pride has made that plain, and the figure of the body which he employs in the next verse makes it plainer still.

4 The human body is one organism. This organism has many members, each with its own function to perform. The body has its unity and functions as a unity in virtue of the fact that each member functions individually, in its peculiarity. It is because the eye functions as eye and because each finger functions as individual finger that a woman can thread a needle. 5 "So we," the Israel of God, the church, we in all the prodigal variety of our heredities and histories, are one body in Christ. We are all baptized, have all died with Christ, and have risen with Him; we have no life but the life that He, our Lord, has given us. We constitute one organism that must function as one. And just here individuality has its place; each member is essential to the whole and to all other members. No member is solitary; no member is expendable. Thus individualism is overcome, and yet there is no deadly uniformity. 6 We have gifts that differ, and that differentiation is the gift of God's enriching grace to each of us. The gifts are God's grace, and they are there for us to *use*, not to evaluate or to discuss. For grace is self-denying and self-imparting, as the grace of Jesus Christ our Lord has made us know. (2 Cor. 8:9)

The gift of prophecy is high in Paul's esteem because it is markedly and preeminently a gift that serves others. "He who prophesies speaks to men for their upbuilding and encouragement and consolation" (1 Cor.

14:3); when the prophet speaks, "all . . . learn" (1 Cor. 14:31). By the prophet's Word the sinner is convicted and converted (1 Cor. 14:25). This gift, the eminent ability, given to some, to "prove what is the will of God" for the church here and now and to declare that will, brings with it its own temptation. It is the temptation to go beyond what God has given us and to muddy the waters of the Spirit with "meditations" of one's own. It is ominously easy to pass from "What the will of God is, that I declare," to "What *I* declare, that is the will of God." The prophet can readily come "to think more highly of himself than he ought." Therefore Paul repeats the basic admonition of v. 3 ("according to the measure of faith which God has assigned him") as a warning for the prophet in particular; his prophecy is to be in proportion to his faith.

7 If God has given a member of the body the gift of "service," the capacity and the will to feed the hungry, clothe the naked, visit the sick, and to express God's own love to the widow and the fatherless, let him serve the whole body by functioning in that service. He need not prophesy or speak with tongues to qualify as a member of the body.

"Teaching" probably refers to instructing men in the Old Testament Scriptures. Paul calls the Old Testament "profitable for teaching" (2 Tim. 3:16) and says that "whatever was written in former days was written for our instruction" (Rom. 15:4). We find the teachers regularly at work in the early church (cf., e. g., Acts 13:1), and these scribes trained for the kingdom of heaven (Matt. 13:52) must have done their work extremely well. The amount and kind of knowledge of the Old Testament Paul presupposes on the part of his readers is amazing; for example, a few words from Genesis are obviously enough to suggest the whole scene of Abraham looking up to the starry skies and reading God's promise of his innumerable descendants there (4:18). The teacher has the gift of teaching; very well, let him teach. 8 The teacher can enrich the mind of faith and give faith a basis for its judgments, but it may be given to another to "exhort," to rouse the wills of men and move them to unanimous action or endurance.

God may have withheld from another the gift of instructive or fervent speech and have given him instead a well-lined purse. Let his purse speak for him; let him give "in liberality" (literally, "in singleness"), in that purity of heart which does not count the cost liberality involves or calculate the praise liberality may win. Another "gives aid"; he espouses a good cause and works for its success. Let him do it with his whole heart, not with half-hearted, routine words and deeds. "He who does acts of mercy" should let his acts of mercy be the free and splendid radiation of the mercies of God, which he himself has received. Let him perform them "with cheerfulness," not with the sullen, gray demeanor that degrades the recipient of the gift and makes ungracious even our most gracious deeds.

The Renewed Life as a Life of Love   *12:9-11*

⁹ Let love be genuine; hate what is evil, hold fast to what is good; ¹⁰ love one another with brotherly affection; outdo one another in showing honor. ¹¹ Never flag in zeal, be aglow with the Spirit, serve the Lord.

9 Paul has already touched on love in the preceding, especially in speaking of contributions, giving aid, and acts of mercy. This is in the nature of the case; faith and love are so intimately related that any line of di-

vision between them is bound to be a fluid one. Love
is to be genuine, not hypocritical. Even within the church
there is, tragically enough, much that passes for love
and yet is but a sorry substitute for genuine love. It is
often sentimental, weak, and therefore basically selfish;
it may make the lover "feel good all over," but it does
not really help those to whom love is shown. The mark
of genuine love is therefore an abhorrence of evil cou-
pled with a holding-fast to the good. Love "does not
rejoice at wrong but rejoices in the right" (1 Cor. 13:6).
Love, to be genuine, must have the courage to call evil
by its name, and to tell a brother his fault in order to
gain the brother (Matt. 18:15; cf. 18:12-14). One can see
why Paul couples "genuine love" with "truthful speech"
in 2 Cor. 6:6-7. The classic example of the uncompro-
mising rectitude and candor of genuine love is the First
Letter of John. 10 Where there is genuine love, there
the church as the family of God is a reality. There all
the brothers of the firstborn Son love one another and
care for one another. Both the words used here, "love"
and "brotherly affection," are taken from the vocabulary of warm, spontaneous family affection.

"Outdo one another in showing honor." Paul speaks
these commands calmly and concisely, as if obedience
to them were self-evident. It is self-evident, but only
under the impetus and inspiration of the mercies of
God. Here particularly the Christians are being summoned to nonconformity with their world. The Greco-
Roman culture which they breathed in as their native
air put no premium on humility. And yet "humility"
is not the adequate word for what Paul is saying here,
for the negative note of self-depreciation is not dominant in his command. The emphasis is on the positive,
on seeing the man beside you with the eyes of the God

of all mercies, as a man of infinite worth, the man for whom Christ died, worth your love and honor, not because he is such and such a man but because he is there, placed there by God. 11 Such love cannot remain a sentiment; it becomes an action, to be carried out with a zeal that never flags. This must be "love of the Spirit" (15:30). The Spirit is the source and power of this love; the energies of our humane goodwill do not suffice for it. It is a service rendered, through the other man, to the Lord Himself. (Cf. Matt. 25:40)

The Renewed Life as a Life of Hope 12:12-21

12 Rejoice in your hope, be patient in tribulation, be constant in prayer. 13 Contribute to the needs of the saints, practice hospitality.

14 Bless those who persecute you; bless and do not curse them. 15 Rejoice with those who rejoice, weep with those who weep. 16 Live in harmony with one another; do not be haughty, but associate with the lowly; *never be conceited.* **17 Repay no one evil for evil, but take thought for what is noble in the sight of all. 18 If possible, so far as it depends upon you, live peaceably with all. 19 Beloved, never avenge yourselves, but leave it** *to the wrath of God; for it is written, "Vengeance is mine, I will repay, says the Lord."* **20 No, "if your enemy is hungry, feed him; if he is thirsty, give him drink; for by so doing you will heap burning coals upon his head." 21 Do not be overcome by evil, but overcome evil with good.**

Or give yourselves to humble tasks *Greek give place*

12 Love and hope belong together. Paul more than once expressly connects the two (1 Cor. 13:7; Col. 1:4-5;

225

cf. Phil. 4:5; Rom. 13:10-11). The command to "rejoice
in hope" seems to come in rather abruptly; perhaps
Paul's first readers, whose life was lived in constant
hope, did not find the transition so abrupt as we do.
The joy which they drew from their hope helped them
to bear the burden of the never-ending claim upon their
love and made their service to the Lord the taking of
a kindly yoke. They drew strength from their hope to
bear up bravely under tribulation. They prayed con-
tinuously, "Our Lord, come!" (1 Cor. 16:22; cf. Rev. 22:
20), and bore up under the pressure of the present until
their Lord should come.

Thus far all fits easily under the caption of "hope";
the combination, "suffering and patience and prayer,"
has in fact occurred before in the context of the Christian hope (8:18, 25, 26). But from here on the precepts
become so miscellaneous, apparently, that many interpreters think it misplaced ingenuity to try to find any
inner unity in them. But it should be noted that the
admonition of v. 19 is again clearly connected with the
future; "*the* wrath" is visited on the transgressor at the
end of days (cf. 2:5; 5:9). And the word "overcome"
in v. 21 is a word that speaks a promise to our hope.
Perhaps the intervening admonitions are related to
hope after all and have a sort of unity. This is not to
say, of course, that there is a strictly logical sequence
in the various admonitions; but, on the other hand, they
are not set down at random.

13 Not only does the Christian hope give courage
and stamina in enduring afflictions (v. 12); it also gives
the Christian that largeness of heart which makes him
sympathetic towards the needs of his fellow saints.
"Hospitality" would be a special form of this active,
sympathetic helpfulness, for hospitality is thought of

here not as a general social graciousness but as a form of aid to be supplied to travelers, especially to exiled or persecuted fellow Christians. **14** If hope gives large-ness of heart toward the persecuted, it also creates the capacity to love and bless one's persecutors. Our Lord's command to love and bless one's enemies and perse-cutors (Matt. 5:44) was not a blank, detached ethical imperative; it has its setting in the hope created by His proclamation of the Kingdom drawn near (Matt. 4:17) and in the promises of the Beatitudes (Matt. 5:3-12). Paul is recalling this command of Jesus here. Peter likewise gives the command to refrain from vengeance and to bless those who revile in a setting of hope (1 Peter 3:9). **15** The largeness of heart created by the Christian hope makes a man open for the joys and sorrows of others generally. Since "the appointed time has grown very short" (1 Cor. 7:29) and the "form of this world is passing away" (1 Cor. 7:31), a man's own joys and sorrows in this age cease to be of ultimate significance. He has a loose hold on the blessings of this age (1 Cor. 7:30). He can enter into the joys and sorrows of his fel-lowman with ready sympathy because he is not shut up in his own concerns. He becomes like his Lord, who manifested His glory in this passing age both by sup-plying wedding wine at Cana (John 2:1-11) and by weep-ing at the grave of Lazarus. (John 11:35)

16 An admonition to unanimity, humility, and gra-cious condescension and a warning against pride are not out of place where present tribulation and the hope that rises above tribulation are being spoken of; Paul's words to the suffering church at Philippi witness to that (Phil. 1:29 – 2:4; cf. 2:14-18; 4:2). Common tribulation and the prospect of a common martyrdom do not of

227

themselves insure unanimity and humility in the troubled church. Indeed vv. 16-17 read like a commentary on the thought of Phil. 4:5a, "Let all men know your forbearance." Paul bids the Christians of Philippi let all men, friends and foes, see in them, the persecuted church, the royal graciousness which springs from consciousness of strength. The church's strength is in her hope; Paul gives the motive and dynamic for this serene forbearance in the words: "The Lord is at hand." (Phil. 4:5b)

17 If haughtiness and conceit are overcome, the desire for vengeance is cut off at the root. Paul is to speak against taking vengeance again, from another point of view, in v. 19. Here he is concerned about the witness given to the world by Christians in their suffering. If Christians present their bodies to God as a living sacrifice, they will present to the world meekly suffering bodies, a noble witness to all sorts of men concerning the God of mercies in whom they hope. **18** Their witness will be not only passive but active also. Mindful of their Lord's beatitude upon peacemakers, they will turn the other cheek, give the cloak to him who sues for the coat, and go the second mile (Matt. 5:39-41). They *will* have peace with all men — "if possible"; they cannot purchase peace at the price of denying their Lord or by obeying men rather than God.

19 A Christian repaying evil for evil is a sorry witness to the world; he is also denying his God, the God of hope. The wrath of God will judge God's enemies at the end of days, after God's mercies have had full scope to do their work. Paul clothes God's claim to be sole Judge and Avenger in the words of Deut. 32:35, quoting freely. Perhaps he was conscious of the words which follow upon the Lord's assertion of His right:

> For the LORD will vindicate his people
>> and have compassion on his servants. (Deut.
>> 32:36)

No sword of vengeance is given to the church; the state is executor of God's wrath in this age. The church does not judge; the church waits and hopes.

20 The only "vengeance" which the Christian has at his disposal is the vengeance of unsought and unmerited love, love shown to his enemy. The only pangs which the Christian can bring upon his enemy are the salutary pangs of contrition; these are the "fiery coals" heaped on his enemy's head. Paul uses the picturesque language of Prov. 25:21-22 to express this thought. The origin of the metaphor of heaping fiery coals on someone's head is obscure, but the interpretation given above seems probable and is confirmed by the following verse.

21 If the Christian allows his natural impulse to carry him away and responds to evil with evil, that is a defeat for him (cf. 1 Cor. 6:7); he is overcome by evil. The flesh has triumphed over the Spirit, and the renewed mind has again become a "base mind" (1:28). If he is led by the Spirit and requites evil with good, that is a victory for him; the victory of Christ, who loved His enemies and interceded and died for them, is being realized in his life. He is overcoming evil as Christ overcame it, in meekness and suffering. His love for his enemy proclaims the Christ to his enemy, confronts his enemy with the invincible love of Christ, and leads his enemy through shame and penitence to faith. This is, of course, the very opposite of the heroic ideal of man. The Christian is not "a man's man," but God's man, with a hope given him by the God of hope who raised Jesus from the dead and gave man a victory over sin and death which quenches in him the desire for any other victories. This thought of victory, or overcoming, is closely associated with the resurrection in Paul (1 Cor. 15:55-57) and in the New Testament with the hope that does not put to shame generally, particularly in Revelation. (Rev. 2:7, 11, 17, 26; 3:5, 12, 21; 12:11; 15:2; 21:7)

The Renewed Life Within the Orders of This World   *13:1-7*

¹ Let every person be subject to the governing authorities. For there is no authority except from God, and those that exist have been instituted by God. ² Therefore he who resists the authorities resists what God has appointed, and those who resist will incur judgment. ³ For rulers are not a terror to good conduct, but to bad. Would you have no fear of him who is in authority? Then do what is good, and you will receive his approval, ⁴ for he is God's servant for your good. But if you do wrong, be afraid, for he does not bear the sword in vain; he is the servant of God to execute his wrath on the wrongdoer. ⁵ Therefore one must be subject, not only to avoid God's wrath but also for the sake of conscience. ⁶ For the same reason you also pay taxes, for the authorities are ministers of God, attending to this very thing. ⁷ Pay all of them their dues, taxes to whom taxes are due, revenue to whom revenue is due, respect to whom respect is due, honor to whom honor is due.

The life which Paul has been describing, this work of faith, this labor of love, this steadfastness of hope (cf. 1 Thess. 1:3), is spiritual worship. Men who thus live on the mercies of God are presenting their bodies to God as a living sacrifice. They are asserting the reality of the new world of God, here and now in the midst of the old world, by proving with renewed mind what is the will of God for every aspect and every portion of their lives, by not conforming to the ways and standards of the old world in which they live.

But there are aspects of life which, it would seem, are not fit material for this worship, portions of life which prove to be stubborn and intractable stuff when men attempt to weave them into the seamless robe of the new life. One of the most obvious and important of such areas of life would be the Christian's relationship to the Roman government, an institution completely identified with this world, a pagan power supported by pagan religious sanctions. To the Jews it seemed a monstrously abnormal thing that God's people should live under pagan Roman rule. The coolly realistic Sadducees might come to terms with the anomaly of Roman rule, the Pharisees submitted to it in resignation as a judgment of God upon His people, the Zealots rejected it as intolerable and passionately rebelled. None found a really positive religious relationship to it. What was the new Israel to do? How was the Christian to find a positive relationship to this all-enveloping and inescapable pagan reality in his life? Paul's language in 12:14, 17, 19 has already made it plain that violence and revolt are out of the question for God's new Israel. But is that all? Is a sort of neutral and resigned passivity the most that the new worship can make of this aspect of men's lives?

1 Paul calls for subjection to the governing authorities, and he lays this obligation on every individual. The motivation for this subjection is not merely prudential but religious. All authority is from God. Paul makes this concrete and practical; he speaks of the authorities "that exist," not merely of authority in gen-

eral or government in the ideal. God is the source of all authority, including the governing authority of Rome. The governing authority that confronts *me* is His. Paul hammers home this point repeatedly in these verses: authority in its concrete manifestations is *God's ordinance.* "God" occurs six times in these seven verses (five times in the Greek; the translators have, correctly, added "God's" to "wrath" in v. 5); and the idea of "ordinance," or "order," is expressed in five words, all having the same root form. One could reproduce this feature of Paul's Greek in bad English somewhat as follows: "Be sub*ordin*ated . . . the authorities that exist have been *ordained* by God . . . (v. 1). He who refuses to sub*ordin*ate himself . . . is resisting God's *ordin*ance (v. 2). . . . Therefore one must sub*ordin*ate oneself." (V. 5)

2 Consequently, resistance to authority is impious, a resistance to an order-of-things established by God. Those who resist will incur the judgment of God; their revolt may prove successful and it may be that no man can call them to account. But they have not, for all that, escaped from God their Judge. 3 Furthermore, this resistance to authority is contempt for, and opposition to, the *goodness* of God. Paul has already spoken of the heinousness of such contempt for God's goodness, how it stores up treasuries of wrath for a man "on the day of wrath when God's righteous judgment will be revealed" (2:4-5). The existing authorities are a manifestation of God's goodness, established by Him to restrain the evil in this evil age; they are His bulwark against the moral chaos which would otherwise engulf mankind.

He who does no evil need not fear the rulers and has no reason to rebel against them. He can count on their "approval" (literally, "praise"). Some men are hard put to find specific evidence for this approval of

232

the good deed in the life of nations. Governments do reward and praise distinguished citizens in various ways, of course. But what "approval" do the unsung, decent, quiet millions ever get? The possibility of "a quiet and peaceable life" (1 Tim. 2:2) created by the ordered vigilance of constituted powers is in itself a mighty piece of praise, a strong approval of the decent man. And when we think of Paul's experience in subsequent years, of how the ponderous machinery of Roman law moved to protect one citizen, Paul, in troubled Palestine and carried him to Rome upon his appeal to Caesar (Acts 22–28), one gets some conception of what Paul had in mind when he spoke of the "approval" of those in authority. 4 In a word, the man in authority is God's servant (whether he knows it or not), for his subjects' good. His divinely given power to punish is therefore in proportion to his capacity for doing good; he can take human life. This servant of God bears the sword to execute God's wrath, God's annihilating reaction against all those who presume upon, or misuse, or spurn His goodness. Paul's use of the word "sword" is explained by the fact that for Romans the sword was the instrument of execution and therefore the symbol of retributive justice; they called the right to inflict capital punishment "the right of the sword." 5 For the Christian, then, the obligation to be subject to governing authorities is based not only, or even primarily, on fear of the evil consequences of disobedience; he obeys "for the sake of conscience." The eye of faith sees in the authorities the hand of God; if he resists that hand, he defiles his conscience, for his disobedience "does not proceed from faith" (14:23) and is sin.

6 Paul reminds his readers that what he is telling them is really nothing new to them: "You also pay

taxes." They are already rendering to Caesar what is Caesar's. Paul can assume that Jesus' word concerning taxes owed to Caesar (Matt. 22:21) is known and obeyed in the churches. If they are paying taxes in obedience to the Lord's command, they are in principle recognizing the place and function of the Roman authorities as "ministers of God," intent upon their duties as His ministers. The word "minister" has religious coloring; it was used of priests and Levites in the Greek Old Testament, and Paul uses it of his ministry as apostle to the Gentiles (15:16). 7 When they pay taxes, they are paying what is due by divine right; they cannot therefore rest content with the mere act of paying tax and revenue. Their hearts must be in it; they must give to the authorities the respect and honor, too, which is their due as servants of God. Thus their life within the this-worldly order of the state becomes a spiritual worship, and their obedient bodies are a living sacrifice:

Behold, to obey is better than sacrifice
and to hearken than the fat of rams. (1 Sam. 15:22)

PAUL AND THE ROMAN GOVERNMENT — EXPERIENCE OR REVELATION?

Paul's words on rulers and authorities are not the ripe fruit of his meditation on the grandeur of the Roman state. True, his experience with Roman authorities had generally been good, and he is writing to the Romans during the first five years of Nero's reign, that good beginning whose promise was to be belied by the excesses of that emperor's later years. But it has been observed that of all the emperors under whom Paul lived there was hardly one who could be called, by ordinary standards of political justice, a "legitimate" possessor of his place and power. Paul could see, in titles like "Augustus" ("revered") and in the divine honors which the emperors accepted from their subjects, especially in the East, the creeping totalitarianism of the imperial state. That totalitarianism would force upon the church the decision between "Caesar is Lord" and "Jesus is Lord." Paul could know that the state can become a Satanic perversion of the preserving ministry of God.

And Paul's experience with the state had not been uniformly good. His rights as a Roman citizen had been outrageously ignored by the magistrates of the Roman colony of Philippi (Acts 16:22, 37; 1 Thess. 2:2). At the time when he wrote his Second Letter to the Corinthians, a few months before his Letter to the Romans, he had been beaten thrice by Roman rods (2 Cor. 11:25). He considers sufferings (8:18), persecution (8:35; 12:14), and the sword (8:35) an ever-present possibility for the church in the Roman Empire; the people of God must reckon with a real possibility of becoming "sheep to be slaughtered" (8:36). And, above all, it was a Roman governor who gave the order for the crucifixion of his Lord; whenever Paul wrote "cross" or "crucified," he had to think of Rome. The "rulers of this age" who "crucified the Lord of glory" (1 Cor. 2:8) were agents of the power of Rome.

These rulers are powers only in this age; "they are doomed to pass away" (1 Cor. 2:6). But meanwhile they are there and are in power, and to see in these rulers and in the sword they bear the work of God, even if it be but the work of God's left hand and no intrinsic part of His unworldly and eternal rule – to see that, a man needs wisdom from on high; he needs revelation to open his eyes to God's hidden governance of all things, for the preservation of mankind and for the good of those who love Him. Paul is speaking what has been revealed to him by the Spirit; he walks by faith here, not by seeing. And when he calls on Christians to obey wholeheartedly these powers as ministers of God, he summons them to an act and a life of faith. If faith is fundamental to life in the church (12:3-8), it is basic also to the Christian life in the world under the state.

The Debt of Love   *13:8-10*

8 Owe no one anything, except to love one another; for he who loves his neighbor has fulfilled the law. 9 The commandments, "You shall not commit adultery, You shall not kill, You shall not steal, You shall not covet," and any other commandment, are summed up in this sentence, "You shall love your neighbor as yourself." 10 Love does no wrong to a neighbor; therefore love is the fulfilling of the law.

8-9 The Christians' attitudes and actions in their relation to the state proceed from faith. Their civic loyalties are therefore of a piece with their whole life of love; all faith is faith which works through love. They pay all men their dues, but that, for them, is minimal. They rise above the orders of this world, not by ignoring them but by doing more than they require. For a man in Christ there is, beyond all that duty may require of him, a debt which never can be noted as "paid in full," the debt of love. His bodily worship of the God of mercies is total, constant, never finished. Once more we hear how Paul's preaching of faith does not overthrow the Law but upholds it (3:31); in him who loves his neighbor with a love which is as whole, as constant, and as active as his instinct to preserve himself the just requirement (8:4) of the Law has been fulfilled. The Law's deepest

236

intention, as Jesus revealed it anew, the intention that man should love his God and his neighbor in an unbroken unity of love, has been fully met. When a man is led by the Spirit and is motivated by the Spirit's love, then his neighbor's marriage, his neighbor's life, his neighbor's goods are as precious in his eyes as his own. 10 Where this love lives and works, there is no wrong against the neighbor which the Law must condemn. The will of God, "what is good, and acceptable, and perfect," has been done.

Life as in the Day   *13:11-14*

¹¹ **Besides this you know what hour it is, how it is full time now for you to wake from sleep. For salvation is nearer to us now than when we first believed;** ¹² **the night is far gone, the day is at hand. Let us then cast off the works of darkness and put on the armor of light;** ¹³ **let us conduct ourselves becomingly as in the day, not in reveling and drunkenness, not in debauchery and licentiousness, not in quarreling and jealousy.** ¹⁴ **But put on the Lord Jesus Christ, and make no provision for the flesh, to gratify its desires.**

The triad of faith, love, and hope dictated the order of the admonitions in Ch. 12; it would seem to be the informing principle in Ch. 13 too. Even though the word "faith" is not used in vv. 1-7, the idea is clearly there. Vv. 8-10 touch on love once more, with particular reference to love as the fulfillment of the Law. And the chapter closes with a passage on hope, one in which the character of the distinctively Christian hope is seen more clearly than before, one of the most beautiful and moving passages in all the writings of Paul. This passage is a carefully constructed hymn of hope, built up in

237

threes. There are three major divisions: the statement of the theme (v. 11a), the development of the theme (vv. 11b-13), and a conclusion (v. 14), which at the same time rounds out the whole thought of Chs. 12 and 13. The central section (vv. 11b-13) again has a triadic structure: three statements of hope (salvation is nearer, the night is far gone, the day is at hand), three exhortations of hope (to cast off the works of darkness, to put on the armor of light, to conduct oneself becomingly as in the day), and three pairs of contrasts to becoming conduct (not reveling and drunkenness, not debauchery and licentiousness, not quarreling and jealousy).

11 The reference to hope reenforces the command to pay the never-ending debt of love (cf. Col. 1:4-5). "Love never ends" (1 Cor. 13:8). As the Spirit is the firstfruits of the world to come (8:23), so the love inspired by the Spirit (15:30) is the manifestation of the new world of God even now, in the midst of the old world; it is destined to endure, when prophecy and speaking with tongues and the piecemeal knowledge of this age shall have ceased (1 Cor. 13:8-9). All these gifts of the Spirit point to the future. When the future becomes full present, these gifts shall have had their day and cease to be. But love shall fill the future too. To know God's "hour" therefore means to walk and work in love.

God's hour, His appointed time of salvation (cf. 3:26), is His gift to men; it is by that very fact also His claim on men. The fulfillment, proclaimed and presented in His Gospel (cf. Mark 1:15), which His hour brings and the sure hope which His hour gives do not call into being men who merely acquiesce in the fulfillment and dream of the future; they set men in motion. To know God's hour is to be roused from sleep. A sleeper does not know where he is or what he is or what hour has struck; he is dead to his duties and his opportunities. He may dream, but does not *know*, and he cannot act. The Christian life is a conscious, a waking and waiting life. When we first came to faith, God's salvation dawned on us — "we *were* saved." But we were saved "in . . . hope," in this hope, that we who are now hidden sons of God shall enter upon the liberty and glory of manifested and transfigured sons of God on that day when the dawn of salvation gives place to the full day of salvation, when the new age which still lies concealed beneath the old shall emerge from hiddenness and be the full and sole and glorious reality of all our lives. Each passing day brings that day closer.

12 The night of this age of sin and death, this age of our suffering and failure, is far gone. The day is at hand. We live in the time since the resurrection of Christ, in which the old age and the new age overlap, and we are exposed to both. The far-gone night is still a power that seeks to make us sons of darkness and of night, doomed to perish with the dying night. To live as in the day therefore involves a struggle; it calls for action, decisive action. We are called upon to cast off the works of darkness that naturally sprout, like fat and noxious weeds, in the night of sin. We are called upon to take up the *armor* of light; the life *as* in the day can be a full reality only in the battle against the forces of night. 13 A casting-off, a putting-on, these things God's day demands. It demands a whole life lived as in the day, a life whose comeliness is a witness to the strong reality of the dawn and to the imminence of the day. This witness is a bodily witness; the men aroused from sleep present their bodies to the God who is Light, in whom "there is no darkness at all" (1 John 1:5); worship and witness are one. The hope that is in them is professed before men in things

as mundane as their attitude toward alcohol and sex, things as common as their ordinary dealings with their fellowmen. Amid the guzzling, wenching, brawling sons of night they walk in radiant decency.

14 Such a life is possible only for men who are clothed in Christ. The Lord Jesus Christ is their armor of light that can overcome all powers of darkness. They have been clothed in Him by Baptism (Gal. 3:27), therefore they can be bidden to take up the given gift, to put Him on anew. Their baptism is to become their daily dress. In Baptism they have participated in His death and resurrection; in Christ they have reached the frontier of the world to come. Only in Him can they find strength to live on that frontier as in the day. In Him they can find strength to speak a constant no to the importunities of the flesh, the futureless flesh with its desires that hold men fast within this world. To "provide for the flesh" is a contradiction in terms; such pro-vision is no foresight at all, for it looks no farther than this dark and dying world.

Christ is mentioned only twice in this section, once in 12:5 and again in 13:14. But Christ is always meant in Paul, even where He is not named. Chapter 13 of the First Letter to the Corinthians is the most striking example of that; in it Christ is not named at all, and yet all that Paul says of love in that chapter gets its color and form from Christ. And here the closing mention of Christ shows how Christ has been in the picture all along. For Paul is repeating the basic thought with which he began (12:1-2). "Put on the Lord Jesus Christ" repeats, with explicit reference to Christ, what was said in 12:2 in the words "Be transformed by the renewal of your mind," just as "Make no provision for the flesh" corresponds to "Do not be conformed to this world." A man clothed in the Lord Jesus Christ presents himself to the Father, to serve Him; if ever a man presented his body as a living sacrifice, holy and acceptable to God, Jesus was that man. If ever a life was an unbroken unity of spiritual worship, it is the life of the Son of God, who served and died and rose and reigns "to the glory of God the Father." (Phil. 2:11)

The Weak and the Strong in Faith United *in One Worship for the Glory of God*   *14:1 — 15:13*

Unanimity is essential to the worship of the new people of God. All must put on Christ and live their lives of faith and love and hope together; there is no room for self-centered individualism. It has already become apparent that this unanimity of the members of the church does not mean that all individuality is suppressed; no monotonous uniformity is imposed on all. Each believer functions in the church and serves the common life of the church "according to the measure of faith which God has assigned him" (12:3). The unanimity and health of the church are maintained by the functioning of "gifts that differ according to the grace given" to each member of the church. (12:6)

Differences in faith manifest themselves in the ministries of the church; they make themselves felt, and create tensions, in another area also. Not all are equally strong in faith. To some believers it is given to see the new life steadily and to see it whole; they apprehend it in all its ramifications and in its implications for all man's decisions and actions. They accordingly walk through life with glad and free self-confidence, with robust courage. These are the strong in faith. Others again have not the power of faith to appropriate

241

for themselves at once and altogether the liberty for which their Lord has set them free (Gal. 5:1). They walk more timidly and circumspectly than their full-blooded brethren, beset by inner blocks, troubled by inhibitions. These are the weak in faith.

In his discussion of the problem of the relationship between the weak and strong in faith, Paul pictures the differences in faith as showing themselves in the believer's attitude toward meat and drink (wine) and holy days. Whether Paul is speaking to an actual situation in the church at Rome or is merely using these instances as typical examples of how differences in the strength of faith manifest themselves, can hardly be made out. Some interpreters think that Paul is speaking to an actual situation in Rome, and they see in the "weak" a Jewish-Christian minority whose religious scruples are being treated cavalierly by their freer Gentile brethren. This is possible, certainly; the term used to describe "unclean" food (14:14) is the Judaic one, found also in the Gospels (Mark 7:15; cf. Matt. 15:11), and men coming out of Judaism with its stringent dietary laws and strict Sabbath observance would naturally be slow to enter fully into the Christian liberty concerning food and holy days. But Paul follows his own advice about "not disputing over opinions" (14:1) and does not go into the thoughts that motivate the weak. Hence we cannot be altogether certain that the scruples referred to are Judaic scruples. Paul had had to deal with a similar problem at Corinth (1 Cor. 8 — 10), and it may be that he is simply taking cases suggested by his past experience as typical, with no direct references to conditions in the church at Rome.

The historical question raised above is relatively unimportant. It does not greatly matter, for our understanding of this section, whether there were vegetarians or not in Rome A. D. 56. Three things that do matter are very clear. First, the weak in faith, though they may be inclined to be censorious of the strong, do not demand that the Law of Moses be imposed upon the new people of God. The problem is not the problem dealt with in the Letter to the Galatians; we hear nothing of circumcision, for instance, and Paul's calm and winning manner here is quite different from his volcanic outbursts in the Letter to the Galatians. The question of the Christian's freedom from the Law is assumed to be, in principle, answered. The only question that remains is: How is that liberty to be employed? Secondly, the difference between the weak and the strong is a threat to the common life of the church. We must remember how significant the common meal, with which the celebration of the Lord's Supper was as a rule closely associated, was for the fellowship of early Christians in both Judaic and Gentile congregations (Acts 2:42, 46-47; Gal. 2:11-21; 1 Cor. 11:21 ff.). Scruples regarding food would tend to disrupt this fellowship and to cast a shadow over congregational fellowship generally. Thirdly, the problem involved *faith;* it was therefore a religious concern. No easy, "sensible" solution, such as dividing the congregation up into like-minded groups or imposing some sort of compromise dietary legislation on all, would do. The question raised by differences in faith had to be answered from the church's central resource, from the Gospel itself. This is how Paul answered it. He speaks to both the weak and the strong and lays the kindly yoke of Christ on both. He addresses first both groups together (14:1-12), then the strong alone (14:13 — 15:6), and finally again appeals to both. (15:7-13)

To the Weak and to the Strong: Do Not Despise!
Do Not Pass Judgment!   *14:1-12*

[1] As for the man who is weak in faith, welcome him, but not for disputes over opinions. [2] One believes he may eat anything, while the weak man eats only vegetables. [3] Let not him who eats despise him who abstains, and let not him who abstains pass judgment on him who eats; for God has welcomed him. [4] Who are you to pass judgment on the servant of another? It is before his own master that he stands or falls. And he will be upheld, for the Master is able to make him stand.

[5] One man esteems one day as better than another, while another man esteems all days alike. Let every one be fully convinced in his own mind. [6] He who observes the day, observes it in honor of the Lord. He also who eats, eats in honor of the Lord, since he gives thanks to God; while he who abstains, abstains in honor of the Lord and gives thanks to God. [7] None of us lives to himself, and none of us dies to himself. [8] If we live, we live to the Lord, and if we die, we die to the Lord; so then, whether we live or whether we die, we are the Lord's. [9] For to this end Christ died and lived again, that he might be Lord both of the dead and of the living.

[10] Why do you pass judgment on your brother? Or you, why do you despise your brother? For we shall all stand before the judgment seat of God; [11] for it is written,

> "As I live, says the Lord, every knee shall bow
>   to me,
> and every tongue shall give praise [u] to God."

[12] So each of us shall give account of himself to God.

[u] Or *confess*

244

1 The weak in faith are evidently thought of as a minority; the church as a whole is told to welcome the "man who is weak in faith." The welcome is to be a genuinely Christian welcome, wholehearted and unreserved. The brother is to be welcomed as he is, in his weakness, and he is to be borne in his weakness until his weakness has been overcome. There is to be no "dispute over opinions"; the thoughts which motivate the weak believer in his actions are *his* thoughts, the operation of his faith and therefore sacrosanct. No one, not even the stronger brother, has the right to invade this hallowed ground, not even for the purpose of providing the weak with better "opinions." The church is not called upon to whip the weak man into shape forthwith with arguments, even though they be well-intentioned arguments. Faith is not fed by logic.

2 This welcome is for the *weak*. Paul does not urge a weak and watery toleration of the heretic, the violater of the truth of the Gospel. He therefore explains what he means by "weak" and "strong." The strong in faith can eat all things; no line of demarcation between clean and unclean foods exists for him. He knows that Jesus Christ his Lord has "declared all foods clean" (Mark 7:19), and so pork is a good gift of God to him. He knows that "the earth is the Lord's, and everything in it" (1 Cor. 10:26; Ps. 24:1). The fact that the meat which he buys in the market has been part of an offering made to a pagan idol does not, for him, erase from it the Creator's mark of ownership; he eats it with a will and thanks the Lord for it. These are the "opinions" which guide him in his conduct. The weak calls Jesus Lord and blesses his Creator too, but the bright glory of his Lord's lordship does not, for him, fall on all meats alike. Therefore he avoids all suspect meats by eating

245

only vegetables. Though set free by Christ, he is not ready yet to use his liberty to the full. Each in his actions seeks to "prove" what is the will of God for him (cf. 12:2), each eats and drinks as he discerns God's will.

3 Each is tempted to look askance at the other. The strong man's temptation is to despise his fumbling, fussy-conscienced brother: What makes a man think he is glorifying God by eating spinach? This contempt need only to be named to be condemned. It has no place in a common life of love, where men are called upon to "outdo one another in showing honor" (12:10). The weak man's temptation is to "pass judgment" on the strong. This "passing judgment" looks more pious than the strong man's contempt; and Paul spends more time on it, to lay it bare for what it is. The weak man passes judgment on the strong on good religious grounds; the strong man's free use of his liberty in Christ looks to him like careless callousness. The strong man is, in his judgment, not taking his religion very seriously. Is not this meat-eating, wine-drinking (14:21), Sabbath-breaking (14:5) man conforming to this evil world? But when the weak man quarrels thus piously with the strong man's liberty, he is really taking up a quarrel with God, "for God has welcomed him," the strong in faith, in this his free strength. Who would dare to impose on him a standard of "spiritual worship" which his God has not imposed? 4 The Lord has purchased him with His own blood (cf. Acts 20:28) and has taken him into His house as His familiar slave. That act has removed him from *our* sphere of judgment; he stands or falls, succeeds or fails, before his Lord. And if the anxious censor should reply, "'Or falls'—that's just the point. I am concerned for him; I fear that his free indulgence in meat and drink may prove to be his fall,"

246

Paul's answer is: "The Lord who welcomed him, the Master who owns him, has power to make him stand. The Lord who gives men freedom gives them strength and wisdom too."

5-6 Whether it be in the observance or nonobservance of certain days or in the eating of, or abstinence from, certain foods, each man is to act on the conviction of *his* mind, the renewed mind which is, in its peculiarity, God's gift to *him*. No man may impose his own convictions on his neighbor, no more than he can live by his neighbor's convictions. Here as in ministry (12:3) a man lives according to the measure of faith which God has assigned him. Only thus can each life be a life of total, spiritual worship; thus each man in his peculiarity is united with every other man in his peculiarity in a common worship. They honor their Lord and give God thanks together.

7-8 We eat or abstain "in honor of the Lord"; that makes both eating and abstaining an integral part of the whole Christian life. We are never autonomous; our whole living is a living "to the Lord." All that Paul has been saying since the beginning of Ch. 12, all that he has said in Chs. 6–8 is involved here. And the Lord's lordship over us does not cease at death. Our dying is no longer blind submission to an inevitable fate. Paul can speak of his own dying as a libation gladly poured out to the Lord (Phil. 2:17-18), as a going home to Him (Phil. 1:23; 2 Cor. 5:8). So then, in living and in dying we belong to Him; He never lets us go. No power, not even the power of that last enemy death, can loose the power of His almighty hand (cf. John 10:28). Our lives do not end in futility, like water seeping away into the sand; they end in personal communion with Him who is in life and death our Lord. **9** By His death He has

247

become the Lord of all, to be acclaimed by every tongue (Phil. 2:6-11). In His risen life He is the Lord, with right and power to rule over all, the dead and the living.

10 We live to Him, we die to Him, we belong to Him who loved us all; He has made us all brothers in the family of God. Within that family there is no room for passing judgment or for contempt. Paul fosters faith by bidding men look back upon the cross and resurrection of the Lord. He also fosters holy fear by pointing men to the Judgment, to the day when God will judge the secrets of men by Jesus Christ (2:16). "We shall all stand before the judgment seat of God"; as surely as we all have one Deliverer, we all shall also have one Judge. We must face Him together, with the marks of all our graceless squabbles graven on our faces. **11** When the Lord, the Creator of the world and Ruler of all history (Is. 45:23; cf. 45:1-22), shall receive the homage of all men, when all shall bow the knee and praise their God, then it will be terrifyingly clear that those differences which seemed so great and so intolerable when we were all cooped up in the cramped chambers of our time were in reality no real differences at all. **12** It therefore behooves each man, whether his sin be passing judgment or contempt, to learn to see these differences in that perspective now; for God will take us one by one, and each of us shall give account to God, not of his contemptible brother or of his loose-living, callous brother, but of himself.

To the Strong: Put No Stumbling Block
in the Way of Your Brother   *14:13 — 15:6*

¹³ Then let us no more pass judgment on one another, but rather decide never to put a stumbling block or hindrance in the way of a brother. ¹⁴ I know

and am persuaded in the Lord Jesus that nothing is unclean in itself; but it is unclean for any one who thinks it unclean. [15] If your brother is being injured by what you eat, you are no longer walking in love. Do not let what you eat cause the ruin of one for whom Christ died. [16] So do not let what is good to you be spoken of as evil. [17] For the kingdom of God does not mean food and drink but righteousness and peace and joy in the Holy Spirit; [18] he who thus serves Christ is acceptable to God and approved by men. [19] Let us then pursue what makes for peace and for mutual upbuilding. [20] Do not, for the sake of food, destroy the work of God. Everything is indeed clean, but it is wrong for any one to make others fall by what he eats; [21] it is right not to eat meat or drink wine or do anything that makes your brother stumble. [r] [22] The faith that you have, keep between yourself and God; happy is he who has no reason to judge himself for what he approves. [23] But he who has doubts is condemned, if he eats, because he does not act from faith; for whatever does not proceed from faith is sin. [w]

[r] Other ancient authorities add or be upset or be weakened
[w] Other authorities, some ancient, insert here Ch. 16:25-27

[1] We who are strong ought to bear with the failings of the weak, and not to please ourselves; [2] let each of us please his neighbor for his good, to edify him. [3] For Christ did not please himself; but, as it is written, "The reproaches of those who reproached thee fell on me." [4] For whatever was written in former days was written for our instruction, that by steadfastness and by the encouragement of the scriptures we might have hope. [5] May the God of steadfastness and encouragement grant you to live in such harmony with

249

one another, in accord with Christ Jesus, ⁶ that together you may with one voice glorify the God and
Father of our Lord Jesus Christ.

13 "Then let us no more pass judgment on one
another." Paul looks back once more to what he has
said to both groups. Both "pass judgment," for the contempt of the strong for the weak is, in effect, a judgment
on the weak. He turns now to the strong and identifies
himself with them (cf. v. 14). The strong must receive
the weak into their fellowship. But their obligation does
not end there, for they are in their freedom a threat
to the faith of the weak, who are brought under the
influence of the example of the strong in their association with them. The free exercise of their strong faith,
their firm conviction that all foods are clean and all
days holy, can prove a block across their weaker brothers' road, to make them stumble and fall. How this comes
about, Paul makes clear in the following.

14 Paul first states his conviction that no food is
in itself unclean. This is a conviction "in the Lord Jesus"
and therefore as true as the truth of the Gospel itself.
It is a conviction based on the revelation, given in Jesus,
that the ancient regulations of the Law concerning food
and drink and festivals were only a shadow of greater
things to come, that in Jesus the substance of these
greater things has been revealed, that the shadows
have no further meaning of their own and cannot bind
men's faith (cf. Col. 2:16-17). Jesus Himself had declared
all foods clean (Mark 7:19). All food is clean; but if a man
eats it in the conviction that it is unclean and that he
disobeys his Lord in eating it, *he* is thereby made unclean. The clean food is unclean to him who looks upon

250

it as forbidden food. **15** Therefore the strong man's freedom can become a stumbling block to the weak. The weak man sees his stronger brother eating food that he has hitherto not dared to eat. He is enticed, or perhaps shamed, into eating what his conscience tells him is forbidden food. Thus he is "injured," made to sin, by what his stronger brother eats. The strong man's eating is no longer innocent, for it has become an act of ruthless lovelessness and destroys his brother. The brother is weak, wrong in his convictions, wrong as wrong can be. But Christ died for him; that makes him, in his foolish weakness, a brother infinitely precious in the eyes of all for whom Christ died (cf. 1 Cor. 8:10-11). To injure him is to sin against Christ Himself. (1 Cor. 8:12)

16 The good, clean food received from God and eaten with thanksgiving by the strong in faith ("what is good to you"), this blessed thing is "spoken of as evil" by the weak man whom it has destroyed. In his sorrow and despair he calls it a Satanic snare that trapped him into disobedience. — This is one way in which this rather obscure verse can be understood, but there is another interpretation which seems to many to be more plausible: Paul is thinking of the effect which these difficulties and tensions within the church may have on outsiders. "What is good to you" would mean the Christians' highest good, that which gives their life its whole content and purpose and sets them apart from all other men. Those who speak of it as evil (literally, "blaspheme it") would be outsiders. Outsiders, observing the friction and heartache occasioned in the Christian community by questions of food and drink, would maliciously assume that food and drink are of supreme importance in the Christian life and would assert ironically that the "kingdom of God," of which the Christians talk so much,

251

involves eating certain foods and drinking certain drinks. This fits in well with what follows.

17 Where God is King and Jesus is Lord, food and drink are not the paramount realities. Jesus told His disciples to seek first God's kingdom and His righteousness and gave them His promise concerning food and drink: "All these things shall be yours as well" (Matt. 6:33). Paul echoes Jesus' words; where men submit in faith to God's reign, there men receive the righteousness of God as God's free gift. There there is peace; men's lives are whole and sound again. There there is joy, joy in the Holy Spirit, who is our foretaste and assurance of the bright new world of God. As Paul puts it elsewhere: "Since we are *justified* by faith, we have *peace* with God through our Lord Jesus Christ . . . and we *rejoice* in our hope of sharing the glory of God" (Rom. 5:1-2). **18** Forgiven men, whole men, men filled with joyous hope, do not destroy the brother for whom Christ died; they serve Christ and do His work in the church. The Father who was well pleased with His only Son is well pleased with these brothers of the firstborn Son. And men, both weak and strong, who see their blessed work and its result, well know their worth. — The Greek words translated "thus" could with equal faithfulness be rendered "in Him," that is, in the Holy Spirit. The thought then would be that the Holy Spirit brings a man under the lordship of Christ and enables him to render pleasing service to God.

19 The duty of the strong is clear. The God of peace who gave to men their Prince of Peace (Is. 9:6) wants peacemakers for His sons (Matt. 5:9). The Christ who builds His church (Matt. 16:18) does His work through men who upbuild one another. Men who make peace and serve their weak brothers are doing "constructive" work in the highest sense of that word. What "disputes about opinions" cannot do, their love can do; it can build up the weak man and enable him to overcome his weakness. The weak brothers, admitted to their fellowship without argument, are edified; they grow strong in the warm sunlight of their stronger brothers' love. 20 This calls for self-sacrifice on the part of the strong; their love must be a self-denying love. Paul therefore once more points out to them what is involved. If they refuse to make the sacrifice and assert their freedom — freedom to eat! — to the full, they will destroy the work of God. The weak whom they despise are God's own workmanship, created by Him in Christ Jesus (cf. Eph. 2:10). The clean food which they confidently eat will turn to poison in their mouths if by their eating they make others sin and fall.

21 The strong may urge that it is "right" for them to evidence the strength and freedom of their faith by eating as they please. Paul's answer is that nothing is so right, so noble, and so manifestly good as love. In love the strong man will show his strength by forgoing the freedom that his strong faith gives him. Because he is strong, he is mobile and can adapt himself; the weak man, immobile in his inhibitions, cannot come to him in his strength. But the strong man can go to the weak and join him in his weakness, as Paul himself did (1 Cor. 9:22). So peace will be maintained; the common life of the church will be sound, unmarred by judging and contempt. So the whole church will be edified. When the weak brother sees how the strong, whom he suspects of callousness and carelessness, lay by their freedom for his sake, when he sees with what radical seriousness these men take the obligations of their faith, how they honor the work of God in the

253

weak — when he sees that, he ceases from censorious-
ness; he may even find the strength, eventually, to
thank God with his stronger brothers over a small glass
of gentle wine.

22 The strong man may honestly regret that he
has by his self-sacrificing course lost an opportunity
to witness; he cannot, he feels, let his light shine before
men if he cannot let men see the freedom for which
Christ has set him free. Paul assures him that no faith
which works by love is ever lost; the God who gave it
sees it. A man is "happy," sure of God's favor, and rich
in the possession of His love when he can do the will
of God as his mind, renewed in faith, has apprehended
it, when he acts in love. Then he has no reason to "judge
himself." A consistent, unbending course of faith that
leaves him with a troubled conscience because he knows
his freedom has made his weaker brother stumble has
no such blessing on it. **23** In fact, such a course condemns him. An act of faith done in doubt and with a bad
conscience is no longer an act of faith; it stands condemned as sin, "for whatever does not proceed from
faith is sin." If it is true that our only righteousness is
"the righteousness of God through faith in Jesus Christ"
(3:22), then all that does not flow from this our faith in
Him is sin. If an act ignores and overrides the redeeming
death of Christ (v. 15), if it withdraws from the royal
reign of God which gives men righteousness and peace
and joy (v. 17), if it contradicts the lordship of the Christ,
who died and rose for us that He might be our Lord in
life and death (vv. 7-9), if it forgets that what we have
received from God we have received in trust and that
"each of us shall give account of himself to God" (vv.
10-12) — any act that forgets all that is sin.

1-2 Paul's theme is still the one church united in

unanimous worship, but from this point on we hear no more of meat and drink and holy days. Paul deals more generally with the relationship between the weak and the strong in the common life and worship of the church. Once more he identifies himself with the strong — "*We who are strong*." In all cases the strong ought to bear with the weaknesses, the failings, of the weak. "Bearing with" the weak is something more positive than toleration of them or indulgence toward them; it means self-renunciation on the part of the strong. They can no longer "please themselves," look out for their own interests, even if that interest is "religious" self-development. They "bear with" the weak by taking the weak upon themselves as their responsibility, by existing for and serving the weak, by imparting their strength to the weak in a gracious ministry that builds him up.

This the strong "ought" to do; they owe this service to the weak. This is not a general "ethical" obligation; it is the personal, religious "ought" of grace, which has its basis in God's redeeming act in Christ. The disciples of Jesus *ought* to wash one another's feet because their Lord and Master has washed theirs (John 13:14); they *ought* to lay down their lives for the brethren because Christ laid down His life for them (1 John 3:16). Paul *owes* the Gospel to all men and *ought* to preach it because he has himself received its grace, the grace of apostleship. (Rom. 1:14; cf. 1:5)

3 The strong ought to serve the weak because the love of Christ constrains them. Christ served the weak. He did not please Himself; He never used His power to serve Himself — the Gospels record no miracle of His that was not a ministry to others. His miracles were Servant's work (Matt. 8:17; 12:15-21; cf. Is. 53:4; 42:1-4), part of the life which was in all its parts a progress

255

toward the cross. He served the weak, the outcast, the branded sinners. He revealed the God of all mercies who desires "mercy and not sacrifice" (Matt. 9:13; Hos. 6:6), the God who seeks the lost (Matt. 18:12-14), the King who forgives His debtor (Matt. 18:27, 32), the Father who receives the prodigal son (Luke 15:20). By His free mercy to the weak and helpless He drew down upon Himself the reproaches of the righteous, who had made their God in the image of their own rigid, righteous, and exclusive selves. They thought they were defending God's honor when they called Jesus the friend of sinners, a glutton and a drunkard who ate and drank in odorous company, a blasphemer who forgave a paralytic his sins on his own authority, a sorcerer in league with Beelzebub; but they were in reality reproaching God, who sent the Son of man to serve and give His life a ransom for many. And so the cry of the singer of Psalm 69, crying to the Lord his God when all men turned against him because he remained faithful to his God, became the cry of God's Anointed: "The reproaches of those who reproached Thee fell on Me." (Ps. 69:9)

It is noteworthy that Paul does not point to the life of Christ to support his statement that "Christ did not please Himself" but instead quotes from the Old Testament. He could evidently presuppose that all the churches knew the way Christ went on earth, as we know it from the gospels; this evidently was a fixed part of the "standard of teaching" to which all members of the church were committed (6:17). What Paul stresses here is the fact that Christ went this way "according to the Scriptures," according to the will of God as revealed in the Old Testament. Paul is emphasizing the fact that the reproach and shame and death which

256

He endured was His revelation of God's love for men. That makes His service to the weak a divinely redemptive act.

4 The Old Testament Scriptures are therefore indispensable to the life of the church; through "prophetic writings" the mystery of Christ is made known to all nations, to bring about the obedience of faith (16:26), and Paul's use of the Old Testament in this letter illustrates how the ancient Word of God sustains and nurtures faith. Paul appropriates Israel's Bible for the new Israel of the last days; all that was written in former days was written for us "upon whom the end of the ages has come" (1 Cor. 10:11). All Scripture looked and pointed toward the last great act of God in Christ; all Scripture therefore serves to instruct the church of Christ "for salvation through faith in Christ Jesus" (2 Tim. 3:15). Through Christ Jesus the Old Testament, this dark, perplexing book, becomes clear and luminous for the eyes of faith; through Him the veil which screens its deepest and true meaning from the eyes of hardened Israel is removed (2 Cor. 3:15-16). Then the Old Testament speaks encouragement and inspires steadfastness; it gives us hope.

5 Indeed, the Old Testament is the voice of God Himself. Paul pointedly applies to God the same two words that he has just used of Scripture, "steadfastness" and "encouragement." God speaks in the Scriptures; it is He Himself who through them gives us hope. This hope is the sure confidence that all His promises, now fulfilled in Christ, will be fulfilled in us. This plants a steadfast courage in our hearts. This gives us that largeness of heart of which Paul has already spoken (12:12-21). This hope, in which we find the strength to bless our enemies, makes us capable of bearing with

257

the failings of the weak. This makes possible a life of harmony between the strong and weak "in accord with Christ Jesus" — He is the source and power of our unity, He whose life and death for us all the Scriptures make luminous for us so that we walk together in their light. **6** This makes the church a united worshiping church, ringing with unanimous doxology to the God and Father of our Lord Jesus Christ.

To All: Welcome One Another   15:7-13

⁷ Welcome one another, therefore, as Christ has welcomed you, for the glory of God. ⁸ For I tell you that Christ became a servant to the circumcised to show God's truthfulness, in order to confirm the promises given to the patriarchs, ⁹ and in order that the Gentiles might glorify God for his mercy. As it is written,
"Therefore I will praise thee among the Gentiles,
and sing to thy name";
¹⁰ and again it is said,
"Rejoice, O Gentiles, with his people";
¹¹ and again,
"Praise the Lord, all Gentiles,
and let all the peoples praise him";
¹² and further Isaiah says,
"The root of Jesse shall come,
he who rises to rule the Gentiles;
in him shall the Gentiles hope."
¹³ May the God of hope fill you with all joy and peace in believing, so that by the power of the Holy Spirit you may abound in hope.

7 After all that he has said in the two previous sections Paul can be succinct in this his third command.

258

He ties it in with the preceding ("therefore"), and three words suffice: "Welcome one another." Paul passes on at once to the motivation for his command: "As Christ has welcomed you, for the glory of God." Christ's "welcome" was so all-embracing that it was the revelation of nothing less than the all-embracing love of God (cf. 5:5-8). In the Christ, in His life and death and in His working through the apostolic word and deed, God is glorified, that is, He is made known, acknowledged, and adored as the one God of all, who "will justify the circumcised on the ground of their faith and the uncircumcised through their faith" (3:30). 8 Christ's love spanned greater and graver differences than those which separate vegetarians from eaters of meat; He gave His costly welcome (it cost His life) to both Jew and Gentile. He ministered, and sent His apostles to minister, to the lost sheep of the house of Israel (Matt. 15:24; 10:5-6), and He was faithful in that ministry unto death. In Him all God's promises to His people were confirmed and ratified; the Gospel of God, promised through the prophets in the Holy Scriptures, became reality in Him (1:1-2). At His coming, Zechariah could bless the Lord God of Israel for His fidelity to His promise (Luke 1:67-75); Simeon, who had looked long for the consolation of Israel, could depart in peace (Luke 2:29-32). Jesus could stand up in the synagog at Nazareth and read the promise written in Isaiah and declare: "Today this Scripture has been fulfilled in your hearing" (Luke 4:21). And Paul could say to the men of Israel at Antioch: "We bring you the good news that what God promised to the fathers, this He has fulfilled to us their children." (Acts 13:32-33)

9 The table which God spread for Israel was rich enough to feed the Gentiles too (Matt. 15:26-27). The

259

risen Christ sent His apostles to all nations, and He was with them. In the Christ proclaimed to the Gentiles God was found by those who did not seek for Him and showed Himself to those who did not ask for Him (10:20; Is. 65:1). Multitudes of Gentiles from the East and West followed in the footsteps of the faith of the centurion of Capernaum (Matt. 8:11) and glorified the God of Israel for His mercy, which gave to them who never sought righteousness the gift of righteousness of God (9:30). Christ's love made all men welcome in His Father's house. The fulfillment of the promises made *to* Israel brought the fulfillment of the promises *for* the Gentiles.

That promise was written in every part of the Old Testament canon, in the Law, in the Prophets, and in the "Writings." When David praised the Lord, his Rock, his Fortress, and Deliverer (Ps. 18), he extolled the Lord "among the Gentiles" (Ps. 18:49); the anointed king, to whom the promise had been given, was minded to have Gentiles join him in his praise. His words were prophetic of the time when Gentiles would find in David's Son and Lord their own Deliverer and would join King David in his song of praise. 10 The song of Moses bade the Gentiles join in the joy of Israel (Deut. 32:43). 11 Psalm 117 called on *all* nations of the earth to praise the Lord. 12 Isaiah spoke of the coming King from Jesse's house, a descendant of David whose reign of righteousness and peace would be a universal reign. Gentiles would fix their hopes on Him, and their hope would not be put to shame. (Is. 11:10; cf. 11:1-9)

13 The God who gave these promises and fulfilled these promises in Jesus Christ is a God of hope. He gives men hope; all men may confidently lay their future in His hands. Paul intercedes with Him: He can give

to the strong and to the weak the joy and peace they need if they are to live and worship together in the church. All joy and peace can be theirs "in believing." Believing is receiving. They find their joy and peace not in themselves but in their God, and He can give them joy and peace in strange and unsuspected ways. He makes all things work together for their good, even the tensions created by the coexistence of the strong and weak in faith. Thus by God's working, by the power of the Spirit who dwells in them, they can *abound* in hope. They can be so rich and strong in hope that they can meet the severest demands made on their love with kindly evenness of mind.

All three of Paul's appeals to the weak and strong for unity have been grounded in the Christian hope (14:9-12; 15:4; 15:13). Here as always in Paul (and the whole New Testament) hope is a power that shapes and guides the church's life. It is just because the church is not conformed to this world that it is a power in this world. We do not as yet see the perfect and perfectly united people of God which one day shall be. We "*believe* one holy Christian and Apostolic Church . . . and . . . look for the resurrection of the dead and the life of the world to come," where the saints shall be "like angels" (Matt. 22:30), absorbed in the rapture of a total and united worship of God. If we believe and hope thus, our actions strain toward that hoped-for goal and promote that hoped-for unity even now. Our worship is true, spiritual worship because it is a worship of hope, against the grain of this world.

Conclusion

Romans 15:14 – 16:27

THE APOSTLE'S PLANS: FROM
JERUSALEM TO ROME TO SPAIN   15:14-33

[14] I myself am satisfied about you, my brethren, that you yourselves are full of goodness, filled with all knowledge, and able to instruct one another. [15] But on some points I have written to you very boldly by way of reminder, because of the grace given me by God [16] to be a minister of Christ Jesus to the Gentiles in the priestly service of the gospel of God, so that the offering of the Gentiles may be acceptable, consecrated by the Holy Spirit. [17] In Christ Jesus, then, I have reason to be proud of my work for God. [18] For I will not venture to speak of anything except what Christ has wrought through me to win obedience from the Gentiles, by word and deed, [19] by the power of signs and wonders, by the power of the Holy Spirit, so that from Jerusalem and as far round as Illyricum I have fully preached the gospel of Christ, [20] thus making it my ambition to preach the gospel, not

where Christ has already been named, lest I build on another man's foundation, ²¹ but as it is written,

"They shall see who have never been told of him, and they shall understand who have never heard of him."

²² This is the reason why I have so often been hindered from coming to you. ²³ But now, since I no longer have any room for work in these regions, and since I have longed for many years to come to you, ²⁴ I hope to see you in passing as I go to Spain, and to be sped on my journey there by you, once I have enjoyed your company for a little. ²⁵ At present, however, I am going to Jerusalem with aid for the saints. ²⁶ For Macedonia and Achaia have been pleased to make some contribution for the poor among the saints at Jerusalem; ²⁷ they were pleased to do it, and indeed they are in debt to them, for if the Gentiles have come to share in their spiritual blessings, they ought also to be of service to them in material blessings. ²⁸ When therefore I have completed this, and have delivered to them what has been raised,^x I shall go on by way of you to Spain; ²⁹ and I know that when I come to you I shall come in the fullness of the blessing ^y of Christ.

³⁰ I appeal to you, brethren, by our Lord Jesus Christ and by the love of the Spirit, to strive together with me in your prayers to God on my behalf, ³¹ that I may be delivered from the unbelievers in Judea, and that my service for Jerusalem may be acceptable to the saints, ³² so that by God's will I may come to you with joy and be refreshed in your company. ³³ The God of peace be with you all. Amen.

^x Greek *sealed to them this fruit*
^y Some ancient authorities insert *of the gospel*

Paul has, by his Letter to the Romans, already in large measure imparted to the Roman Christians the "spiritual gift" he had promised to impart to them when he came to them (1:11). He, "called to be an apostle" (1:1), has set before them once more, "by way of reminder" (15:15), what it means to be "called to be saints" (1:7). He has reminded them of the new status that God's forgiving verdict has given them. He has pictured for them the new divinely given life that is theirs to live. He has portrayed the new people of God in which God's grace has implanted them. He has summoned them to full participation in the new worship that the Gospel of God has created for God's new Israel, in which Gentile and Jew unite to praise the God and Father of the Lord Jesus Christ. Now he can disclose to them more fully (cf. 1:10-13) his plans and can invite the church of Rome, strengthened by his spiritual gift (1:11), to a "partnership in the Gospel" (Phil. 1:5) with himself.

14 Paul's appreciative words concerning the endowments of the Roman Christians, their goodness, their knowledge, their ability to instruct one another, are more than urbane tact or gracious modesty; they are genuinely apostolic. Paul honors the "work of God" (cf. 14:20) in Rome. These words are written in the spirit of his words to the Corinthians: "Not that we lord it over your faith; we work with you for your joy, for you stand firm in your faith" (2 Cor. 1:24). The hallmark of genuinely apostolic authority is its selflessness (cf. 1 Cor. 3:5-9). **15** Only a man wholly selfless in his authority could designate the huge theological riches of his letter as a "reminder" of what the saints in Rome already knew. One wonders whether Paul would be greatly pleased by our modern admiration of his "originality." He himself lays no claim to it (cf. 1 Cor. 15:11). A selfless man may speak very boldly, as Paul has spoken on some points, for his boldness is not that of a man seeking to establish *his* power; it is the boldness of a man intent upon channeling the grace which he has received to others, for *their* strengthening. (Cf. 1:5; 12:3)

16 God gave him grace for ministry; the work of God is to be done through him. Paul cannot be emphatic enough in asserting that it is just that, the work of God. The apostle is an instrument in the hands of the Trinity; he is "a minister of *Christ Jesus*," the Gospel which he preaches is the "Gospel of *God*," the offering which his priestly ministry presents to God is "sanctified by the *Holy Spirit*." Within this framework of doxology to the triune God, Paul can "magnify" his ministry; as in 1:9, he speaks of it in priestly terms. He is a priest performing a sacrificial ministry in proclaiming the Gospel; the offering which he presents to God is a living sacrifice, the Gentiles whom his preaching calls to be saints of God. His word is an inspired Word; in it the Holy Spirit works to consecrate men, to make them an acceptable offering to God. **17** Paul can be proud of his work, his priestly ministry, for God—but only "in Christ Jesus," for the basic sacrifice, the only sacrifice of expiation which the Gospel knows, is His (cf. 3:25). Because God has put Him forward "as an expiation by His blood, to be received by faith" (3:25), men can in faith offer acceptable sacrifices of devotion and thanksgiving. Thus Paul can describe the Philippians' gift to him as "a fragrant offering, a sacrifice acceptable and pleasing to God" (Phil. 4:18), he can bid men present their bodies as a living sacrifice to God (Rom. 12:1), and he can here call his apostolic ministry a priestly

265

ministry of sacrifice. **18** He can be proud, he can boast only in Christ, for he is the chosen instrument of Christ (Acts 9:15). Christ works in his every word and deed; Christ Himself confronts the Gentiles in Paul's apostolic ministry and brings them under His Lordship in the obedience of faith.

19 That is *the* miracle, the fact that Christ speaks and acts in His apostle, that the treasure of His creative grace is conveyed in the dying bodies of men (2 Cor. 4:7-12). The "signs and wonders" performed by Paul are but varied manifestations of this one great miracle, concrete embodiments of this one overwhelming grace. Paul spoke of the *grace* of his apostolate in his first words to the Romans (1:5); he has not spoken of "the *signs* of a true apostle" (2 Cor. 12:12) until now. The sequence is significant. It is significant, too, that he speaks of the mighty deeds which he has done first as "signs" and then as "wonders." They *are* "wonders"— extraordinary, supernatural, startling; but the important thing is that they are "signs"—they signify, they reveal, they speak of the almighty grace of God. The New Testament never speaks of the mighty deeds of either Jesus or His apostles merely as "wonders"; the term "wonder" occurs only in combination with other terms which point to the significance, the revelatory character, of these deeds, and the Gospels do not directly use the word "wonder" of the deeds of Jesus at all. Paul goes on to set his miraculous powers in the larger framework of "the power of the Holy Spirit." His signs and wonders, like those of Jesus Himself (Matt. 12:28; Acts 10:38), are a part, an important and significant part but only a part, of the outpouring of the Spirit of God on all flesh in the world's last days, an operation of the liberating law of the Spirit of life in Christ Jesus. (8:2)

266

Up to this point Paul has been speaking of his apostolate theologically, revealing the religious bases of his life and work; he has been underscoring and expanding what he had said of himself in the opening paragraph of his letter (1:1-7). Now he speaks of it historically. The impetus of the grace given him by God has carried him in a wide arc from Jerusalem to Illyricum in northwestern Greece. Why Paul should name Jerusalem as the eastern terminus of his activity is not quite clear. If he were speaking chronologically, Damascus or Arabia (Acts 9:19-20; Gal. 1:17) would be more accurate; and from all we know from both Acts and Paul's letters he never did spend much time in Jerusalem in the first years following his conversion (Gal. 1:18-19; Acts 9: 26-30). Paul is evidently not interested in a strict chronology or in giving a minute chronicle of his career. He is, rather, indicating the unity of his work and that of the other apostles. His ministry has been a part of the whole fulfillment of Jesus' prediction and command "that repentance and forgiveness of sins should be preached in His name to all nations, *beginning from Jerusalem*" (Luke 24:47). According to the prophets, knowledge of the true God was to proceed, "in the latter days," from Jerusalem to all the nations:

> For out of Zion shall go forth the law,
>> and the word of the LORD from Jerusalem.
>> (Is. 2:3)

His "full" preaching of the Gospel in Antioch, in Ephesus, in Macedonia, and in Corinth has been a radiation of the Light that broke men's darkness in Jerusalem. This appreciation of Jerusalem is reflected in Paul's interest in the collection for the Jerusalem saints (15:25-28; 1 Cor. 16:1; 2 Cor. 8-9) and in his practice of reporting to the

267

church in Jerusalem at the conclusion of his missionary journeys (Acts 18:22; 21:15; cf. Gal. 2:1-2). Whether "as far round as Illyricum" means that Paul preached in Illyricum or only that his activity carried him as far as the borders of Illyricum, can hardly be determined. Acts records no activity of Paul's in Illyricum.

20 In what sense did Paul "fully preach" the Gospel in the eastern Mediterranean lands? In the apostolic sense; his business as an apostle is to lay foundations (1 Cor. 3:10). The superstructure of the church he can leave to others. If the Word of the Lord has been planted in the great centers and can grow and spread from them, the apostolic preaching has been fully done. The apostle's faith in the Word of God as a power which will continue to work in believers and sound forth, inevitably, from them is apparent here (cf. 1 Thess. 2:13; 1:8). Where Christ is "named," that is, where He is known and worshiped and obeyed (cf. 2 Tim. 2:19), the apostolic church will carry on the apostolic task (cf. 1 Thess. 1:6). **21** The Old Testament word that illumines the words and deeds of Christ (Is. 52:15) sheds light on the ministry of His apostle too. Isaiah's word concerning the Servant of the Lord, who is set "to be a light for the Gentiles" (Acts 13:47; Is. 49:6), presses on toward its fulfillment and urges Paul, the servant of that Servant, on to lands and nations that have never heard of Him. (Is. 52:15)

22 This "necessity" which was laid on Paul (1 Cor. 9:16), the necessity of proclaiming Christ where He was not named and known before, has tied him to the East and hindered him from coming to Rome. The foundations had to be laid in the East, where God wanted them laid, before he could turn to Rome and the West. **23** But now that task is done; now he can fulfill his long-cherished strong desire and come to them "by God's

will" (1:10; 15:32). Now God has work for him in the
West. **24** Rome cannot, obviously, be the goal of his
journey, for there the foundation has long since been
laid, and Christ is named in Rome. Paul's goal is the
western extremity of the Mediterranean Roman world,
Spain, the most thoroughly Romanized of the Roman
provinces. He will see the Romans "in passing" and
enjoy their company for a little, to strengthen them and
to be encouraged in his task by them (1:11-12). But he
looks to them for more than encouragement, valuable
as that gift is to him. He wishes to be "sped on his
journey" by them. This expression (literally, "send on,"
"send forward") is a missionary term; passages like
Titus 3:13-14 and 3 John 6 make it plain that this "speed-
ing on" could include very substantial support of the
men who were sped on their journey (cf. also 1 Cor. 16:6,
11; 2 Cor. 1:16). Paul is soliciting the support of the
Romans for his new venture in Spain. He will need,
perhaps, letters of recommendation, guides, informa-
tion, money. Paul probably hopes to make Rome his
base for operations in the West to serve him as Syrian
Antioch had in the East.

25 There is one more ministry which Paul must
perform in the East before he can turn toward Rome
and Spain. He is going to Jerusalem "with aid for the
saints," for the poor in Jerusalem. Paul never forgot
what James, Peter, and John had laid on his heart in
Jerusalem years before when they gave him the right
hand of fellowship, that he should "remember the poor"
in Jerusalem (Gal. 2:10). Moreover, this "minister of
Christ Jesus to the Gentiles" (15:16) never became
a specialist in Gentile missions; he never forgot the Jew
or Judaic Christendom. He worked and suffered to the
end that there might be one new Israel of God, one

tree of God's planting to burgeon to His glory. He magnified his mission to the Gentiles in the hope that he might win his Jewish kinsmen also (11:13-14), and he kept his Gentile churches mindful of the debt they owed to their Judaic brothers. His references to the collection for the Jerusalem saints in his letters (1 Cor. 16:1-4; 2 Cor. 8 – 9; cf. Acts 24:17) show what store he set by this expression of unity between Gentile and Jew, that "inexpressible gift" of "the surpassing grace of God." (2 Cor. 9:14-15)

26 The Gentile churches of Macedonia and Achaia paid their debt to Jerusalem gladly. **27** "They were pleased to do it," in free graciousness; Paul's words in 1 Cor. 8:1-5 in praise of the self-sacrificing generosity of the Macedonian churches is the best commentary on this verse. They were pleased to do it, and it was an obligation resting on them; they are debtors to the saints of Jerusalem, for the Gospel came to them from Jerusalem. Again we have that same combination of obligation and free resolve which is the mark of genuine love (cf. 1:14-15). **28** So highly did Paul value this contribution as an expression of the unity of the church and as a means of strengthening this unity that he resolved to accompany the bearers of the gift himself (cf. 1 Cor. 16:4), although he did so at the risk of his life (cf. 15:31 and the note there). As the footnote indicates, Paul uses figurative language to describe his act of delivering the Gentile gift: he will "seal this fruit" to the saints of Jerusalem. Since Paul uses "seal" and "sealing" generally to denote the mark of ownership (Rom. 4:11; 1 Cor. 9:2; 2 Tim. 2:19; 2 Cor. 1:22; Eph. 1:13; 4:30), and since he has just spoken of the Gentiles' debt to Jewish Christians, the difficult expression probably means that Paul will tell the saints of Jerusalem, "This gift belongs to you; it is the product of the Gospel which went out from you." The fruit accrues to the original giver.

When Paul has completed this last ministry in the East, he can turn westward with a light heart, having done all he could "to maintain the unity of the Spirit in the bond of peace" (Eph. 4:3). **29** His coming will, he is assured, be fraught with blessing for the saints in Rome; the Christ who works mightily through him by word and deed (15:18) will work through him bountifully in Rome.

30-31 Paul looks with some foreboding toward his voyage to Jerusalem; he knows from experience to what lengths the inveterate hatred of his unbelieving countrymen can go, and the event more than justified his forebodings (Acts 20:3; 21:27-31; 23:12). He also knew that, though he enjoyed the confidence of the leaders of Judaic Christendom, he was suspect in the eyes of many Jewish Christians, who would view his coming, even if he came with gifts, with a jaundiced eye (cf. Acts 21:20-26). Paul therefore draws the church of Rome into his apostolic activity even now, before he has seen them face to face. He asks for their intercessions on his behalf; the solemnity of his appeal, by their common Lord and by the love with which the Spirit binds all the servants of the Lord to one another, underscores the reality of the danger which Paul faces and the seriousness with which he makes this his first request of them. **32** Then, when their prayers for him have been heard, he can come with joy and be refreshed in their midst, in the full assurance that his coming is God's will. **33** A benediction closes the main body of the letter. Chapter 16 is a long postscript.

Paul reached Rome two years later than he had

planned and in a fashion different from the one he had
planned; he came as a prisoner, to stand trial in Rome.
But even so he came in the assurance that he came by
God's will (Acts 23:11). And his coming was not without
joy; when the brethren of Rome came down to the
Forum of Appius and Three Taverns (30 miles!) to meet
him, "Paul thanked God and took courage" (Acts 28:15).
His letter had borne fruit. Whether Paul ever carried
out his plan to go to Spain must remain doubtful; two
early sources, the First Epistle of Clement (A. D. 96)
and the Muratorian Canon (A. D. 170) indicate that he
did, but the tradition of the churches of Spain knows
nothing of Pauline activity in Spain.

COMMENDATION
AND GREETINGS   16:1-16, 21-24

[1] I commend to you our sister Phoebe, a deaconess
of the church of Cenchreae, [2] that you may receive
her in the Lord as befits the saints, and help her in
whatever she may require from you, for she has been
a helper of many and of myself as well.
[3] Greet Prisca and Aquila, my fellow workers
in Christ Jesus, [4] who risked their necks for my life,
to whom not only I but also all the churches of the
Gentiles give thanks; [5] greet also the church in their
house. Greet my beloved Epaenetus, who was the
first convert in Asia for Christ. [6] Greet Mary, who
has worked hard among you. [7] Greet Andronicus and
Junias, my kinsmen and my fellow prisoners; they
are men of note among the apostles, and they were
in Christ before me. [8] Greet Ampliatus, my beloved
in the Lord. [9] Greet Urbanus, our fellow worker in
Christ and my beloved Stachys. [10] Greet Apelles,

272

who is approved in Christ. Greet those who belong to the family of Aristobulus. [11] Greet my kinsman Herodion. Greet those in the Lord who belong to the family of Narcissus. [12] Greet those workers in the Lord, Tryphaena Tryphosa. Greet the beloved Persis, who has worked hard in the Lord. [13] Greet Rufus, eminent in the Lord, also his mother and mine. [14] Greet Asyncritus, Phlegon, Hermes, Patrobas, Hermas, and the brethren who are with them. [15] Greet Philologus, Julia, Nereus and his sister, and Olympas, and all the saints who are with them. [16] Greet one another with a holy kiss. All the churches of Christ greet you.

[21] Timothy, my fellow worker, greets you; so do Lucius and Jason and Sosipater, my kinsmen.

[22] I Tertius, the writer of this letter, greet you in the Lord.

[23] Gaius, who is host to me and to the whole church, greets you. Erastus, the city treasurer, and our brother Quartus, greet you. [b]

[b] Other ancient authorities insert verse 24, *The grace of our Lord Jesus Christ be with you all. Amen.*

Paul's letter of commendation for Phoebe, deaconess of the harbor town to the east of Corinth (vv. 1-2), his greetings to members of the Roman church (vv. 3-16), and the greetings from his co-workers and companions (vv. 21-23) give us a glimpse into the energetic and many-sided life of the early church.

Paul's warm and generous characterizations of the men and women whom he singles out for special greetings are tantalizingly brief, but even so they serve to clothe the saints in Rome with historical flesh and blood. The names themselves tell us something of the composition of the church. There are Greek, Latin, and Jewish names in the list, most of them common enough, especially among slaves and freedmen (liberated slaves). Some of these slaves and freedmen are connected with great houses ("who belong to the family of," vv. 10, 11). The Aristobulus of v. 10 may be the grandson of Herod the Great of that name who spent his life in Rome; he was probably already dead at the time of the writing of the Letter to the Romans, but his slaves and freedmen would continue to be identified by his name. "Narcissus" (v. 11) may refer to the freedman who became powerful and influential under Emperor Claudius and was executed by Nero A. D. 54; his slaves had probably become a part of the emperor's household. Servants of the Lord Jesus in the servants' quarters of Lord Caesar!

Some of those named had worked with Paul and had suffered with him (vv. 3, 4, 7, 9); all knew him and could tell the Roman Christians what manner of man was coming to see them and was soliciting their sympathy and aid for his work in Spain.

The number of women in the list is remarkable, and the characterizations attached to six of the seven names mentioned are no less remarkable. If women kept silence in the public worship of the church (1 Cor. 14:34), they certainly did not remain inactive in the work of the church. Paul uses the same word ("worked hard") to describe the activities of Mary, Tryphaena, Tryphosa, and Persis (vv. 6, 12) that he uses to describe his own strenuous apostolic life (1 Cor. 15:10). He pays tribute to the unwearying love and devotion of Rufus' mother by calling her "his mother and mine" (v. 13). Phoebe, the bearer of the Letter to the Romans, deaconess of Cenchreae, has afforded help and protection to many Christians passing through that busy port, Paul among them (vv. 1-2). And Prisca is a woman of heroic stature; she is named with her husband Aquila as fellow worker of Paul. She has put all the Gentile churches in her debt by her services and has risked her neck to save Paul's life, perhaps at Ephesus, where Paul's ministry was marked by trials and dangers. (Vv. 3, 4; cf. Acts 20:19; 19:23-40; 1 Cor. 15:32; 2 Cor. 1:8-10)

The church at Rome apparently had no special house of worship. The Roman Christians met in homes. The church in the house of Prisca and Aquila is specifically named (v. 5), and vv. 14 and 15, in each of which five persons are named with the addition "and the brethren who are with them" and "and all the saints who are with them" respectively, probably refer to house churches too. This was normal; we hear of other house churches in the New Testament (Acts 12:12; 1 Cor. 16:19; Col. 4:15; Philemon 2). In the first two centuries the churches had no buildings of their own.

The people named by Paul were a mobile lot; whether this holds of early Christians generally or only of Paul's closer friends, who would be drawn into the orbit of his restless energy, one cannot say. Then too, Rome was the center of the Roman world, and many Christians would be drawn there by their business interests. The edict of Claudius banishing Jews from Rome A. D. 49 (cf. Acts 18:2) affected the movements of Aquila and Prisca; perhaps some of the other Jewish Christians also had left Rome because of the edict, had lived for a time in the East, and had now returned to Rome. Phoebe is on her way from Cenchreae to Rome, on business that can justly claim the aid of the Roman Christians (vv. 1-2). Aquila, born in Pontus (Acts 18:2) in the north, has with his wife ranged from Rome to

Corinth and to Ephesus and is now in Rome again (Acts 18:2, 18, 26); later we find him in Ephesus again (2 Tim. 4:19). Epaenetus, the first convert to Christ in the province of Asia, is now in Rome (v. 5). Andronicus and Junias were in Christ before Paul (v. 7); they are Jewish Christians, then, and probably charter members of the Jerusalem church. Something depends on how one understands the phrase "men of note among the apostles" (see below), but on any understanding of the words it is certain that these two men have previously worked and suffered with Paul in the East and are now active in Rome. Rufus (v. 13), "eminent in the Lord," is probably to be identified with the Rufus of Mark 15:21, the son of Simon of Cyrene, who bore Jesus' cross. Paul has known him and his mother in the East; his tribute to Rufus' mother makes it likely that he was a frequent guest in her house. With so many Christians in motion, letters of commendation such as Paul writes for Phoebe were probably no rarity. (Cf. 2 Cor. 3:1)

We learn very little of churchly offices or organization. The reference to the deaconess Phoebe is our earliest reference, perhaps the only one in the New Testament, to this office. (Some see a reference to deaconesses in 1 Tim. 3:11 also.) It would be interesting to know just how this woman had been "a helper of many" and just what business took her to Rome. One can conjecture, but guesses are not history.

Andronicus and Junias are described as "men of note among the apostles" (v. 7). This may mean that they were well known in the circle of the apostles, in Jerusalem, outstanding members of the first church. Or, they may themselves be apostles, members of that larger circle (which Paul calls "all the apostles," 1 Cor. 15:7, a group larger than "the Twelve," 1 Cor. 15:5) of men to whom the risen Lord appeared and gave apostolic authority, men like James the brother of the Lord (Gal. 1:19; cf. 1 Cor. 15:7). This seems more likely. Still a third possibility is that they were authorized and commissioned messengers of a local church, like the men mentioned in 2 Cor. 8:23; but since such "apostles" never constituted an identifiable or a compact group, it is difficult to see how anyone could be spoken of as being a "man of note" among them.

Whatever their organization, these men and women had a strong feeling of solidarity. "In the Lord," "in Christ," the phrase which occurs a dozen times in this chapter, was no empty phrase for them; it designates a power, a person, that welded them together. Not only Paul's fellow workers and companions at Corinth, including his secretary Tertius, send their greetings to Rome (vv. 21-23); Paul can say: "All the churches of Christ greet you" (v. 16) – all the churches know of his plans, all accompany him with their prayers, all bespeak a welcome for him in Rome.

The picture of an early Christian service of worship shimmers through vv. 16-20. The assembled congregation has heard Paul's apostolic Word; the service of the Word is concluded, and the solemn celebration of the Lord's Supper is about to begin. The church marks and expresses its solidarity in the Lord by the exchange of the holy kiss (cf. 1 Thess. 5:26; 2 Cor. 13:12; and especially 1 Cor. 16:20-22), which is found as a fixed part of the liturgy in 2d-century sources. Having spoken a corporate yea to the Lord, whose body and blood, given and shed for them, they are about to receive, the members of the church speak the inevitable nay to all who will not call Him Lord and exclude them from their communion. In 1 Cor. 16:22 we hear such an anathema: "If any one has no love for the Lord, let him be accursed." Here, in the Letter to the Romans, the anathema takes the form of a stern warning against those who serve not our Lord Christ but their own appetites. (Vv. 17-20)

THE APOSTLE'S WARNING   16:17-20

[17] I appeal to you, brethren, to take note of those who create dissensions and difficulties, in opposition to the doctrine which you have been taught; avoid them. [18] For such persons do not serve our Lord Christ, but their own appetites, [z] and by fair and flattering words they deceive the hearts of the simple-minded. [19] For while your obedience is known to all, so that I rejoice over you, I would have you wise as to what is good and guileless as to what is evil; [20] then the God of peace will soon crush Satan under your feet. The grace of our Lord Jesus Christ be with you. [a]

[z] Greek *their own belly* (Phil. 3:19)
[a] Other ancient authorities omit this sentence

17 Paul alerts the Roman Christians to a danger more subtle and more destructive than any which he has yet mentioned, against men "who create dissensions and difficulties." The stern and peremptory tone of these verses shows how deep Paul's concern is; he has seen what havoc creators of "dissensions and difficulties" wrought in Galatia and in Corinth. Apparently they have not yet appeared in Rome; the fact that the warning appears so late in the letter is evidence of that. If they were an immediate threat, we should expect that Paul would have dealt with them in the body of his letter. The language of the warning is, moreover,

278

quite general; Paul is forewarning against a possible attack, not meeting a specific attack as in his Letter to the Galatians.

The activity of these men disrupts the unity of the church ("dissensions") and endangers or destroys the faith of believers ("difficulties"); the word translated "difficulties" here is found also in 9:33 ("a stone *that will make men stumble*"), 11:9 ("a pitfall"), and 14:13 ("a stumbling block *or hindrance*") and denotes that which tempts or entices men to sin or apostasy or false belief. They create dissensions and difficulties by false teaching, "in opposition to the doctrine" which the Romans have been taught (cf. v. 18, "fair and flattering *words*"). Their teaching runs counter to and seeks to override the "doctrine," that "standard of teaching" to which the Roman Christians "have become obedient from the heart" (6:17), that Gospel which set them free from sin and made them slaves of righteousness, God's own slaves (6:18, 22). Their very existence as servants and sons of God is at stake where these men do their work. Therefore they must "note" them, so as to recognize them, and they must "avoid" them when they have recognized them; there is no room for such men in the fellowship sealed with the holy kiss. **18** They must avoid such men, for such men are not servants of their Lord Christ; they do not "pursue what makes for peace and for mutual upbuilding" (14:19; cf. 18) but the exact opposite, dissensions and difficulties. Their devotion is to themselves, "their own appetites." Paul lists "dissensions" among the "works of the flesh" in Gal. 5:20 (along with "party spirit") and calls the men who created dissensions and difficulties in the Galatian churches "those who want to make a good showing in the flesh" (Gal. 6:12). "Avoid" is a rigorous word, but Paul's words

279

in Galatians indicate that he meant it to be rigorous; no compromise or accommodation is possible, for "a little leaven leavens the whole lump." (Gal. 5:9)

The second half of v. 18 shows why Paul put such emphasis on "noting" such men; discrimination is needed, for the false teachers sound dangerously like true ones. They bubble blessings and are winsome in their speech. The simple-minded, who have had no experience with the fair forms that evil can assume, are deceived by them. Their "different Gospel" (2 Cor. 11:4; Gal. 1:6) does not sound so different as to be recognized at once as being "in opposition to" the doctrine which they have been taught.

19 What happens in Rome is news in all Christendom (cf. 1:8). Paul therefore rejoices over this city set on a hill, whose obedience of faith is known to all. But just because the Romans are such conspicuous witnesses to the Gospel, Paul is also concerned for them; if the light that is in them becomes darkness, a shadow will fall on all Christendom. He would therefore have the Romans be wise, not with the kind of wisdom which creators of dissensions had propagated at Corinth, but with that true wisdom which can look evil in the face and yet know and love the good with uncorrupted innocence. Paul seems to be echoing Jesus' word concerning the wisdom of serpents and the innocence of doves. (Matt. 10:16)

20 These weeds that look like wheat are the planting of the Enemy (Matt. 13:28); Satan disguises himself as an angel of light, and his servants disguise themselves as servants of righteousness (2 Cor. 11:13-15). But the Serpent (cf. 2 Cor. 11:3) can deceive only those who want to be deceived (cf. 2 Thess. 2:9-10); and so Paul's last word is a triumphant word of assurance. "Then,"

280

if they will receive and use the wisdom God gives them through the apostolic Word, they need not tremble at this Satanic counteroffensive in the church. The God of peace will put an end to dissensions and difficulties and will crush Satan, the ultimate author of them all, under their feet (cf. Gen. 3:15), "soon," on His great Day that ushers in the everlasting peace. (For this "soon," cf. Rev. 1:1; 22:6.) Until that Day the grace of the Lord Jesus Christ is with them and will keep them safe.

Concluding Doxology   16:25-27

25 Now to him who is able to strengthen you according to my gospel and the preaching of Jesus Christ, according to the revelation of the mystery which was kept secret for long ages 26 but is now disclosed and through the prophetic writings is made known to all nations, according to the command of the eternal God, to bring about the obedience of faith — 27 to the only wise God be glory for evermore through Jesus Christ! Amen.

25 Paul began the body of his letter with the proclamation of the power of God at work in his Gospel (1:16). What wondrous things that power can do and does, his whole letter has set forth in unparalleled fullness. Paul closes with a hymn in praise of the God who has power; He is a God at hand, able to sustain the Romans in their conspicuous and responsible place, able to strengthen them for the greater tasks that Paul's coming will open up to them. He is a God at hand, and His Word is near them. Paul's Gospel is itself that Word, but not because it is Paul's; it can strengthen them because

281

Jesus Christ Himself is preaching in Paul's Gospel. "And Christ is God's" (1 Cor. 3:23); Christ is the disclosure of the "mystery" of God, the revelation of His long counsels of salvation that worked in strange and secret ways for long ages, all through the dark and inconspicuous history of His little people Israel. 26 In Christ that mystery has been disclosed; God's plan now works on the stage of universal history, from Jerusalem to Rome, and will work on to Spain and to the ends of the earth. All nations now shall know the God who hid Himself so long in Israel. God's ancient Word, "the prophetic writings," do their part to make Him known; they are the interpretive witnesses to what the eternal God has revealed in Christ, His righteousness (3:21). Thus by God's own working and by God's command, men will be brought to the obedience of faith. The Romans need not fear; whatever tasks they undertake, they shall not undertake in vain. 27 They need but bow in adoration before the God whose wisdom guides all history toward His goal, to the glory of His grace. Faith sees that goal and glory even now and gives God glory through Him in whom God's glory has appeared, through Jesus Christ.

For Further Reading

Bruce, F. F. *The Epistle of Paul to the Romans*. Tyndale Bible Commentaries. Grand Rapids: Eerdmans, 1963.

An outstanding commentary which brilliantly achieves the aim of the Tyndale series, that of providing "commentaries which avoid the extremes of being unduly technical or unhelpfully brief." Both Bruce's introduction (which is full and informative, dealing with all the major questions concerning the epistle) and his commentary (an exposition of the thought of each section, followed by more detailed verse-by-verse comments) are marked by sound scholarship, a clear and gracious style, and a profound reverence for the apostolic Word. The student who has worked through a commentary like the present one will find Bruce's somewhat more technical work a sound and challenging next step in his study. Even the more advanced students, like the theologically trained pastor, will find the book not only a good refresher course in the Epistle to the Romans; they will find that Bruce is a scribe trained in the Kingdom who brings forth from his treasure things both old and new. There is a good bibliography, confined to works in English. The Tyndale series uses the King James Version as its basic text; Bruce constantly compares other versions, especially the Revised Standard Version and the New English Bible.

Brunner, Emil. *The Letter to the Romans,* trans. H. A. Kennedy. Philadelphia: Westminster Press, 1959.

For the student who is sufficiently at home in the thought of the Letter to the Romans and Paul generally to use this work critically, the famous Swiss theologian's brief but pithy commentary can provide stimulus and some fresh insights. Brunner has not, in my opinion, always remained faithful to the thought of Paul; for example, his treatment of Baptism does not do full justice to the fact that in Baptism God acts upon us (p. 49) and the "groaning creation" of Chapter 8 receives rather cavalier treatment (pp. 74 – 75), to mention just two examples. But again and again the thought of the introduction, that "in this letter of Paul to the Romans God Himself wants to speak to us," breaks through powerfully. The translation, unfortunately, does not do full justice to the vigorous and racy German of the original.

Erdman, Charles R. *The Epistle of Paul to the Romans.* Philadelphia: Westminster, 1925.

This brief (160 duodecimo pages) commentary is clear, pointed, and meaty; it is often warmly devotional in tone and spirit without neglecting the main business of exposition. The author does not do full justice to Paul's treatment of Baptism in Chapter 6 and makes Paul say more concerning the salvation of "all Israel" in Chapter 11 than Paul, in my opinion, actually says. But apart from these (and a few other very minor) deficiencies, it is a useful and edifying little book, written by a man obviously very much in love with his book and its Gospel message.

Hunter, A. M. *The Epistle to the Romans*. Torch Bible Commentaries. London: SCM Press, 1955.

This 134-page commentary, based on the English Revised Version, is written by a scholar who can write in a sprightly style without sounding flippant or frivolous and combines solid learning with deep reverence for the apostolic Word. "Here we encounter a man," he says of the Epistle to the Romans, "claiming to have 'the mind of Christ,' who sees the Saviour's finished work with eyes unsealed and purged by the Holy Spirit, so that he can view it in the whole vast context of God's ways with man in history. Romans thus becomes for us a master-key to the Gospel of God in Christ" (p. 18). He slips out of this attitude of reverent submission to the apostolic Word of God occasionally. One wonders whether it is true to Paul's thought to speak of faith as an "experiment" (p. 21) – "experiment" suggests that if this way (of taking God at His word) fails, we can always try another. For Paul there is no other way. But perhaps Hunter did not wish to suggest that either. More serious is the freedom which Hunter takes over against Paul's teaching concerning Adam and Christ (pp. 20, 59–60) and Paul's stress on the sovereignty of God in Chapter 9 (pp. 90–92). Similarly he feels free to dissent from Paul's judgment on pagan idolatry (p. 32) and his hope for the renewal of all creation in Chapter 8 (p. 83). And it would seem that he is not altogether faithful to Paul's thought in his treatment of "propitiation" (p. 46) and of the second half of Chapter 7. (P. 74)

But despite these occasional concessions to modern thought and modern individualism, Hunter's book is basically a reverent and sympathetic exposition. Hunter has sober and sound things to say, for example, on the reality of the wrath of God (pp. 31 – 32) (which goes against the grain of much modern thought), on "objective atonement" (p. 47), and on the continuing relevance of Romans for today (pp. 17 – 22 of the Introduction, and in occasional comments throughout the commentary). The Introduction covers all essential points adequately and is marked by sober judgment and graceful writing.

Luther, Martin. *Commentary on the Epistle to the Romans, A New Translation by J. Theodore Mueller.* Grand Rapids: Zondervan, 1954.

As the translator states in the preface, this translation of Luther's historic lectures of 1515 – 16 on the Epistle to the Romans "is a digest rather than a complete, scholarly edition. Its purpose is to present to the reader the most important thoughts of the great Reformer. . . . I did not endeavor to produce a literal translation. My object was to reproduce the sense of Luther's notes in clear and concise language." (Pp. 6 – 7)

Luther: Lectures on Romans, Newly Translated and Edited by Wilhelm Pauck. Library of Christian Classics, Vol. XV. Philadelphia: Westminster, 1961.

The significance and value of a complete and annotated edition such as this is well summed up by the translator and editor toward the close of his long Introduction. The importance of this commentary, he says, "consists in this, that it shows Luther on the road to the Reformation—at a time when, as these lectures also clearly demonstrate, he was bound with all the fibres of his soul to the Roman Catholic Church, hating nothing so much as heresy and arbitrary defiance of clerical authority . . . They prove that Luther became a reformer . . . because his basic understanding of the Christian gospel led him to oppose teachings and practices that he found irreconcilable with it. . . . What his basic understanding of the gospel was and how he achieved clarity about it—this is impressively and movingly displayed in these lectures on the letter to the Romans, more so than in any of his other writings."(P. lxv)

Nygren, Anders. *Commentary on Romans,* trans. Carl C. Rasmussen. Philadelphia: Muhlenberg, 1949.

This is a scholarly rather than a strictly popular work and can be read with profit only by one already pretty well at home in the thought world of the Epistle to the Romans. For such, the book can prove stimulating and helpful. The strength of the book lies in the originality of its approach; Nygren regards the section 5:12-21 as the heart of the epistle and interprets its whole message in the light of it, often with great force and brilliance. His exposition of the section dealing with the wrath of God is masterly, and his exposition of Chapter 7 revives the insights of Martin Luther (whose influence is apparent throughout the work) and of the Reformation generally. The weakest section is, unfortunately, the exposition of 3:21-31, where Nygren seems almost to be arguing against Paul rather than interpreting him. To me the section on the Christian life (12:1 — 15:13) does not seem to sustain the high level of the earlier chapters.

Taylor, Vincent. *The Epistle to the Romans*. Epworth Preacher's Commentaries. London: The Epworth Press, 1955.

This brief (100 pages) commentary by a famous British scholar, on the Revised Version, has much to commend it: a profound appreciation of basic Gospel proclaimed by Paul, a persistent emphasis on the "by grace alone" of man's salvation, a consciousness of the fact that the ancient Gospel is relevant to man's need in our century. The work is marred by the fact that the author assumes that we of the 20th century have the power and the right to criticize this apostolic witness to our Lord, the words of the man in whom Christ speaks (2 Cor. 13:3). He therefore, for example, fails to do justice to Paul's use of the Old Testament (pp. 13—14: Paul is "a child of contemporary Judaism," p. 23: Paul "puts his own meaning into" Hab. 2:4); he seems to imply that Paul's speaking of "the direct judgment of God" in the history of man is merely a "Jewish tendency" (p. 25), "the tendency to find the primary cause of all things in God *to the neglect of what we today recognize as secondary causes*" (p. 64, italics mine); he is somewhat skeptical about Paul's "signs and wonders" (p. 94: "strange things happened . . . but their precise character can no longer be determined"), and he fails to do justice to the hard truth of Chapter 9. The last paragraph on page 59 states the author's conviction on what constitutes "authority in Christian belief" and explains his failure to submit wholly to the voice of Christ in the apostle. But for those able to use the work critically it has some real values; not least among them are the author's suggestions for preaching.

Index to Notes